Dissecting Irish Politics

Brian Farrell

Dissecting Irish Politics

Essays in Honour of Brian Farrell

edited by

TOM GARVIN

MAURICE MANNING

RICHARD SINNOTT

UNIVERSITY COLLEGE DUBLIN PRESS
Preas Choláiste Ollscoile Bhaile Átha Cliath

First published 2004
by University College Dublin Press
Newman House
86 St Stephen's Green
Dublin 2
Ireland

www.ucdpress.ie

ISBN 1-904558-12-7

Cataloguing in Publication data available
from the British Library

Typeset in Ireland in Adobe Garamond, Janson
and Trade Gothic by Elaine Shiels, Bantry, Co. Cork
Text design by Lyn Davies
Index by Jane Rogers
Printed on acid-free paper in England
by MPG Books, Bodmin, Cornwall

The editors and publishers gratefully acknowledge
financial support from the National University of
Ireland Publications Scheme and the Academic
Publications Committee of University College Dublin

The editors wish to express their thanks to Daniel Sinnott
for his picture research in the RTÉ Stills Library.

Contents

Contents

Contributors to this volume

JEAN BLONDEL founded the Department of Government at the University of Essex in 1964 and co-founded the European Consortium of Political Research in 1970 and directed it up to 1978. From 1985 until 1994 he was Professor of Political Science at the European University Institute in Florence, and is attached to its Schuman Centre. He is Visiting Professor at the University of Siena.

JOHN COAKLEY is an Associate Professor of Politics at University College Dublin and is director of the Institute for British–Irish Studies. He has edited *The Social Origins of Nationalist Movements* (Sage, 1992); *Politics in the Republic of Ireland* (with Michael Gallagher, 3rd edn, Routledge, 1999); *Changing Shades of Orange and Green: Redefining the Union and the Nation in Contemporary Ireland* (UCD Press, 2002); and *The Territorial Management of Ethnic Conflict* (2nd edn, Frank Cass, 2003).

STEPHEN COLLINS is the political editor of the *Sunday Tribune*. He graduated with an MA in Politics from University College Dublin, and worked with the Irish Press Group before joining the *Sunday Tribune* in 1995. He has written a number of books about Irish politics including *The Cosgrave Legacy* (1996) and *The Power Game: Ireland under Fianna Fáil* (2001).

DAVID FARRELL is a Jean Monnet Professor of European Politics at the University of Manchester, and is an editor of the journal *Party Politics*. He has just completed a book-length study on Australia's preferential electoral systems.

THEO FARRELL is senior lecturer in international relations at the University of Exeter and associate editor of the *Review of International Studies*. He was college lecturer in politics at University College Dublin in 2001–2.

vii

PETER FEENEY is head of public affairs policy in RTÉ. He was the editor of current affairs from 1990 to 1997.

GARRET FITZGERALD retired from the post of Research and Schedules Manager in Aer Lingus in 1958 to undertake a career as an academic, consultant and journalist. He entered politics in 1965 and was appointed Minister for Foreign Affairs in 1973. From 1977 until 1987 he was leader of Fine Gael and was Taoiseach in 1981–2 and 1982–7. Since then he has been a lecturer, consultant, journalist and company director, and, since 1997, Chancellor of the National University of Ireland.

TOM GARVIN is Professor and Head of the Department of Politics at University College Dublin. He has published extensively on Irish politics and is the author of *The Evolution of Nationalist Politics* (1981), *Nationalist Revolutionaries in Ireland 1858–1928* (1987) and *1922: The Birth of Irish Democracy* (1996). His *Preventing the Future: Politics, Education and Development* is to be published in 2004.

NIAMH HARDIMAN is a senior lecturer in the Department of Politics at University College Dublin, and convenor of the Governance Research Programme at the Institute for the Study of Social Change at UCD. She is working on a book about the Irish state, facilitated by a Senior Research Fellowship from the Irish Research Council for the Humanities and Social Sciences.

RONAN KEANE has been Chief Justice since 2000. Previously he was Ordinary Judge of the Supreme Court (1996–2000), Judge of the High Court (1979–96), and President of the Law Reform Commission (1987–92). He is author of *The Law of Local Government in the Republic of Ireland, Company Law in the Republic of Ireland*, and *Equity and the Law of Trusts in the Republic of Ireland.*

BRIGID LAFFAN is Jean Monnet Professor of European Politics and Director of Research, Dublin European Institute, University College Dublin. She has published widely on the dynamics of European Integration in scholarly journals, notably *the Journal of Common Market Studies* and the *European Journal of Public Policy*. She is academic director of a six country cross-national research project entitled Organising for Enlargement.

PETER MAIR studied History and Politics in University College Dublin, and is currently Professor of Comparative Politics at Leiden University in the Netherlands. He is co-editor of the journal *West European Politics*.

MAURICE MANNING lectured in Politics at University College Dublin and was a member of Dáil Éireann and Leader of Seanad Éireann. He has written several books on Irish politics, including *James Dillon: A Biography* and in 2002 became President of the Irish Human Rights Commission.

MICHAEL MILLS was appointed Ireland's first national Ombudsman in 1984, serving two terms before reaching retirement age in the mid-1990s. Previously he worked in the *Irish Press*, which he joined in 1954 and was appointed political correspondent of in 1964. During that time he was also a regular commentator on radio and television.

RICHARD SINNOTT is Associate Professor in the Department of Politics and Director of the Public Opinion and Political Behaviour Research Programme at the Institute for the Study of Social Change, University College Dublin.

Abbreviations

ESRI   Economic and Social Research Institute

GS   General Staff

IPA   Institute of Public Administration

IRTC   Independent Radio and Television Commission

NAI   National Archives of Ireland

NESC   National Economic and Social Council

NLI   National Library of Ireland

RTÉ   Radio Telefís Éireann

TCD   Trinity College, Dublin

UCD   University College Dublin

CHAPTER ONE

Brian Farrell: political scientist, teacher, broadcaster and colleague

MAURICE MANNING

—

This series of essays written by friends, colleagues, former students and admirers of Brian Farrell is testimony not to one, but to three extraordinarily full and satisfying careers. In an age of ever increasing specialisation and ever narrowing focus, it is doubtful if many – or any – today would manage to combine in one lifetime the role of inspirational teacher, pioneering academic and outstanding public service broadcaster.

Brian Farrell is first and foremost an academic, and above all else it is his published work that will be his legacy. Beginning at a time when Irish political science was in its infancy, and in an era when publishing was an optional extra for most academics, his contributions to the literature on Irish politics have been original, reflective, outward looking – and numerous. They were and continue to be of enormous help to students, to an increasingly aware civil service and to a growing number of overseas academics turning their attention to Ireland. It is an extraordinary fact that, with the exceptions of Warner Moss[1] in the 1920s, J. L. McCracken[2] in the 1950s and James Hogan's[3] venture into electoral studies in the 1940s, there was virtually no scholarly political science literature. For those who were students in the 1960s the appearance of Basil Chubb's *Source Book of Irish Politics* was a sensational addition to the almost non-existent literature of the time and, a few years later when Brian Farrell's publishing career began, the contributions of Chubb and Farrell started to make a real and enduring difference.

The start of Brian Farrell's academic career in 1966 coincided with the early days of Irish television. It was easy in those days to look askance at academics who left the comfort of the Common Room to engage in politics or television. Brian Farrell, like his good friend Garret FitzGerald, had no such inhibitions. Indeed, the present writer recalls vividly the reaction of one senior colleague to the news that Garret FitzGerald was entering politics: 'Oh dear, what a shame! He could have made a good academic.' Farrell like FitzGerald, however, saw that there could be an enormous synergy between academic and public life, and that one of the strongest traditions of University College Dublin was an active involvement in the public life of the new state, whether through Dáil and Ministerial service or through vigorous contribution to debates on the major policy issues of the day.

In Brian Farrell's case television was the medium he chose, and it was an inspired choice. Technically, he became one of the greatest ever broad-casters. His rapport with a very capricious medium was total. Whatever the circumstances, no matter how disastrously things were going off-air, no matter that the skies were falling all around, Brian Farrell was calm, magisterial and in command. Words were never fluffed, intros never muddled, conclusions never – well, rarely – rushed or abrupt. In a word, Brian Farrell's sense of auth-ority on air was total. He was aggressive and terrier-like, especially when faced with prevarication, evasion or spin. He was rude on occasions, but usually only when such was needed to get a straight answer. He was also a great ceremonial broadcaster – no visit of a US President from John F. Kennedy on, no State funeral, no major crisis was complete without his elegant, insightful, reassuring presence.

Over time he became a national figure, known by name and repute to virtually every citizen in the land. But it was more than mere recognition. His perceived sense of fairness, his personal authority, his lack of deference persuaded viewers that he was on *their* side, representing the public interest in seeking to get answers. In the extent of public trust and credibility reposed in him, he was Ireland's Walter Cronkite or Richard Dimbleby.

All of this reinforced the synergy between Brian Farrell, the political scientist whose first discipline was history, and the television pundit reporting, analysing and interpreting the world of politics and politicians. The longer view, the context was ever present. The people he was interviewing, the situ-ations he was analysing, the outcomes he was dissecting were the raw material for his academic studies, each enriching the other. Brian Farrell likes politicians and sees them as real people, not numbers to be crunched. He has enormous respect for the centrality of the democratic political process, a very clear grasp of the checks and balances, the constitutional constraints within which politics operates. It is this sense of context, the clear-eyed view of the ethical and constitutional rules underpinning politics that, above all, gives his television work its distinctive edge.

Another, less glamorous and largely forgotten area where he was willing to bring academic values to the market place was his early work in promoting extra-mural studies at University College Dublin. In a pre-online age, in the intellectually barren years of the 1950s and 1960s and before regional third-level institutions had been established, there was a hunger in rural Ireland for access to further education – in most cases for education as a good in itself, rather than as a means of professional advancement. University College Dublin had a long history of sponsoring and validating lectures and diploma courses for communities that were willing to provide the basic infrastructure – a job usually done by the local vocational education committee. In particular there was a special demand for courses in sociology, politics, history and literature. The lectures may at times have provoked Patrick Kavanagh to write dismissively of

Spreading in Naas and Clonakilty/News of Gigli and JM Rilke[4]

but the reality was that they gave a taste for third-level education to people who never had that opportunity. They were a broadening, liberating experience for many. One had only to attend a diploma conferring ceremony or see the splash such events made in local media coverage to realise just how big was the impact in local communities. Brian Farrell was enormously generous in the time he gave to these courses, travelling the circuit, lecturing, and most of all encouraging.

There were other significant aspects to Brian Farrell's academic career. He was – and is – in an old fashioned way, very much a 'College Man'. He was proud to be a part of University College Dublin, never doubting its role as a major national institution. It was his second home, the place where much of his best work was done.

And high among that best work was his teaching. He was, as might be expected from such a communicator, a superb teacher. Unlike many academics, he took his teaching seriously. Each lecture was a performance, a drama to be enacted, and enacted with enthusiasm and passion. Sometimes he overdid it – over theatrically 'hamming' it, a feature some of us attributed to his thespian days in the Dramsoc and the Gate Theatre, and undoubtedly some of that unused thespian potential resurfaced in the lecture theatre. One way or another the students loved it, and appreciated being lectured to by somebody 'who was in the know'. And they appreciated too the hours of quiet counselling, the ever helpful advice and most of all the encouragement he gave, and not just vague encouragement, but help of a very practical nature. And those of us who were his colleagues will recall the acts of generosity, the friendship and the sense of fun and the pride he took in the achievements of his colleagues, especially during his time as Head of Department.

But his central life's work has undoubtedly been his publications. His first two books, *Chairman or Chief? The Role of Taoiseach in Irish Government* and *The Founding of Dáil Éireann: Parliament and Nation-Building*, published in quick succession in 1971, set the tone. *Chairman or Chief?* may have been slight in volume but was groundbreaking in content. It was the first academic study of the role of prime minister in the Irish system, the first attempt to assess the relationship of prime minister to cabinet and parliament. In this book Farrell is the first serious scholar since Warner Moss in the early 1930s to judiciously mix interview material and documentary sources. In doing this, he raised some eyebrows, but his judgement has stood the test of time. The book also provided a starting point for his later biography of Seán Lemass. It is no secret that Lemass was Farrell's great political hero. Lemass, the no-nonsense Dubliner, the visionary pragmatic appealed to Brian Farrell's own restlessness with the status quo. The book captured the essential Lemass and, in passing, told us much about the author's own political values.

Parliament, in various manifestations, is at the centre of much of Brian Farrell's writing. Beginning in 1971 with *The Founding of Dáil Éireann*, followed two years later by *The Irish Parliamentary Tradition* and, in 1994, *The Creation of the Dáil: A Volume of Essays from the Thomas Davis Lectures* and with many journal articles in between, Brian Farrell expounded his belief in the centrality of parliament to the democratic political process and to the development of the modern Irish state. His first such publication, *The Founding of Dáil Éireann*, was sharp and insightful in an area hitherto neglected by scholars; *The Irish Parliamentary Tradition* was a vigorous antidote to the then dominant emphasis on a revolutionary interpretation of Irish politics, while *The Creation of the Dáil* was an elegant and thoughtful celebration of 75 years of Irish parliamentary autonomy. These three books and Farrell's several essays and journal articles on various aspects of parliament represent the single most important contribution to Irish parliamentary studies by one author. The essays and articles include socio-economic analysis of Dáil membership, coalition-building, clientelism, government formation and ministerial selection, and much more. Brian Farrell undoubtedly led the way in Irish parliamentary studies; the great regret must be that his pioneering work has not been fully taken up by others and we still lack a full-blown study of the modern Irish parliament. But that this has not happened is not the fault of Brian Farrell. His contribution led the way for others to follow.

Other important publications include Farrell's attempt in 1970 to put the Irish party system into an understandable international context – something not previously attempted, and his sustained series of electoral studies, many of them in the Washington-based American Enterprise Institute series and his media studies.

This catalogue is not complete but it illustrates not just the range and depth of Brian Farrell's publications, but also the fact that in so many areas he was first into the field, prepared to take a risk and chart a course. This set of essays recognises that fact, that Brian Farrell was one of the pioneers who developed modern Irish political science. In a distinguished career as a teacher, television commentator and public figure, it is his publications that will remain, and deservedly remain, a lasting monument to his contribution.

Notes

1   Warner Moss, *Political Parties in the Irish Free State.* New York: Columbia University Press, 1933.
2   J. L. McCracken, *Representative Government in Ireland: Dáil Éireann 1919–1948.* Oxford: London University Press, 1958.
3   James Hogan, *Elections and Representation.* Cork: Cork University Press, 1945.
4   Augustine Martin to author.

CHAPTER TWO

Cogadh na gCarad: the creation of the Irish political elite

TOM GARVIN

—

The Republic of Ireland is unusual among the older English-speaking western democracies in being not only democratic, but in being born of violent revolution. Apparently democratic politicians like Kevin O'Higgins went together with apparently romantic revolutionaries like Michael Collins. Only the United States among this small group of post-England countries has a similar post-revolutionary heritage. Further, the Irish revolution was heavily informed by its American predecessor, a fact that has been often overlooked.

The Fenians of the 1860s, for example, used songs derived from the songs of the soldiers of the American Civil War; Fenian leaders were often prominent American Civil War veterans, and were 'the men in the square-toed boots', or men who wore Yankee Army (Government Issue, or GI) shoes. Again, Charles Stewart Parnell, a man with an Anglophobe American mother, counted heavily on American-Irish goodwill and dollars. American money also fuelled the Irish War of Independence; Kevin O'Sheil, one of the first Dáil judges, wrote a history of the American revolution in the middle of the Irish revolution (O'Sheil, 1920). He was very clearly fascinated by the analogy between the Yankee Minutemen of 1776 and the IRA of his own time.

The fact that violence played an important part in the formation of the Irish democracy between 1913 and 1923 has had serious consequences for Irish political culture. For example, the romantic rhetoric of militarist nationalism had to be paid homage to by civilian, elected politicians long after the militaristic phase of the revolution was over. Even more recently, three quarters of a century on, the way in which the Rising of 1916 should be commemorated in 1991 was not quite a dead issue.[1]

The further fact that nationalist violence during that period was a rather reluctant reaction to the Ulster rebellion against Home Rule in 1912 has also been significant; in effect, unconstitutional violent traditions gained a temporary advantage over the dominant constitutional and democratic tradition within Irish nationalism.

The most obvious consequence of the violence incurred during the birth of the Irish Free State was the split between those who supported the use of non-violent, constitutional means of political action and those who saw violence as the principal way in which nationalist aspirations could be achieved. I have argued in my *1922: the Birth of Irish Democracy* (Garvin, 1996) that the split reflected a profound division in the Irish political mind between a romantic republicanism and a hard-headed pragmatic nationalism. The former was ambivalent about electoral democracy, whereas the latter was almost depressingly in favour of a dull, everyday democratic order. Eamon de Valera was to spend much of his career in trying to bridge that division, either by trying to legitimise the revolution or by trying to avoid the issue completely (Cronin, 1972: 151–74).

The leaders who created the revolution, and who both led the armed struggle and created a democratic order, shared this deep ambivalence about politics and violence. They were often simultaneously national democrats and national insurrectionists, and the division was commonly inside each leader's mind. Michael Collins, for example, was a man of often ruthless violence who made an astonishing transition to something like statesmanship in 1921–2; Eamon de Valera, the hero of 1916, was to make a slower, but fundamentally similar, transition between 1919 and 1936. The general pattern of younger gunman evolving into older politician is very striking.

Origins of the Irish revolutionary elite

The tradition the revolutionary elite came from was that of the Irish Republican Brotherhood (IRB). This Fenian Brotherhood dated back to 1858, and was founded by three men who met in Langan's Timber Yard in what is now Fenian Street in Dublin. The word 'Fenian' itself recalled hazily notions of the Fianna of Fionn Mac Cumhaill. The Fenians had enjoyed extensive support among Irish emigrants in the United States in particular. Many of its founders had emigrated to the US, commonly in the shadow of the Great Famine. Many of these early Fenians were imbued with a vision of Ireland as a country that England, as an empire, had ruined. An abortive rising was staged by some Fenians in 1867. Later, Fenian activists were heavily involved in agrarian politics and nationalist movements of all sorts. One could claim that old Fenians constructed much of the modern Irish party system.

7

By the end of the nineteenth century, however, the Fenian movement appeared to be moribund, and was seemingly dominated by old men who reportedly bored their younger fellow countrymen with reminiscences of their rebel youth. Young men were more interested in joining the British Army, getting an education or simply emigrating to America. Yet political events in the period after the fall of Parnell revived the old movement's flagging fortunes.

First of all, Parnell's destruction appeared to discredit, and certainly weakened, constitutional nationalism of the kind that he had offered the nationalist Irish. Secondly, the split was very rancorous, and the bitterness was intensified by the activities of Catholic leaders such as T. M. Healy. Thirdly, the rise of two key organisations, one sporting and one cultural, gave the IRB leaders a fresh chance. The sporting organisation was, of course, the Gaelic Athletic Association, founded in Thurles in 1884 and dedicated to the revival and development of Gaelic games. The IRB quickly penetrated this organisation and used it as a propaganda vehicle and as a way of getting into the minds of young people. In particular, the GAA was used to drive a wedge between the young men and the police, as well as segregating the young men from British armed forces personnel. Members of these forces were excluded by the GAA from its activities, and the GAA also prohibited its members from participating in what were called 'foreign games' – games such as rugby and soccer (Garvin, 1981: 135–59).

This division between young men who 'took the King's shilling' and those who refused to take it, sometimes because they could afford not to, became very deep, and often served as an alibi for murdering ex-servicemen in 1919–23.[2] This same division tended, despite the IRB's essential ideological liberalism, to coincide with the older Catholic versus Protestant divisions on the island. Radical Catholics became attracted to republicanism or republican, anti-imperial socialism; radical Protestants became attracted to liberal unionism or 'British' socialism.

The cultural organisation was the Gaelic League, founded in Dublin in 1893. The League was dedicated to the rediscovery of Gaelic Ireland, and to the revival of as much of Ireland's traditional culture as was feasible. Also, it wished to clean up aspects of Gaelic culture that were unacceptable to late Victorian morals. The version of Gaelic culture that it offered had at best a tangential relationship to the real, semi-pagan, Gaelic culture that it claimed to be defending. The Gaelic League became very popular after 1900, having been mainly a Dublin and Trinity College coterie up to then. Eventually this organisation was to come under the control of the IRB in 1911, a power-grab being engineered by Thomas Ashe and Sean T. O'Kelly. This was much to the distress of the League's founder, Douglas Hyde, who profoundly disliked his organisation being penetrated by politics. In essence, the IRB activists ousted Hyde in a coup that was in part generational: young men displaced the old (Garvin, 1987a; Lynch, 1957).

Another event that gave new heart to the younger nationalist revolutionaries was the Boer War. The spectacle of two small Boer republics fighting the British Empire to a standstill seemed to indicate that the age of imperialism might be coming to an end. Britain was a superpower, but was not without rivals. Germany constituted a major, and growing, menace on the European mainland, and the US was already showing signs of developing the military and industrial might which later permitted it to slip into Britain's seat as the new hegemonic world power in the twentieth century.

The IRB, the Gaelic League, the Dungannon Clubs and the Gaelic Athletic Association attracted large numbers of young men and women in the first years of the new century, much as was happening to similar organisations elsewhere in Europe. The decade before 1914 was a time of a youth cult throughout Europe. In Germany, romantic nature-loving organisations such as the *Wandervoegel* proliferated. In England, young people joined extra-mural educational schemes, recorded lovingly in the writings of, for example, H. G. Wells. In Ireland, the IRB and similar organisations, both unionist and nationalist, recruited many energetic young men, disillusioned with politics and possessed of a cult of heroism and violence. Young women followed enthusiastically after, often urging the young men on.

Meanwhile, constitutionalism had become shipwrecked yet again in Ireland. In 1912, Ulster prepared openly to resist Home Rule by force if need be, with support from elements in the British Army. Ulster Unionism also had the help of many senior Tories. A major historical irony is provided by the fact that Ulster 'loyalists' were also aided by the Imperial German Government, fishing in the troubled waters of a potential enemy. Ulster loyalism, perennially trumpeting its fidelity to the Crown, originated in the deepest of treasons. Many heroic supporters of Ulster loyalism and unionism were massacred during the First World War, most spectacularly at the Battle of the Somme, in mid-1916.

In 1913, the Irish Volunteers, heavily penetrated by the IRB, arose to counter the Ulster Volunteers. The Irish Volunteers were explicitly inspired by their Ulster counterparts. The coming of the Great War left the secret society in control of about 5,000 separatist and anti-War Volunteers. This military organisation was the immediate ancestor of the Irish Republican Army and, strangely, of the Army of the independent Irish state that emerged in 1922.

The IRB, a small group of men, now had its own little army, but inside this conspiratorial group lay a further conspiracy, centred on Patrick Pearse. This even smaller group staged a rebellion in Dublin in 1916, against the wishes of the majority of the IRB leadership. After the executions and the attempt by London to impose conscription in 1918, separatism in the form of Sinn Féin swept nationalist Ireland. The new party won virtually all seats in Ireland outside eastern Ulster in the British general election of December 1918. The new MPs refused to take their seats in Westminster, and declared themselves to be the democratically elected rulers of a putatively independent Ireland.

Independence and the Irish political elite

Dáil Éireann was founded in January 1919 (for details, see Farrell, 1971, 1973). Guerrilla war followed, and was accompanied by a systematic takeover of the apparatus of government by the Dáil between 1919–22. In 1922 Britain conceded effective independence to 26 of Ireland's 32 counties. This compromise split the independence movement totally, and a short civil war in the South resulted in the defeat of the insurrectionists by the compromisers.

In the remainder of this chapter, I present a social analysis of the IRB, Sinn Féin and IRA elite as it was on the eve of coming to state power in 1922. I define the elite as including all Sinn Féin and Republican Labour TDs elected in 1918 or 1921, in republican reckoning the First and Second Dála; all IRA leaders listed in the standard *Who's Who in the War of Independence*; all Cumann na mBan leaders similarly included; all members of the Supreme Council of the IRB, 1920; and all 16 leaders executed in 1916. The elite thus defined comes to 304 people.[3]

One salient feature of the nationalist leadership was, unsurprisingly, youth. Most were born in the 1880s and 1890s, with a noticeable bias in favour of the later decade. Most were male, and they were nearly all Catholic. Proportionately speaking, the group was far more Catholic than was the population of the island of Ireland at that time, as nearly one quarter of that population was Protestant, mainly, but not entirely, concentrated in Ulster. The elite was very clearly non-northern; the six counties that came to make up Northern Ireland were dramatically under-represented, and this was so even if only the Catholic population of the area were to be taken into account.

A very large proportion of the leaders had had some experience in the Gaelic League, which provided them with an ideology of loyalty to the past, to cultural roots and to the idea of reviving the ancestral Irish culture. Most paid at least lip service to the project of making the Irish language once again the main spoken language of the island. Many went further than that, and became very proficient speakers of the language and enthusiastic, even fanatical proponents of its revival.

The Gaelic League appears to have had a huge 'spiritual' or psychological impact on that generation of young men and women. It was, in a sense, their university and their movement of personal liberation. In old age, veterans of the movement would reminisce wistfully about the expeditions to archaeo-logical sites, the ceilidhes, the language classes and the national conventions that brought thousands of young men and women together in Dublin every year. In a country that was rather dull, conformist and repressive, the League appeared to supply a way of sharing patriotic projects, an intellectual life and a cultural rediscovery. It was also a means of getting away from parental control and the restrictions that priests and employers attempted to impose on young people. As Denis McCullough, a senior IRB leader, was to put it years later:

> We lived in dreams always; we never enjoyed them. I dreamed of an Ireland that never existed and never could exist. I dreamt of the people of Ireland as a heroic people, a Gaelic people; I dreamt of Ireland as different from what I see now [in 1966] – not that I think I was wrong in this (quoted in Garvin, 1987b: xi).

Even if we leave the six counties of what is now Northern Ireland out of account completely, the leadership was pronouncedly southern in origin. That is, it was southern even in relation to the twenty-six county area that became the Irish Free State. The southern province of Munster was noticeably favoured as the place of origin of the revolutionary leaders. The Dublin area was the birthplace, or place of early rearing, of only one sixth of the leaders; the rest of Leinster had a proportionate number of birthplaces, but Munster, with well over one third of the leaders, was very heavily over-represented. Cork was, even in Munster, heavily over-represented, and west Cork was particularly pro-minent as a producer of leaders: Michael Collins, Gearoid O'Sullivan, J. J. Walsh, Diarmuid O'Hegarty and Tom Barry were among the most conspicuous members of this very conspicuous group. At the time, the importance of west Cork was recognised, and people spoke casually of the group as a sort of 'mafia'.

As in many other nationalist movements, leaders tended to come from either rural areas or very large towns. Relatively few came from the small towns that dominated so much of the country commercially and militarily, serving as they did as bases for military garrisons and the barracks of the Royal Irish Constabulary. Sinn Féin's top leaders, often first generation city folk, joined hands with rural activists against the towns. Ernie O'Malley, author of what is perhaps the most literary IRA reminiscence of that time, *On Another Man's Wound*, wrote 'in the country the small farmers and labourers were our main support, and in cities the workers with a middle-class sprinkling; towns we could not rely on' (O'Malley, 1979: 144).

This pattern was repeated in the financing of the movement. Contributions to the cause of Irish independence were noticeably more generous in the province of Munster, Limerick being particularly open-handed. This southern bias was not new. It appears to echo the distribution of the Gaelic League, in many ways the key founding organisation, which was very strong in Munster. Munster had been the home of the early GAA, and had a tradition of rural agitation and violence that dated back to the middle of the eighteenth century. Whiteboyism, an extraordinary series of agrarian organisations, for example, started in Tipperary, in central Munster, in 1761, in the middle of the Seven Years War. Munster was also the province of origin of the Christian Brothers, an educational order that had an immeasurable effect on the minds of thousands of young, able and ambitious men in the last decades of British rule. This salience of the south was popularly caricatured in *Dublin Opinion* at the time in a famous cartoon entitled 'The Night the Treaty was Signed', which depicted a horde of doubtfully qualified office-seekers rushing along the road from Cork to Dublin in their night attire.

Rurality was a noticeable feature of Irish political organisations in general. Many Sinn Féin or IRA leaders tended to have local power bases in country areas where they had many relatives and friends and were regarded as part of the local community. If they left their native areas, it was not to go to neighbouring counties where they might be resented as blow-ins, but rather to go to Dublin or further afield. Eamon de Valera goes from Bruree to Dublin; Collins goes from Sam's Cross to London; O'Malley goes from Mayo to Dublin; P. S. O'Hegarty from Cork to London. Country-born men in Dublin had the advantage relative to native-born Dubliners of being 'county men', with access to an informal freemasonry based on links of kinship, schooling and place. There were, and still are, formally organised county associations which organised social gatherings and kept these links alive.

In many ways, Munster was the part of Ireland which had become closest to true independence prior to 1914. The novels of Charles Kickham and Canon Sheehan, which enjoyed an enormous popularity at that time, extolled the virtues of the rural, familial and yeoman-farmer society that had emerged in Munster in particular in the post-Famine era. In some ways, this ideological preference for rural and familial society echoed Thomas Jefferson's similar idealisation of the American yeoman farmer a century previously. To an extent, Sinn Féin became dominated by Munster elements. It was in Munster that the IRA campaign against British authority became most intense; it was the fighting men of Munster who resisted most stubbornly the Treaty settlement; and it was in western Munster that the anti-Treatyites made their last stand in 1923. On the other hand, the 'west Cork mafia' centred on Michael Collins was a crucial support for the infant Free State at the beginning.

Occupationally, the leaders of the independence movement were middle class, as is usual among revolutionary leaders everywhere. Furthermore, those who were of humbler origin were evidently clever, energetic and very upwardly mobile. The professions were heavily represented, both the higher professions such as medicine or law, and the lower professions such as teaching and journalism; these were people who dealt in ideas and in publicising such ideas. Civil servants and shopkeepers were noticeably well represented. Farmers were not as well represented as might be expected from their presence in the general population. Over half the population of the 26 counties were engaged in farming at that time, but only one fifth of the leaders seem to have been farmers. However, a very large proportion of the leaders had parents who were farmers.

To sum it up, the leaders were non-agrarian and middle class, highly educated by the standards of the time, socially mobile and probably unusually energetic and intellectually able. Nearly half had received some third-level education, a statistically extraordinarily high proportion at that time. However, this disproportionately high level of education would be typical of most nationalist revolutionary elites in the twentieth century. Many Sinn Féin and IRA leaders were students at, or recent graduates of, the new university colleges and teacher training institutes that had sprung up to give a first generation of Catholics a third-level education of a kind acceptable to their religious beliefs.

Another feature of the leaders was their relative cosmopolitanism. Perhaps half of the leaders had lived outside Ireland for significant portions of their lives, usually in Britain or the US. The 'returned emigrant' syndrome, so conspicuous in the Fenianism of the 1860s, was very noticeable in the leadership of the movement. Foreign experience does seem to have had a stimulating effect on these young men; Collins was a voracious reader of the kind of English literature an intelligent young man of the time would have read: Wells, Galsworthy, Bennett and Shaw. P. S. O'Hegarty, another Corkman and one-time employee of the Post Office in London, was secularised by his experiences; unlike many of the leaders, he supported a complete and unambiguous separation of Church and State, and ascribed his opinion to his experience of living in secular London, away from the religious collectivism of his native Cork.

In many cases, living in England moderated the young men's inherited Anglophobia. It may be, for example, that Collins's extraordinary turnaround on the Treaty issue was partly due to his understanding of, and liking for, the English leaders, an understanding and liking which de Valera apparently did not share. De Valera had never lived in England, whereas Collins had spent nearly ten years in London. De Valera had had the possibly doubtful advantage of a Blackrock College education. Collins had had the clear advantage of an education in the brilliant national school system of the time.

Cogadh na gCarad

The split of 1922 seems to have been only mildly conditioned by these socio-logical characteristics of the leaders. In fact, the best predictor of the vote on the Treaty was sex; all six women TDs voted against the Treaty in January 1922, and a lot of incidental evidence indicates that women activists were far more likely to oppose the Treaty than were men. Why this was so is hard to say, but may have had something to do with political selection. In the Victorian culture of the time, it was unusual for women to engage in public political activity. Any woman who did choose to do so would, therefore, be defying a strong taboo, and be perhaps more adventurous or radical than the average male activist. Certainly, the radicalism of the women was noted at the time; the anti-Treatyites became known humorously as 'The Women and Childers Party'. Erskine Childers, a famous half-English activist, was typed, together with the 'republican women', as a prime wrecker of the Treaty. It is intriguing to speculate as to how much of the intense reaction against women in public life after 1922 was gener-ated by the behaviour of the 'republican women' in 1921–3 (Garvin, 1996: 96–9).

Another striking aspect of the split of 1922 was the power it had to divide families. For example, brothers in the MacNeill family fought on opposite sides, as did brothers of the well-known west Cork Hales family, to take two random instances of a common phenomenon. Older leaders supported the Treaty more firmly than did the young.

Overall, the impression given is that the Treaty divided people by personal loyalty to one or other of the top leadership rather than by social origin.

Collins's acceptance of the Treaty was the main factor that induced his famous squad to accept it too and form the core of the new Free State Army. A common remark was to the effect that 'if it's good enough for Mick, it's good enough for me'. Similarly, de Valera's abrupt rejection of the Treaty turned many key figures against it. Harry Boland actually admitted he opposed the Treaty because he could not let de Valera down in his time of crisis. A certain feminist solidarity with her fellow woman TDs seems to have persuaded Dr Ada English to oppose the Treaty. De Valera's personal trust in the advice of Erskine Childers, together with his evident fondness for the Englishman, seem to have been significant factors in prompting him to reject the settlement (Garvin, 1996: 159–61).

Personal loyalties have as much to do with collective political action as do ideological systems of belief or class solidarities. The split of 1922 was partly ideological, but seems to have been an intensely personal division between people who had been comrades together in a collective revolutionary experience that was extraordinarily intense. The split was experienced not just as a parting of the ways, but as a moral collapse, the destruction of a great solidarity which would never be rebuilt.

The other side of the coin in such a subculture was, of course, disloyalty, whether actual or perceived. Each side increasingly accused the other not of being misguided, but of disloyalty, whether that be disloyalty to the Republic or to a Treaty that was held to be in Ireland's national interest. Dialogue between the two sides became impossible, as mutual distrust took over from the extraordinary comradeship of the previous six years. Irish democracy had a bloody birth in 1922, as the new Army of the Irish Free State under Collins and Richard Mulcahy crushed an IRA that was seen as being in mutiny against a democratically elected Dáil Éireann.

Subsequently, the two sides formed stable political parties which have dominated the politics of independent Ireland ever since. The bitterness caused by the Civil War took fifty years to fade, and it was a bitterness of an intensity that can only arise out of a falling out among firm friends. Irish speakers termed the Irish Civil War Cogadh na gCarad, the 'War Between Friends'. However, behind the hatreds there does seem to have been a certain sense of collective shame, as though the Irish Civil War had been unnecessary, a disaster that had befallen both sides.

Furthermore, almost like quarrelsome children, they had broken the toy that they had all coveted and over which they had quarrelled: the vision of an independent, 32-county Ireland. Whatever slim chance there was of the Treaty settlement achieving some all-Ireland arrangement disappeared in the violence of a Civil War that was mainly fought in Munster, a province that was physically and mentally remote from Ulster.

The gradual realisation of the elementary proposition of the futility of the Civil War sobered the new Irish national political elite mightily, and helped to turn visionaries into sadder, bitterer but perhaps wiser men and women. These new elites set themselves to build a consensual democracy, with all its faults and limitations, on the part of the island of Ireland they had inherited (Garvin, 1996: 156–88; Fanning, 1983). However, because of this embittered past, Dublin politicians proved incapable of handling the Northern Ireland problem until that first generation of elites had died out; and new politicians, who did not know about or care about the ephemeral issues of 1922, eventually took over.

Envoi

Parallel with the formation of the Irish political elite was the formation of the Irish state. States in Europe typically have one of two origins: they are either dynastic or external. England or France offer classic examples of states which were founded by local royal dynasties which accumulated power to themselves, constructed administrative apparatuses, systems of coercion and taxing powers. Other examples of similar state-building processes would be Muscovy/Russia, Spain or Sweden. Externally created states are actually created by dynastic states to govern other territories, usually dependent or perhaps colonised. European examples of such states would be Finland, Norway and Ireland. Outside Ireland, most of the states of Africa and what used to be the British Caribbean are of external origin.

The Irish state was completely rebuilt by the British government in the decades after the Famine, and in many ways the present Irish state bears the hallmarks of that birth. Irish law and administrative practice are based on British Victorian precedent. The state's external and colonial origins are reflected in particular in its extreme centralisation and an equally extreme weakness of local government. Everything goes up to Dublin, and goes down again. Police, health and welfare services are all subject to central controls. Parliament is weak, and backbenchers tend to fall into the role of local grievance-monger to the central powers in Dublin.

The revolutionaries of 1916–22 often had ambitions and wide-ranging schemes of reform, involving the encouragement of local initiative, decentralisation of government and ensuring that Dublin did not dominate the polity (Farrell, 1975). However, the underlying structural logic of the system has been such as to render most such initiatives impossible or unrealistic. What happened, as revolutionary élan faded after the Civil War, is that in effect a parochial democratic process was married to the post-British state apparatus. Parish-pump politics tempered post-colonial state structures.

Since those early decades, of course, things have changed. Parastatal organisations, or 'semi-state bodies', have proliferated: public transport, Aer Lingus, the Bog Development Board and the postal and telecommunications systems are all semi-state in structure. Also, Ireland has gone from being a post-peasant rural society to being a suburban 'post-industrial' society, without ever going through a classic 'smokestack industry' phase. It is as though the country passed from the nineteenth century to the twenty-first century while skipping the twentieth. Irish democracy has had to deal with many problems, and has done reasonably well. Whether it can cope with Northern Ireland remains undetermined.

Notes

1   This chapter is a heavily expanded and rethought version of a Thomas Davis lecture delivered by the author on RTÉ radio in 1994. A version was published in Farrell (1994). The standard book on the emergence of the Free State is Curran (1980), which has never been published in Ireland. This has since been supplemented by Mitchell (1993). See also Garvin (1987b, 1996). Also see the essays in Dorgan and ni Dhonaghadha (1991).

2   On ex-servicemen as targets, see Hart (1998).

3   Elite sources: Stationery Office (1929, 1932, 1939, 1945); Boylan (1999); O'Farrell (1980). On elite analysis, see Garvin (1987b: 33–55); Cohan (1972).

Bibliography

Boylan, H. (1999) *Dictionary of National Biography*. Dublin: Gill & Macmillan.

Cohan, A.S. (1972) *The Irish Political Elite*. Dublin: Gill & Macmillan.

Cronin, Seán (1972) *The McGarrity Papers*. Tralee: Anvil.

Curran, Joseph (1980) *The Birth of the Irish Free State*. Alabama: Alabama University Press.

Dorgan, Theo and Mairin ni Dhonaghadha (1991) *Revising the Rising*. Derry: Field Day.

Fanning, Ronan (1983) *Independent Ireland*. Dublin: Helicon.

Farrell, Brian (1971) *The Founding of Dáil Éireann: Parliament and Nation-Building*. Dublin: Gill & Macmillan.

Farrell, Brian (ed.) (1973) *The Irish Parliamentary Tradition*. Dublin and New York: Gill & Macmillan/Barnes & Noble.

Farrell, Brian (1975) 'The legislation of a "revolutionary" assembly: Dáil Decrees, 1919–1922', *Irish Jurist*, 10 (1).

Farrell, Brian (1994) *The Creation of the Dáil*. Dublin: Blackwater Press.

Garvin, Tom (1981) *The Evolution of Irish Nationalist Politics*. Dublin: Gill & Macmillan.

Garvin, Tom (1987a) 'The politics of languages and literature', *Irish Political Studies* 2: 49–64.

Garvin, Tom (1987b) *Nationalist Revolutionaries in Ireland*. Oxford: Oxford University Press.

Garvin, Tom (1996) *1922: The Birth of Irish Democracy*. Dublin: Gill & Macmillan.

Hart, Peter (1998) *The IRA and its Enemies*. Oxford: Clarendon.

Lynch, Diarmiud (1957) *The IRB and the 1916 Insurrection*. Cork: Mercier.

Mitchell, Arthur (1993) *Revolutionary Government in Ireland*. Dublin: Gill & Macmillan.

O'Farrell, P. (1980) *Who's Who in the Irish War of Independence*. Dublin and Cork: Mercier.

O'Malley, Ernie (1979) *On Another Man's Wound*. Dublin: Anvil.

O'Sheil, Kevin (1920) *The Birth of a Republic*. Dublin: Talbot Press.

Stationery Office (1929) *Flynn's Parliamentary Companion*. Dublin: Stationery Office.

Stationery Office (1932) *Flynn's Parliamentary Companion*. Dublin: Stationery Office.

Stationery Office (1939) *Flynn's Parliamentary Companion*. Dublin: Stationery Office.

Stationery Office (1945) *Flynn's Parliamentary Companion*. Dublin: Stationery Office.

CHAPTER THREE

The Governor-General and the Boundary Commission crisis of 1924–5

RONAN KEANE

—

It would be an understatement of some magnitude to say that the Anglo-Irish Treaty of 1921 left much unfinished business in its wake. Lloyd George was neither the first nor the last British prime minister to find that whether solutions to the Irish question work in practice cannot be decided in the immediate aftermath of what may seem at the time to be historic watersheds. The turbulent episode of the Boundary Commission demonstrated that the ambiguities and uncertainties which the Government of Ireland Act 1920 – conveniently but not entirely accurately described as the 'partition act' – and the Treaty left unresolved had not come to an end with the victory of the Irish Free State government in the civil war or the survival of the new statelet of Northern Ireland through the same period.

The history of the Boundary Commission has been the subject of two magisterial studies by Dr G. J. Hand: his introduction to the body's long suppressed report when it was first published in 1968 (Hand, 1969), and his essay on the role of the Free State nominee to the Commission (Hand, 1973). This essay considers the part played in the episode by Timothy Michael Healy, the first Governor-General of the Free State.[1]

The first Westminster statute to provide for the exclusion of six of the Northern counties from the area of a Home Rule Parliament was the Government of Ireland Act 1914, given the royal assent on the eve of the outbreak of the First World War but suspended in its operation until the end of the war. That exclusion was, however, to be only for a limited period: the critical changes effected in 1920 were that the exclusion was to be permanent and the six counties were to have their own parliament. The Act of 1920 was, of course, stillborn so far as Southern Ireland was concerned because of the refusal of the Sinn Féin MPs, now commanding the support of the overwhelming majority of voters in the area, to take their seats. The Treaty, having provided for the establishment of the Irish Free State and the right of the parliament of Northern Ireland to resolve that the powers of the Parliament and Government of the Free State should not extend to Northern Ireland, went on in Article XII to say that if such resolutions were passed:

> a Commission consisting of three persons, one to be appointed by the Government of the Irish Free State, one to be appointed by the Government of Northern Ireland and one who shall be chairman to be appointed by the British Government shall determine, in accordance with the wishes of the inhabitants, so far as may be compatible with economic and geographic conditions, the boundaries between Northern Ireland and the rest of Ireland, and for the purposes of the Government of Ireland Act 1920, and of this instrument, the boundary of Northern Ireland shall be such as may be determined by such Commission.

According to Lionel Curtis, 'the engagements to which the Irish signatories attached the greatest significance were those implicit in Article XII'.[2] But, in the words of a leading British judge, Lord Buckmaster, they were also 'full of grave and dangerous ambiguity'.[3]

During the Treaty negotiations, members of the Irish delegation had received private assurances from the British side that the effect of these provisions would be to detach so much territory from Northern Ireland as to render inevitable the absorption of the rump in the Free State. Arthur Griffith, in particular, was confident that the Free State would receive 'most of Tyrone and Fermanagh and part of Londonderry, Down etc.' (Longford, 1972: 167–78).[4]

The outbreak of the civil war just over six months after the signing of the Treaty meant that the new government in Dublin had other more urgent preoccupations than reminding the British about the Commission. Michael Collins, who seems to have had no faith in it despite the blandishments to which Griffith had been subjected during the Treaty negotiations, had done his own deal with Craig in March 1922, when both men agreed that the question should be settled between Dublin and Belfast without any Commission being established, an agreement which was to be short lived. The Executive Council established a North-Eastern Bureau under the direction of Kevin O'Sheil, a barrister and civil servant, to assemble the material that would be required when the Commission came into existence. But Collins's successor, W. T. Cosgrave, showed no inclination at first to press the British on the implementation of Article XII.

Even with the end of the civil war in July 1923, there were reasons for caution, not least owing to the political situation in Britain. A period of unusual instability had resulted from the fall of the Lloyd George coalition, the reduced strength of the divided Liberal Party and the increased parliamentary representation of the infant Labour Party led by Ramsay MacDonald. Dublin initially had to deal with a Conservative government headed by Andrew Bonar Law, who had also been the leader of the militant Conservative opposition to the Home Rule Bill in 1912 and was unlikely to be of much assistance to a Dublin government hoping for fruitful results from the setting up of the Commission. Nor could much more be expected from Stanley Baldwin who succeeded him in May 1923.

Among those warning the Cosgrave government against pressing for the establishment of the Commission at this point was Healy, who had moved into the viceregal lodge some months earlier. A memorandum circulated to the Council on 11 July reported that

> the Governor-General is concerned by the fact that, in the opinion of a leading personage in political and journalist circles in England, the last Prime Minister of that country is not friendly disposed towards the Dublin government and as long as he wields his present influence, quarters that might otherwise be friendly will not be inclined to assist us openly.[5]

Healy's nomination as Governor-General had defused one of the many problems that the Treaty settlement had bequeathed to both governments. The requirement that a representative of the crown in Ireland should be appointed with the same powers as the Governor-General of Canada was, next to the oath of allegiance and membership of the Empire, the most unpalatable feature of the Treaty in the eyes of the Irish delegation. Collins had told the committee assigned the task of drafting the new Constitution of the Free State to omit any reference to these provisions of the Treaty, but at British insistence they were incorporated, the Treaty itself indeed being annexed to the document as a schedule. The Irish gloomily contemplated the possibility of a Tory grandee or, even worse, minor royalty reigning in Dublin Castle.[6] For their part, the British had to reckon with the Irish nominating someone whom they would regard as a murderer to act as the King's deputy.

Healy was acceptable to a broad spectrum of Irish opinion, since his nationalist credentials were impeccable: he had been one of the most effective members of the Irish parliamentary party during the days when it seemed so close to bringing at least a measure of self-government to Ireland. The fact that he had also been the most vituperative of all Parnell's opponents during the terrible days of the split would not have damaged those credentials in the slightest in the eyes of the Catholic hierarchy and a large number of those who had taken the pro-Treaty side.[7] Moreover, although Healy's political career and reputation had been badly tarnished, not merely by the savagery of his invective at the height of the split, but by his inglorious politicking in the years afterwards, he had rehabilitated himself to some extent in Sinn Féin eyes during the post-1916 period by being willing to defend IRA prisoners (Sexton, 1989: 76). Finally, and perhaps conclusively, he was Kevin O'Higgins's uncle.[8] At the time, O'Higgins was Minister for Home Affairs and rapidly establishing himself as the strongest figure in the cabinet.

From the British point of view, there could undoubtedly have been worse choices: as a parliamentarian of long standing at Westminster who had never been directly involved in sedition, Healy would have had considerable advantages in their eyes. They must certainly have been reassured by the remarkably obsequious letter he wrote to the Duke of Devonshire, the Secretary of State for the Colonies in Bonar Law's government, after his nomination in which he told the Duke that he would ensure that the Free State government and parliament observed the restrictions on their powers imposed by the Treaty to the letter, a communication of which Cosgrave and his colleagues knew nothing (Sexton, 1989).

Healy did carry with him into the viceregal lodge one important quality for a ceremonial head of state. The viciousness of his public image was not mirrored in his private life: he seems to have been a kindly and gentle man who charmed all who knew him.[9] Those qualities are reflected in the cabinet papers of the time: a picture emerges of an avuncular figure, genuinely concerned that the young ministers struggling with awesome responsibilities should have the benefit of his wisdom and experience.

Although Healy's tenure of the office was marked by at least one major disagreement with the Executive Council,[10] it was nothing like as serious as those in which his successor, James MacNeill, became embroiled when Fianna Fáil took office in 1932, and which led almost immediately to the latter's resignation. He was, moreover, in a significantly stronger position than successive holders of the office of President of Ireland in having a relatively detailed knowledge of the day-to-day decisions of government, particularly in the sensitive area of relations with London and Belfast.

Observance of the Treaty requirement that Healy should fulfil a role equivalent to that of the Governor-General of Canada meant that all decisions of the

Executive Council – as distinct from individual ministerial orders – were trans-mitted by him in the form of a despatch to the Secretary of State for the Colonies in London. The practice was for the Secretary to the Council to send a draft dispatch to the viceregal lodge, embodying the relevant decision for signature by the Governor-General. It was, of course, little more than a rubber stamp procedure but it ensured that Healy was aware of all the communications – many of them confidential – between the Dublin and London governments.[11] It was knowledge of which he was to make use when Dublin at last decided that the issue of the Boundary Commission would have to be confronted.

Towards the end of 1923, the British proposed the holding of a conference in London to discuss the implementation of Article XII. But before the conference took place, dramatic changes occurred in the political scene at Westminster. Bonar Law's successor, Stanley Baldwin, was defeated in the general election in November and a Labour government under Ramsay MacDonald took office for the first time. It was a minority administration dependent for its con-tinuance in office on the support of the Liberals and, while there must have been hopes in Dublin that more could be expected of such a government than those led by Bonar Law and Baldwin, the Labour ministers were also something of an unknown quantity. Healy, from his days in the Commons, knew some of them well and took the opportunity to impress his views on Cosgrave and his colleagues as to how they should handle the British side in the delicate negotiations ahead.

At a meeting in Cosgrave's office on 30 January 1924, also attended by O'Higgins, the Attorney General, Hugh Kennedy and O'Sheil, Healy warned the ministers against expecting too much from the Labour government.[12] That they were well intentioned, he had no doubt: he spoke particularly highly of Arthur Henderson, who had led a Labour mission of investigation to Dublin during the Black and Tan period. But they were also, he said, 'absolutely igno-rant' about Irish affairs and did not understand the situation in the north-east. Their preoccupation with 'trade union affairs and continental internationals' had left them little time to get a grasp of Irish affairs.

Pointing out that the Government of Ireland Act 1920 had been enacted without a single Irish vote, nationalist or unionist, being cast in its favour at Westminster, Healy urged the ministers to lay particular stress on what was happening in the north-east:

The treatment of the Catholic minority in the Six Counties is another matter we should stress, laying particular emphasis on the pogroms, the imprisonment of large numbers of Catholics without trial, the absolute immunity extended to criminals who were not Catholics, the driving out of their homes of Catholic men for no conceivable reason, many of whom could not be accused of belonging to any political party, the special consideration meted out to irregulars and those who were opposing the Government of the Saorstat (e.g., Frank Aiken permitted to wander about County Armagh unmolested and to consolidate his plans against us: he attended Mass and funerals openly all during the trouble of last year and at present cycles openly along the open country in County Armagh).

The ministers should draw the contrast with the Free State in which there was 'perfect religious and civil freedom'. And they should not neglect to urge strongly the 'historical argument' against partition:

At no time in history was (Ireland) ever divided or partitioned, certainly never in the present disgraceful manner. The Six Counties are especially Irish, County Down contains St Patrick's grave and St Brighid's; Shane O'Neill's grave is in County Antrim and in Tyrone and Fermanagh are the memorials of many battles and cultures sacred to Irish memory.

The Irish delegates should be 'stiff and unyielding', Healy declared, not giving an inch. Their model should be none other than Craig: 'He is like a piece of iron. He never yields, for he knows that should he yield he would be torn to pieces in Belfast within twenty-four hours afterwards.'

Reminding the ministers that Craig and his government were 'exceptionally intimate' with British political and social circles, the Governor-General concluded by advising them to be 'as sweet as honey' with MacDonald and his colleagues, but in conference to be 'as hard as granite'.

The London conference opened on February 1 under the chairmanship of the new colonial secretary, J. H. Thomas. It was inconclusive and was adjourned until April. Whatever prospect there was of Conservative ministers successfully influencing Craig, who proved just as immovable as Healy had predicted, there was even less in the case of the Labour government. The unionist attitude was that, since they had not been a party to the Treaty, they were not bound by the provision for a boundary commission. Serenely indifferent, as always, to the inconsistency of, on the one hand, wishing to remain part of the United Kingdom and, on the other, rejecting the sovereignty of the Westminster parliament that had ratified the Treaty, they adamantly refused to nominate a representative to the Commission.

Thus the first of the 'grave and dangerous' ambiguities, to which Lord Buckmaster had referred, came to the surface. The Treaty had not provided for the possibility that one of the nominating governments might refuse to play its part. The inexperienced Labour government, sinking into a political and legal quagmire, grasped thankfully the lifeline offered by their law officers and referred the problems that had arisen to the judicial committee of the Privy Council. Could the Commission function without a Northern Ireland nominee? If not, could the Governor-General of Northern Ireland be ordered by the British government to nominate a representative without the advice of his masters? If not, could the British government fill the gap? If the Commission had to be composed of three persons, would the views of the majority prevail?

When the reference was made to the judicial committee, the Irish Free State was invited by the Registrar of the Privy Council to be represented at its hearings. But Cosgrave's government had adopted the attitude that it was for the British government to fulfil their obligations under the Treaty and that they were not in any way concerned with the advice being sought by that government. Consistently with that posture, they declined the invitation to be represented at the hearing on 22–23 July 1924.

Their decision not to be represented was contrary to the advice of the Governor-General through whom the invitation was transmitted to the Executive Council. In a letter to the Secretary of the Council, Healy urged that the invitation should be accepted and that counsel on behalf of the Free State should submit that the judicial committee had no jurisdiction to entertain the reference.[13]

Healy's view that the reference was *ultra vires* was based on a literal interpretation of the Judicial Committee Act 1833 under which it was purportedly made. It would take us too far afield to consider how well founded that view was. Healy, although a parliamentarian and platform orator of acknowledged brilliance, had not much of a reputation as a lawyer.[14] Cosgrave and his colleagues obviously preferred to rely on the advice of Hugh Kennedy, unquestionably a very fine lawyer.

It is tempting to speculate on what might have happened if Healy's advice had been taken. It would certainly have created a new situation if the Judicial Committee had been persuaded to decline jurisdiction. Would MacDonald and Thomas have glumly accepted the inevitable and proceeded with the Commission in the absence of a representative of Northern Ireland? It is difficult to see what the Free State government had to gain from absenting themselves from the Privy Council proceedings.

As it was, the Judicial Committee advised that the British government had no power to appoint the third member of the Commission and that the Commission could not lawfully proceed in the absence of a Northern Ireland nominee. They also concluded that a commission of this nature could act by a majority. The London and Dublin governments agreed on the enactment of amending legislation to enable the British government to appoint a member of the Commission on behalf of Northern Ireland.

The Cosgrave government had announced, as far back as May 1923, that their nominee to the Commission was to be Eoin MacNeill, the Minister for Education, a distinguished scholar in the field of Celtic studies who had also played an influential role in the transformation of Sinn Féin into a revolutionary movement. Since in addition to being a minister he was also a Northerner and a Catholic, he met what Cosgrave considered were three essential preconditions for the Free State commissioner (Hand, 1973: 210). The British government, for their part, had much difficulty in settling on a chairman: eventually in June 1924, just before the Judicial Committee's deliberations began, the appointment was announced of Mr Justice Richard Feetham of the Supreme Court of the Union of South Africa. The British government, the necessary legislation having been passed, appointed as the Northern Ireland representative Joseph R. Fisher, a barrister, sometime editor of the *Northern Whig* and dedicated unionist.

The subsequent history of the Commission is too well known to require detailed retelling. Feetham made a private tour of the border areas in advance of its sittings: he passed through Dublin on his way, but a suggestion from Curtis that he should stay at the viceregal lodge and be introduced by the Governor-General to Cosgrave and his colleagues was rejected by Healy as 'not politic', being likely to cause offence in Belfast.[15]

When the Commission's membership was complete, the commissioners made a tour of the Northern counties and then began their hearings in London. Counsel for the Free State submitted that the Commission was not empowered to decide that any territory should be ceded by the Free State.[16] This was in accord with the view strongly held by Kennedy, who had been succeeded as Attorney-General, on his appointment as chief justice, by John O'Byrne. Although there were good legal grounds for that view, it was rejected by Feetham, with whom, predictably, Fisher agreed. Even more crucially, Feetham took a narrow view of the Commission's dangerously ambiguous terms of reference, again supported by Fisher: they could only effect rectifications of the existing county boundaries, rather than the transfer of large areas which would significantly alter the territory of 'Northern Ireland' as defined by the 1920 Act. The territory resulting from their labours, they held, should be capable of maintaining the government and parliament envisaged by the Act and the Treaty.

MacNeill, under the protocol adopted by the Commission, felt obliged to keep his colleagues in Dublin in the dark as to the road down which the commission was travelling (Hand, 1973: 232). Fisher had no such qualms, keeping his unionist friends in Belfast well briefed on developments. MacNeill has been criticised both for his meticulous adherence to confidentiality and his somewhat passive attitude towards Feetham and Fisher, but there is no reason to suppose that a more resolute attitude on his part would have made any real difference to the outcome of the Commission's deliberations.[17] In the event, following the leak of the Commission's findings in the *Morning Post* on 7 November 1925 (probably attributable indirectly to Fisher), MacNeill resigned and Cosgrave negotiated a new agreement with Baldwin, who had replaced MacDonald in Downing Street.

The Commission's award had provided for the incorporation of part of South Armagh, with a population of 14,500, into the Free State and the transfer to Northern Ireland of part of Donegal. The Free State was the net gainer in terms of both territory and population, but the changes failed to meet even the most modest expectations of Northern nationalists: the retention of Newry and South Down in Northern Ireland was a particularly bitter blow. Cosgrave and Baldwin agreed at Chequers that the award should not be published, the boundaries should be left as they were and, as a quid pro quo, the financial provisions of the Treaty should be modified in favour of the Free State.

The transfer of part of Donegal to Northern Ireland had been anticipated in Dublin and it was thought that this might include the Inish Owen peninsula. Healy, who was on holiday in the appropriately regal surroundings of Biarritz as the Commission's work drew to its close,[18] wrote to the Council from there on 10 October warning that 'Feetham might join with Fisher to effect such an amputation'. He suggested that the Commissioners should recommend that the peninsula and Derry City should form a single constituency to avoid the risk of gerrymandering. Ultimately, the award provided for the retention of the peninsula in the Free State.

O'Sheil had recommended to the Executive Council in a report on 5 June 1923, that their optimum position should be the incorporation in the Free State of 'all Ireland except Co Antrim, the extreme North Eastern corner of Donegal, portions of North and mid-Armagh (excluding Armagh City) and North and mid-Down'.[19] His hope was that, faced with even the possibility of this drastic loss of territory, Craig and the Ulster unionists would settle for Irish unity with a local parliament for the north-eastern area.

There was never any likelihood that Article XII of the Treaty would fulfil the high hopes placed on it by so many nationalists north and south of the border. Even if the Commission had awarded the county and city of Derry, Tyrone, Fermanagh, South Armagh, South Down and Newry to the Free State, was it even remotely possible that Craig and his followers would have acquiesced quietly? And in those circumstances was a British government under Baldwin and MacDonald going to risk confrontation and civil war?

The Cosgrave government can hardly be criticised for insisting on the British government adhering to the procedures of Article XII: any other strategy would have left them exposed to the reproach of having abandoned the Northern Catholic minority to their fate. It is more difficult to understand their unwillingness to accept the fact that the combination of the unionist refusal to accept rule from Dublin and the reluctance of British governments to coerce them into joining the Free State made the immediate achievement of a united Ireland an improbable dream. In both their public and private utterances, the constant emphasis was on the 'die-hards' and 'irreconcilables' who would ultimately find themselves so weak and isolated as to ensure their incorporation in the Free State.[20]

No one was in a better position to warn them against the ultimate futility of such nationalist dreams than Healy. As a member of the Irish party at Westminster, he had been at the centre of affairs when Gladstone's two home rule bills perished. He had seen Asquith prevaricate endlessly in the face of Orange militancy encouraged by the conservatives under Bonar Law. He cannot have been surprised when Lloyd George capitulated finally and settled for the Northern Ireland solution. No one should have known better than he how unachievable in practical terms the inclusion of the heartland of Ulster unionism in an independent Ireland was in 1924 and 1925. Not merely were there weak minority governments in office in London: the Northern Ireland state was now an accomplished fact. Its leaders, as Healy himself admitted, were men of resolution, determined to keep it in place, who could count on the support of powerful friends in England. Like many others of the nationalist tradition in Ireland, Healy in his role as elder statesman preferred not to confront the logical consequences of these uncomfortable realities. In his approach to the Boundary Commission, he was thus at one with the basic precepts of that tradition, ultimately reflected in the 'Hibernia Irridenta' articles of the Constitution of 1937, holding fast to the belief that 'the historical argument' must eventually prevail.

Notes

1   There is much valuable material on the Boundary Commission in the records of the Executive Council of the Irish Free State transferred to the National Archive (hereinafter NA) by the Department of the Taoiseach. Healy's memoirs (1928), although written during his period in the Viceregal Lodge, are silent on the episode. On Healy's tenure of the Governor-Generalship, see Sexton (1989) and Callinan (1996: Ch. 27).

2   Memorandum cited by Hand (1973). Curtis, a member of the famous Milner 'kindergarten', was an adviser of Lloyd George during the Treaty negotiations.

3   House of Lords debates, series V, col. 757 (22 March 1922).

4   A first hand account of the discussions with the Irish delegates on the topic is to be found in Jones (1970: 155–8).

5   NA, Dept of Taoiseach, S1801.

6   Countess Markievicz, in a remarkable flight of fancy during the Treaty debates in the Dáil, had claimed that there was a plot on foot to marry off the bachelor Collins to the King's only daughter, Princess Mary, later the Princess Royal, and install him as Viceroy. See Dáil Éireann (Treaty Debates) 184, 3 Jan. 1922.

7   It should, of course, be said that there was also a sizeable body of opinion, in both the pro- and anti-Treaty camps, which would have regarded his conduct, particularly in the period after Parnell's death, as unforgivable

8   Sexton (1989) cites a conversation with Patrick McGilligan, a colleague of O'Higgins in Cosgrave's government.

9   See, for example, the account of him in O'Connor (1925: 82) and O'Brien (1974).

10   When he initially refused to sign the Intoxicating Liquor Bill, 1923, on technical legal grounds. See Sexton (1989: 93).

11   The procedure was based on the principle that the Governor-General was not merely the representative of the Crown in the Irish Free State: he also represented the British government. It ended in 1927 when the British finally accepted the Irish claim that he should be solely the representative of the Crown.

12   The account that follows is based on 'Rough Notes' of the conference taken by O'Sheil, NA S1801.

13   Letter of 5 July 1924, NA S1801.

14   Sir James O'Connor said of him that he was the sort of advocate whom clients rather than solicitors asked for, since he zestfully excoriated the other side, while unfortunately losing the case in the process; see O'Connor, 1925: 80

15   NA S1801.

16   There is a complete record of the submissions of counsel on behalf of the Irish Free State in Appendix 1 to the Report.

17   MacNeill, it should be remembered, unlike his two colleagues, suffered from the disadvantage of being a part-time commissioner, since he retained his portfolio in the Executive Council.

18   NA S1801. Biarritz was the favourite winter resort of Queen Victoria.

19   NA S1801.

20 J. J. Lee (1989: 148) points out that it was in any event by no means clear that the Unionist heartland needed the periphery to survive economically.

Bibliography

Callinan, Frank (1996) *T.M.Healy*. Cork: Cork University Press.

Hand, G. J. (ed.) (1969) *Report of the Irish Boundary Commission 1925*. Shannon: Irish University Press.

Hand, G. J. (1973) 'MacNeill and the Boundary Commission', in F. X. Martin and F.J. Byrne (eds), *The Scholar Revolutionary: Eoin MacNeill 1867–1945 and the Making of the New Ireland*. Shannon: Irish University Press.

Healy, T. M. (1928) *Letters and Leaders of My Day*. London: Butterworth.

Jones, Thomas (edited by Keith Middlemas) (1970) *Whitehall Diary: Vol. III, Ireland 1918–25*. Oxford: Oxford University Press.

Lee. J. J. (1989) *Ireland 1912–1985*. Cambridge: Cambridge University Press.

Longford, Lord (Frank Pakenham) (1972) *Peace by Ordeal: An Account from First-Hand Sources of the Negotion and Signature of the Anglo-Irish Treaty, 1921*. 2nd edn. London: Sidgwick & Jackson.

O'Brien, Conor Cruise (1974) *States of Ireland*. Herts.: Panther.

O'Connor, James (1925) *History of Ireland, 1798–1924*. London: Arnold.

Sexton, Brendan (1989) *Ireland and the Crown, 1922–1936: The Governor-Generalship of the Irish Free State*. Dublin: Irish Academic Press.

CHAPTER FOUR

De Valera and democracy

PETER MAIR

—

Almost thirty years ago, in June 1973, at the age of 91, Eamon de Valera left public office for the very last time. By then he had served 14 years as president of the Irish Republic, and was almost certainly the world's oldest democratically elected head of state. By then, however, it also seemed that he enjoyed only a modicum of popular respect and affection, and, if anything, it was with a sense of relief that his last exit was marked. Six months earlier Ireland had become a fully fledged member of the then EEC, and it seemed fitting that this ageing symbol of Ireland's past was now finally being put out to grass. In summer 1973 it was the future that beckoned.

Two years later, in August 1975, de Valera died. And while his state funeral was marked with all the trappings of public respect and homage, he has since become quite a marginal and forgotten figure. Indeed, when not forgotten, he has tended to be denigrated. Lacking the obvious charisma and heroic qualities of his old rival Michael Collins, being linked to an image of Ireland which has always clashed uncomfortably with the prevailing notions of modernity and progress, and being marked forever by his role in the provocation of civil war, de Valera has tended to inhabit the grey areas and gloomy shadows of the national political culture. The more lasting sense is that of a dark and foreboding presence on the political stage, a figure of guile rather than of integrity, a leader who seemed as likely to inspire suspicion as trust, and one whose memory is rarely celebrated, except perhaps, and then only occasionally, within his own Fianna Fáil party circles.[1] In this regard Tim Pat Coogan's conclusion is quite typical, when at the end of his long and often valuable biography, he judges de Valera to be wanting: 'on the great challenges which confronted him in his years of office, de Valera did little that was useful and much that was harmful' (Coogan, 1993: 693).

But however typical, such an evaluation is clearly inadequate. Even leaving aside de Valera's contribution to the policy profile developed in post-independence Ireland – and even here, as Tom Garvin (1998a, 1998b) has more recently suggested, de Valera's record was not always as bad as it is painted – his contribution to the polity itself was immense.

Part of his achievement was purely personal, of course, in that his own political career was marked by a longevity and a capacity to endure that remains without parallel in the democratic world. Moreover, this was despite being a relatively late starter. It may be difficult to appreciate now, but de Valera was already in his mid-30s when he first won election as a Sinn Féin MP in 1917, and was just six months short of his 50th birthday when he first became head of government in 1932. He then continued to hold the post of Taoiseach through to 1948, and then again in 1951–4, and 1957–9, eventually shifting across to the presidency at the age of 77.

To put this into a broader perspective, when de Valera first won elected office, Woodrow Wilson was president of the United States; when he finally retired in 1973, Richard Nixon was still in the White House. In terms of international politics, his political career began at the time of the First World War [2] and ended shortly before the American defeat in Vietnam. In domestic terms, it ran from the Easter Rising to Europeanisation.

De Valera's political success was more than simply personal, of course. Indeed, the party which he founded, Fianna Fáil, went on to become one of the most successful parties in twentieth-century Europe. The party was founded in 1926, and first entered the Dáil in mid-1927. Since then, across 24 elections and close to 80 years, it has managed to poll an average of almost 45 per cent of the popular vote. It has fallen below 40 per cent on only three of these 24 occasions – in its first electoral contest as a Dáil party in September 1927, and again in the 1990s, in 1992 and 1997. It has actually exceeded 50 per cent twice – in 1938 and 1977. There are few if any parties competing in multi-party systems in western democracies that can match that record of enduring electoral success. Moreover, by June 2003, the anniversary of de Valera's retirement, Fianna Fáil had notched up a total of almost 55 years in government office, the large part of which has been served as a single-party administration. As in the case of de Valera himself, there are obviously those who may dislike the Fianna Fáil party and what it stands for; but no-one can fail to appreciate its sheer success in electoral and governmental terms – indeed, in this sense it is virtually without equal across the western democratic universe.

Given de Valera's obvious political successes, both personal and partisan, why then does he continue to be sidelined? In the main, there are four elements involved here. First, and most simply, he polarised opinion. In other words, as well as engendering strong personal loyalties, which did tend to fade with time, he also provoked deep hostility, and even if the details of his political life have been forgotten, this inherited hostility has tended to persist.[3] Second, the vision of Ireland with which he is most closely, if often inaccurately, associated – the cosy homesteads, the comely maidens, the athletic youths, and so on (see the classic radio 1943 broadcast, printed in Moynihan, 1980: 466–9) – quickly came to be seen as both outdated and embarrassing. Far better, it seemed, to hark back to the more modernised and urban visions of Lemass,[4] a political leader who now tends to receive a much more favourable retrospective evaluation than de Valera (see, for example, Horgan, 1998). Third, he is seen as too 'political' a figure in the Machiavellian sense of the term, that is, he is seen as a political leader lacking in any real sense of principle or integrity.[5] This is the view that has also done so much to inspire the unfavourable comparison with his erstwhile contemporary, Michael Collins, a comparison that not only underlies the two best-selling Coogan biographies (1990, 1993), but also the *Michael Collins* film by Neil Jordan. Fourth, and most important of all, in his rejection of the Treaty settlement in 1922, and, thereby, through his role in precipitating the Civil War in 1922, de Valera has come to be considered as somebody who both betrayed and endangered democracy in the new Irish state – a betrayal which is seen to be all the worse given the majority vote in the Dáil in favour of the Treaty, given the substantial electoral victory recorded by the pro-Treaty forces in the 1922 election, and given especially that it was his own emissaries who had agreed to sign the Treaty in the first place. In other words, not only did he refuse to accept responsibility for his own actions, but he also refused to recognise and accept a democratic outcome. It is in this sense that he is seen to have both betrayed and endangered democracy, and it is principally for this reason that his memory is no longer widely cherished.

It is not my intention to deal with the specifics of the first three of these arguments. Within limits, each is valid to a degree. To be sure, there are also other arguments, and against these three points can be weighed the additional personal and party political achievements which I mentioned above, and his role more generally as the constitutional architect of the modern Irish republic – warts and all. In that sense, and even allowing for the negative judgements, it is still perhaps surprising that he does not receive a better contemporary evaluation, and that he is not placed at the same level as other conservative state-builders, such as, for example, de Gaulle or Adenauer.

Be that as it may, it is the fourth argument that concerns me, since it is largely incomplete, and for that reason it is also misleading. Indeed, what I will suggest in this paper is that as well as once undermining democracy in the early 1920s, de Valera also did much to cement and consolidate democracy, albeit at a later stage in his own development as well as in that of the state. In other words, by looking at his first years in power, in 1932 and 1933, I am seeking to redeem de Valera's reputation as a democrat, and to pay due recognition to what was, in fact, his decisive role in ensuring that democracy survived in the new Irish state – against the odds.

Holding power in 1932 and 1933

First it is necessary to review the events leading up to and including those first years of power, since, as will become apparent, the particular sequence is important. De Valera's Fianna Fáil party was founded in 1926 as a result of a split in Sinn Féin, with the new organisation being distinguished by virtue of its more pragmatic approach to participation in the institutions of the Irish Free State. The first election in which it competed was in June 1927, when, still following an abstentionist strategy and refusing to swear the oath of allegiance, it polled 26 per cent of the vote, and won 44 of the then 153 Dáil seats. This election was followed by the assassination of Kevin O'Higgins, which prompted the Dáil to pass a new law requiring all candidates to commit themselves to accepting the oath of allegiance. On this basis, Fianna Fáil chose to enter the Dáil in August 1927. A new election was then called for September 1927, and Fianna Fáil, for the first time a fully participant party, polled 35 per cent of the vote and won 57 seats. This was not enough to displace Cumann na nGaedheal, but it was enough to allow Fianna Fáil to dominate the opposition in the new parliamentary session. The next election came in 1932, and this time Fianna Fáil polled 45 per cent of the vote and won 72 seats, leaving it as the biggest single party but without an overall majority. On 9 March 1932, Fianna Fáil formed a minority government with Labour support, and de Valera became head of government for the first time. Less than one year later, de Valera called a snap election, in which Fianna Fáil went on to increase its vote to almost 50 per cent and to win an overall majority of 77 seats.[6]

What we see here, on the face of it, is nothing unusual. The sequence of events suggests that this is more or less a conventional story. A party comes from a period in opposition to win office as a minority government, feels understandably vulnerable because of its lack of an overall majority, and then calls a snap election in the hope that it can build on its momentum, wrong-foot the opposition, gain extra seats, and thus win a firmer grasp on power. Moreover, in this case the strategy clearly did succeed. And again, this is not in itself unusual, whether the story be played out in Ireland or elsewhere. De Valera himself called another snap election in 1938, and yet again in 1944. Harold Wilson followed the same strategy in the UK in 1966 and 1974, as did François Mitterrand in France in 1981, and Helmut Kohl in Germany in 1983.

But while this now may be seen as a conventional political strategy, in the context of Ireland in the early 1930s it was nothing short of remarkable. Why so? Simply because, having just been elected to office, and being then faced with the prospect of an uncertain and potentially vulnerable hold on power, de Valera chose to cement and reinforce his control by *electoral* means – that is, by democratic means. In other words, in seeking to consolidate his own and his party's position in the new Irish state in 1933, de Valera did *not* opt for a non-democratic solution. Seen within a context of a long international history of democratic consolidation and breakdown, this was de Valera's great historic achievement.

The challenge to democracy

If there is one single weakness in the work of those historians and political scientists who have addressed the development of the modern Irish state since independence, it is that they have tended to take democracy in Ireland, and its survival, more or less for granted.[7] That Ireland has remained democratic is, or so it appears, a normal, or almost natural development. Reference is made to the strong parliamentary tradition that grew out of Irish involvement in Westminster, to Ireland's location within the so-called 'democratic universe', and to the powerful precedents established by the first Cumann na nGaedheal administrations. Moreover, since Irish cultural understandings, and much of the historical perceptions, have inevitably developed within an English-speaking, Anglo-American environment, it has always proved relatively easy to take democracy as a given – much more so, for example, than is the case within the continental European tradition. Of course, the story goes, these early politicians were democrats – what else could they have been? Even then, to cite a conclusion that is now very familiar to students of contemporary politics, it seemed that democracy was the only game in town.

But consider de Valera's context in the early 1930s. Or rather, consider his two contexts – one the broad European context; the other, the specifically Irish context. Let us look at the European context first. The immediate point to underline here is that Europe at that time had only recently discovered full democracy – as indicated by free and fair competition between political parties, on the one hand, and by the right of all adult citizens to participate in elections regardless of their class, income or gender (Dahl, 1971). The Irish Free State had established such a system in 1922. A number of other European countries had established such a system in the period 1918–20 in the wake of the trauma of the First World War. Some – including Belgium, France, Switzerland and the UK – had by then also taken all the steps with the exception of gender equality.[8] If we leave aside this last criterion, then when Ireland established democracy in 1922, it joined a club of 22 other democracies. By current standards, this was not a large club. By the standards of 1922, it was also a very new club – most of the members having experienced democracy for just a handful of years.

By 1922, in other words, democracy was a new and relatively uncommon system – albeit one that had begun to spread rapidly in Europe in particular. But what is perhaps more important to underline, is that by the early 1930s, when de Valera was settling into power, this new system of democracy was already a system under threat. In other words, many of these newly established democracies were proving unable to survive.[9] Italy had already succumbed to an authoritarian regime in 1922 – the same year that Ireland established its own democratic regime; Portugal followed in 1925, and then Poland and Lithuania in 1926; Germany and Austria fell to authoritarianism in 1933, Estonia and Latvia in 1934; Greece in 1936 and Spain in 1939.

To be sure, a majority of Europe's new democracies did survive, at least until either German occupation or war, and in spite of often strong internal authoritarian opposition: Belgium survived, as did Czechoslovakia, Denmark, Finland, France, Norway, The Netherlands, Sweden, Switzerland and the UK. But two things are particularly striking about this experience. First, in terms of the sheer numbers of cases, the chances of surviving as a democracy in inter-war Europe was little more than one in two; in other words, and thinking in terms only of the number of regimes, there was something more than a 40 per cent chance of living under an authoritarian government during the inter-war period.

Second, as even a quick glance at the list indicates, it was particularly in Catholic Europe that the chances of surviving as a democracy were slight – or at least it was slight among those countries where Catholics made up a large proportion of the population, that is, in Austria, Germany, Italy, Poland, Portugal and Spain. In fact, Ireland itself, together with Belgium, Czechoslovakia, and France, were the only mainly Catholic countries in Europe where democracy remained intact, even if it was sometimes seriously challenged (Capoccia, 2001). Democracy, itself a relatively new phenomenon, was therefore especially vulnerable in Catholic Europe in the 1920s and 1930s. There, at least, it was *not* the only game in town. Other games could be played, and what is noteworthy about the Irish case at least is that these other games were not played – or at least not successfully. This is not only noteworthy, it is also remarkable. And this is where the second of de Valera's contexts becomes relevant: Ireland itself.

The 1932 change of government had been the first real change of government in the state – the first direct transfer of power from one party to another. This moment, when it occurs peacefully, and when it follows the accepted democratic procedures, is crucial in any new democracy. Indeed, as Huntington (1991: 266–7) has suggested, it is really only with this first transfer of power that we can speak of the beginning of democratic consolidation. In the Irish case, however, it was especially crucial, since it involved the former losers in a civil war replacing the former winners. Less than ten years after having being defeated in an armed conflict, the losers were now finally coming to political power.

The anxiety that prevailed at the time has since been well documented, of course. Fianna Fáil had only recently spoken of itself as being still just a 'slightly constitutional' party, and not long before it was to come to power it had not only set itself up in opposition to the incumbent Cumann na nGaedheal government, but it had also sometimes sought to deny that government its legitimacy. The bitterness that prevailed was also more than evident. The civil war had not just been nasty on the ground, as it were – a feature where concern could perhaps be confined to the behaviour of the actual protagonists involved in the armed conflict, the state security forces on the one hand and the IRA on the other – it had also been nasty in terms of state policy, a policy characterised by multiple executions, sometimes without even the facade of a prior trial, and by the extensive use of military tribunals. Harassment had also continued for some time after the war itself had ended, often with scant regard for civil liberties. Indeed, it is worth recalling that de Valera himself had been arrested in 1923, on the eve of the election of that year, and was released only in July 1924 – three years before he was to enter the Dáil.

Democracy tends to be taken for granted in Ireland. What is even more to the point, however, is that the transfer of power in 1932 also tends to be taken for granted, as does the election of 1933, when de Valera sought to strengthen his vulnerable position by democratic means. So much for granted, in fact, that in both the contemporary and subsequent accounts of these years, extraordinarily little attention has actually being paid to these crucial events.[10] Moreover, when the transfer of power is discussed, which is only rarely, the focus is usually on just two topics, one of which is largely irrelevant, and the other somewhat misplaced.

The largely irrelevant topic concerns the short-term political questions that were involved – questions such as whether any Fianna Fáil deputies, fearing a Cumann na nGaedheal coup, really did carry guns into the Dáil on the day government was due to be transferred, or the nature of the deal agreed by Labour in return for its promise to support Fianna Fáil's minority government. Both are secondary questions, of course. The second topic that comes up in this context is more serious, however, in that a number of commentators on the period have been concerned to emphasise the apparent magnanimity of William T. Cosgrave and Cumann na nGaedheal in 'allowing' the change of government to take place – that is, Cosgrave and his party's magnanimity in not actually staging a coup. Indeed, in most accounts of this first crucial transfer of power, the message that clearly comes across is that which gives most of the credit to Cosgrave and his colleagues, and which therefore offers particular testimony to Cumann na nGaedheal's democratic credentials. As Joe Lee (1989: 175), himself a sometime defender of de Valera, has observed in his major history of twentieth-century Ireland, 'Nothing so became Cosgrave in office as his manner of leaving it.' Tom Garvin (1992: 226–7), another occasional defender of de Valera, also echoes this view, noting for example, that 'the securing of the adhesion of the bulk of the anti-Treaty forces to the institutions of the state in the form of Fianna Fáil in 1927 represented a real breakthrough in the process of legitimising the new system', but then going on immediately and somewhat incongruously to add that '[This] was an extraordinary triumph for William Cosgrave's statesmanship'. In other words, the credit for paving the way for the peaceful transfer of power, and hence for the consolidation of Irish democracy, was Cosgrave's rather than de Valera's. It was the former who deserved praise for accepting the rules. But on Fianna Fáil and de Valera there is almost nothing. They won, they took office, they called a subsequent election, and that was that. What else could have been expected?

In fact, quite a different outcome might easily have been expected. For what is really striking about this set of circumstances is not what de Valera and Fianna Fáil did in 1932 and 1933, but what they did *not* do. This was, in fact, an extraordinary moment. Those who had been defeated in a bitter civil war less than a decade before had now won office and had displaced those who had defeated them. And once in office, they were to proceed to follow all of the rules of the game – and more. And all this was to take place in the 1930s, when

Catholic Europe seemed otherwise quite content to abandon its newly found engagement with democracy. In theory at least, this was not what might have been expected.

Against the odds

Some 40 years ago, the leading comparative political scientist Gabriel Almond (1960: 41–2) suggested that the problems confronting new states in their immediate post-independence period could well lead nationalist groups in those states to push for authoritarian solutions. Although Almond was mainly concerned with the well-known cases of Turkey and Poland, the conditions that he identified could also be seen to have applied to Ireland, and, within Ireland, to Fianna Fáil. Indeed, in the particular circumstances that prevailed in Ireland in the 1930s, with its recent civil war past, and with a strong and persistent pattern of political polarisation – not to speak of the influence of the ideas coming from Catholic Europe – this option must surely have seemed attractive at times.

Moreover, and this can most evidently be stated with the benefit of hindsight, we are also now in a position to apply to Ireland in the 1930s the lessons that comparative research has recently begun to tell us about processes of regime change, and about the establishment – as well as the breakdown – of democracy. In the past, much of the scholarly understanding of these processes was heavily sociological and often deterministic. The 'choice' between authoritarianism and democracy was primarily seen as a function of particular social and economic circumstances, with the nature of regimes being largely determined by the structure and stresses within the wider society. Following this line of reasoning, for example, we could seek to account for the Irish escape from authoritarianism in the 1930s by reference to the 'democracy-inducing' social and economic conditions that prevailed at the time.[11]

More recently, however, and in quite a convincing fashion, the comparative literature has begun to lay much more stress on the contingent circumstances that are involved in such regime transitions. As a result, we have learned to become much more aware of the importance of voluntarism and activism in determining whether the path that is chosen is authoritarian or democratic (e.g., Kitschelt, 1992; Doorenspleet, 2001). This new perspective also obviously implies that the choice of regime in the Irish case had probably much less to do with the particular social environment in which the leaders found themselves, and much more to do with their own personal and strategic choices and predispositions. Actors are now seen to count, and it is in this sense that the decisions taken by de Valera – as well as those by Cosgrave – assume much greater weight.

The authoritarian option was certainly open at the time. It may also have been given some serious consideration. Indeed, to have followed that particular path would certainly not have confounded expectations. John Coakley (1995: 636), for example, has noted almost in passing that '[i]n view of the fate of post-1918 democracies in Eastern and Central Europe with which Ireland shared so many historical, cultural, political, and socio-economic characteristics, it would not have been surprising had the new Irish state succumbed to a powerful authoritarian or fascist-type movement in the interwar period'. The same point is alluded to by Brian Farrell (1988: 30; see also Smith, 1995) in his overview of the 1937 Constitution. 'In the wrong hands', noted Farrell, 'Ireland could have gone the way of other European states in the dangerous Europe of the mid-thirties. De Valera [by 1936] had abolished the Senate, had an overall majority in the Dáil and a totally flexible constitution with neither effective judicial review nor the requirements of a popular referendum to restrain his will. He could, by simple act of the single parliamentary chamber dominated by his party, make whatever constitutional changes he wished. It was a classic opportunity to establish a dictatorship.'

In the event, of course, and as we now know, Ireland was to remain a democracy. Indeed, it was a democracy which, following de Valera's 1937 constitution, acquired a complex of institutions that proved remarkably open, consensual, and democratic (see below, pp. 43–4). In social terms, of course – and it is on these aspects that most of the attention of subsequent commentators has been focused – the constitution was far from being open and pluralistic. Indeed, by virtue of the strong promotion of Catholic social teaching, it can even be argued to have had its own authoritarian elements. But once we move beyond the social sphere and look instead at the institutional design – which is, after all, the core of the constitutional framework, even if taken for granted – and especially when we take account of the political context from which that institutional design emerged, it is the democratic configuration which most impresses, not least by virtue of its exceptionality.

But why did de Valera and Fianna Fáil follow this path? Why did they commit themselves so clearly to what was a very whole-hearted democratic alternative? Even leaving aside the conditions which might or might not have fostered a full-blooded fascist movement in Ireland at the time, why did de Valera never seem seriously tempted to follow, say, the Polish example, or that of Latvia, where centrist, authoritarian and Catholic forces forcibly held power in opposition to both the right and the left? Authoritarianism in inter-war Europe took many forms, and some at least of these must have seemed appealing to de Valera and Fianna Fáil once they had finally come to power.

But what did de Valera do when he finally won office, and yet still felt his position to be vulnerable? We know the answer, of course: he called another election, and he then went on to establish a constitution which enjoyed many more safeguards against abuse than that which it replaced.

It is impossible within the scope of this brief chapter even to attempt any explanation of this remarkable and usually unacknowledged development. In fact, there are no quick or ready answers. The surface of de Valera's political ideas has still scarcely been scratched, and the nature of his attitudes towards democracy and democratic institutions still remains enigmatic. What is necessary to underline, however, is that de Valera and Fianna Fáil proved democratic, and they did so against the odds, whether these be tallied up domestically or internationally.

What is equally puzzling, of course, is why this question is so rarely addressed, even within contemporary political science research (though see Kissane, 2002), and especially why de Valera's achievement in this respect seems so widely disregarded. Certainly if we look at the history of inter-war Europe, and more generally at the large and growing volume of literature dealing with transitions to and from democracy, it seems more and more obvious that the Irish experience in the 1930s is both remarkable and under-appreciated.

Of course, there is one easy answer as to why de Valera followed the path he did: his actions resulted from the influence of what Brian Farrell (1973) once identified as 'the Irish parliamentary tradition'. Elite political culture in Ireland was forged in Westminster, and even after independence it remained closely tied to British terms of reference. And just as Britain proved one of the very few countries in Europe to escape any significant fascist or authoritarian mobilisation during the 1930s, so Ireland remained automatically, as it were, or naturally, committed to democracy. No other alternative would have been considered.[12]

But this answer is inadequate, and it misses at least three important counterarguments. In the first place, this supposed commitment to parliamentary politics had obviously failed to convince just ten years earlier, in 1922. Indeed, the civil war itself was precipitated in part through the explicit rejection of democratic procedures by a significant element of the political class – led by de Valera. Second, as Tom Garvin (1996) has convincingly shown, it is perhaps only with great difficulty that we could speak of some widespread sense of democratic culture prevailing at the popular level at the time – indeed such a sense remains quite limited today. In other words, there was little in the popular culture at the time that might have been seen to oblige the elites to follow the democratic alternative. The probability is that had de Valera actually opted for a non-democratic solution in the early 1930s, it would not have provoked much real outrage on the ground. Popular democracy was still in its infancy in Europe, and there were a sufficient and indeed growing number of examples from comparable nations to convince the Irish citizenry that it was also probably not even required.

Third, and perhaps most importantly, it is worth recalling that the most powerful anti-democratic impetus that did emerge in Ireland in the 1930s came precisely from those who were apparently *most* closely wedded to the British tradition – that is, from the Blueshirt/Cumann na nGaedheal elements, whose opposition to the social and economic programme pursued by de Valera led them to form quite a sizeable semi-fascist oppositionist movement in 1933 and 1934 (Manning, 1972; Regan, 1999). In other words, if elements within the most pro-British of the two political camps found it so easy to flirt with a fascist alternative, then it is likely that the much vaunted influence of British democratic culture on the other camp has been seriously over-estimated. Yet again, then, it seems that de Valera followed the democratic rules of the game against the odds.

De Valera and democracy

Perhaps this was all just lip service. Recall the famous Machiavellian streak. Perhaps if de Valera had lost the 1933 election, things might have been different. In other words, it might be suggested that de Valera followed the democratic path in 1933 simply because he was convinced that he could win by these means. For de Valera at least, it might be suggested, this could hardly have been a matter of principle.

Two points are important here, one brief, one more lengthy. First, all elections are sources of uncertainty. However popular he might have believed himself to be, de Valera had no cast-iron guarantee that the 1933 election would go his way. Hence, if he was considering an authoritarian solution, he would likely have taken it in 1932, and not risked defeat at the polls in 1933. Indeed, as Coakley (1995) and Farrell (1988) suggest, the option was still there even after 1933, and it was still not taken up.

Second, any sense that he was playing another game was surely dispelled by his new constitution of 1937. That constitution is of course well known, at least in its old, pre-amended form. And it is, or was, principally known by virtue of its social and ideological character – the territorial claim to Northern Ireland; the repeated commitment to the Catholic Church and Catholic social teaching; the ban on divorce, and so on. This was not a pluralist document. It was a document of the majority and for the majority.

But it was also a document *by* the majority – and this is something that we now tend to neglect. That is, it was put to the electorate for their approval, even though there was nothing in principle to prevent de Valera from adopting it by means of a parliamentary vote alone. And again, as in 1933, there was no guarantee of success. Indeed, the document was approved by only a relatively narrow majority. At the same time, however, and this is a most crucial point, it was not a constitution that sought to impose a majoritarian model of democracy. On the contrary, it set out an institutional framework which imposed many more effective constraints on the exercise of executive authority than had been the case in the 1922 Constitution *as practised*, and which also limited government control much more significantly than was the case in many other of the surviving European democracies, including the United Kingdom. Indeed, in strict institutional terms, the now much maligned and battered document which de Valera laid before parliament and people in 1937 bore many of the features which Arend Lijphart (1984) was later to associate with what he termed a *consensus* democracy, and which have also recently been highlighted in the renewed attention devoted to Madisonian democracy in particular, and to classic republican notions of democracy more generally (e.g., Pettit, 1997).

By way of conclusion, let me turn briefly to that constitution, a constitution which defined the political system as established by de Valera, and which in 1937 – one year after Metaxas had assumed dictatorial powers in Greece, and two years before Franco's final victory in Spain – also served to underline his commitment to a democratic path.

What were the key characteristics of this document, at least as far as this present discussion is concerned? What, if anything, does it tell us about de Valera's commitment to, and conception of democracy? Keeping this brief, there are six elements that need to be emphasised, since in each case they indicate a more or less firm willingness on his part to disperse – and at the same time therefore to constrain – the exercise of political power.

First, as noted, there was the constitution's mode of adoption: despite Fianna Fáil's effective majority in the Dáil, the decision to adopt the constitution was not to be the prerogative of parliament; rather it was put to the people in what was to be Ireland's first referendum. Second, once adopted, it was designed to prove relatively invulnerable to elite manipulation. Here again, power was given away, in that any future amendments to the constitution would require majority approval in a popular vote. Third, it created a new head of state, a President, whose role, to be sure, was largely symbolic and ceremonial, but whose appointment, most strikingly, derived also from a popular vote. Here too, this might be seen to run against expectations, since the selection of a largely symbolic head of state in non-monarchical party democracies is often retained as the prerogative of members of parliament and party leaders. That it should be deemed an elected office, particularly during that late inter-war period, appears to reflect a very powerful commitment to popular democracy.

Fourth, the constitution reinstituted a bicameral legislature, with, it is true, a weak upper house, and without the legitimacy provided by direct election. But even allowing for that, it did still indicate a willingness to disperse the levers of power. Fifth, it cemented constitutionally a proportional electoral system in which, almost exceptionally, voters were afforded an opportunity to choose not just between parties, but also between candidates within and across political parties. Here too, it seemed that the emphasis then lay on constraining the prerogatives of elites and their control over the selection and appointment of the members of the political class. Finally, it established a potentially highly independent Supreme Court, the tasks of which were not only to safeguard the Constitution as such, but also to serve as a watchdog over, and act as a constraint on both executive and legislature. And again, particularly at a time when most European states were strongly resisting what they felt to be an encroachment by judges into politics (see Stone Sweet, 2000: 31–8), this was a remarkable initiative.

This was in many respects the blueprint for a consensus-style democracy – at least as far as the structure of the political system was concerned (Lijphart, 1984). While maintaining a system that was highly centralised in a territorial sense, within that all-powerful centre it nevertheless created a framework for the dispersal of power across a number of autonomous institutions. It also established a variety of important limits to the exercise of executive power, including plebiscitarian procedures. Since then, of course, the day-to-day practice of Irish politics has proved strongly majoritarian, with a largely deferential parliament, a quite exceptional level of party discipline, and a persistent resort to narrowly based majority cabinets. But given that such obvious majoritarian impulses already existed in the politics of the time, and given that many of these impulses had already emerged with even greater force under the Cumann na nGaedheal administration (see Kissane, 1998), what remains striking in the 1937 constitution is the extent of its insistence that power be *formally* circumscribed. This need not have been so.

In sum, and however we might seek to explain his actions in 1922, the de Valera of the 1930s – de Valera in power – emerges as a democrat. Moreover, he emerges as a democrat against the odds. This is something that, in hindsight, we should not take for granted. Moreover, given the often-tragic political history of twentieth-century Europe, the fact that the political leadership of the Republic rested for so long in democratic hands is something that should not now be undervalued. This has been by any standards a major achievement, and it should be recognised as such.

Acknowledgements

An earlier version of this chapter was presented at the launch of the Research Centre for Contemporary Irish Politics at the University of Ulster in 1999. I am grateful to Henry Paterson, Tom Garvin and Bill Kissane for their comments on that earlier version, even though the usual disclaimer applies. I was originally encouraged to look at this topic by a stimulating lecture given by Brian Farrell in Limerick in the mid-1970s. Apparently he has forgotten the lecture. I never did.

Notes

1 In one quite recent Fianna Fáil party *Festschrift*, de Valera, Sean Lemass and Jack Lynch each receive eight pages of evaluation, with 19 being given to Albert Reynolds and 20 to [the pre-tribunal] Charles Haughey. See Hannon and Gallagher (1996).

2 The Clare by-election which brought de Valera to national prominence in 1917 was precipitated by the death of William Redmond MP, who died in action in Belgium, and who was reputed to have then been the oldest man to command a company in the line.

3 I personally first became aware of this as a young boy in 1963, on a visit to Dublin with my parents, when the news came that Pope John XXIII had died. 'Isn't it a shame' remarked somebody to my father, 'that old saint in Rome dying, and that old bugger in the Park still going on as strong as ever'.

4 Lemass appeared to have little time for pastoral scenes and dancing at the crossroads. 'I find it hard to have patience with those people who see beauty only in hills and valleys and none at all in "men at work"', he once responded when asked about the possible environmental damage that could be caused by locating industries in areas of scenic or artistic interest. 'In my view one of the most beautiful sights in the world is a busy modern factory, employing Irish workers supporting happy Irish homes, no matter where it is located.' See his interview in *Hibernia*, 23 Sept. 1960.

5 Note Eamon McCann's (1974: 26) glib depiction of de Valera as 'the old Fagin of the political pickpockets'. McCann's description also recalls the more xenophobic attacks on de Valera as being not really 'Irish', but instead Spanish/Jewish/foreign, and hence someone who could not really be trusted.

6 This proved to be a particular source of celebration among Fianna Fáil supporters, since 77 was also precisely the number of persons executed by the Free State government during the Civil War.

7 One very recent and valuable exception to this tendency is Kissane (2002).

8 Gender equality in voting was introduced in the UK in 1928, and in Belgium and France at the end of the Second World War. It was also finally introduced in Switzerland in 1971.

9 For some recent assessments, see Karvonen (1993), and Berg-Schlosser and Mitchell (2000). For a valuable overview of the defence of democracy at the time, see Capoccia (2001).

10 For one significant exception, see Munger (1975).

11 This approach is very comprehensively assessed with specific application to the Irish case in Kissane (2002).

12 Munger (1975: 23–4) also gives quite some weight to this factor.

Bibliography

Almond, Gabriel A. (1960) 'Introduction: a functional approach to comparative politics' pp. 3–64 in Gabriel A. Almond and James S. Coleman (eds), *The Politics of Developing Areas*. Princeton: Princeton University Press.

Berg-Schlosser, Derk and Jeremy Mitchell (eds) (2000) *Conditions of Democracy in Europe, 1919–39*. Basingstoke: Macmillan.

Capoccia, Giovanni (2001) 'Defending democracy: reactions to political extremism in inter-war Europe', *European Journal of Political Research* 39 (4): 431–60.

Coakley, John (1995) 'Ireland' pp. 634–8 in Seymour Martin Lipset (ed.), *The Encyclopedia of Democracy*, vol. 11. Washington D.C.: Congressional Quarterly.

Coogan, Tim Pat (1990) *Michael Collins: A Biography*. London: Hutchinson.

Coogan, Tim Pat (1993) *De Valera: Long Fellow, Long Shadow*. London: Hutchinson.

Dahl, Robert A. (1971) *Polyarchy: Participation and Opposition*. New Haven: Yale University Press.

Doorenspleet, Renske (2001) 'The Fourth Wave of Democratization: Identification and Explanation'. PhD thesis, Leiden University.

Farrell, Brian (ed.) (1973) *The Irish Parliamentary Tradition*. Dublin: Gill & Macmillan.

Farrell, Brian (1988) 'From First Dáil through Irish Free State', pp. 18–32 in Brian Farrell (ed.), *De Valera's Constitution and Ours*. Dublin: Gill & Macmillan.

Garvin, Tom (1992) 'Democratic Politics in Independent Ireland', pp. 222–33 in John Coakley and Michael Gallagher (eds), *Politics in the Republic of Ireland*. Galway: PSAI Press.

Garvin, Tom (1996) *1922: The Birth of Irish Democracy*. Dublin: Gill & Macmillan.

Garvin, Tom (1998a) 'The ambivalence of de Valera', *The Irish Times*, 9 April.

Garvin, Tom (1998b) 'The enigma of Dev – the man from God knows where', *The Irish Times*, 10 April.

Hannon, Philip and Jackie Gallagher (eds) (1996) *Taking the Long View: 70 Years of Fianna Fáil.* Dublin: Blackwater Press.

Horgan, John (1998) *Sean Lemass: The Enigmatic Patriot.* Dublin: Gill & Macmillan.

Huntington, Samuel P. (1991) *The Third Wave: Democratization in the Late Twentieth Century.* Norman: University of Oklahama Press.

Karvonen, Lauri (1993) *Fragmentation and Consensus: Political Organization and the Interwar Crisis in Europe.* Boulder, Co.: Social Science Monographs.

Kissane, Bill (1998) 'Majority rule and the stabilisation of democracy in the Irish Free State', *Irish Political Studies* 13: 1–24.

Kisssane, Bill (2002) *Explaining Irish Democracy.* Dublin: University College Dublin Press.

Kitschelt, Herbert (1992) 'Structure and process driven explanations of political regime change', *American Political Science Review* 86 (4): 1028–34.

Lee, J. J. (1989) *Ireland 1912–1985: Politics and Society.* Cambridge: Cambridge University Press.

Lijphart, Arend (1984) *Democracies: Patterns of Majoritarian and Consensus Government in Twenty-One Countries.* New Haven: Yale University Press.

McCann, Eamonn (1974) *War and an Irish Town.* Harmondsworth: Penguin.

Manning, Maurice (1972) *The Blueshirts.* Dublin: Gill & Macmillan.

Moynihan, Maurice (ed.) (1980) *Speeches and Statements by Eamon de Valera, 1917–1973.* Dublin: Gill & Macmillan.

Munger, Frank (1975) *The Legitimacy of Opposition: The Change of Government in Ireland in 1932.* London: Sage [Contemporary Political Sociology Series, vol. 1, no. 6].

Pettit, Philip (1997) *Republicanism.* Oxford: Oxford University Press.

Regan, John M. (1999) *The Irish Counter-Revolution, 1921–36.* Dublin: Gill & Macmillan.

Smith, Murray (1995) 'The title *An Taoiseach* in the 1937 Constitution', *Irish Political Studies* 10: 179–84.

Stone Sweet, Alec (2000) *Governing With Judges: Constitutional Politics in Europe.* Oxford: Oxford University Press.

CHAPTER FIVE

The suicidal army: civil–military relations and strategy in independent Ireland

THEO FARRELL

—

Ireland won statehood by feat of arms. The Irish Republican Army (IRA) pursued a guerrilla campaign, operating independently of civilian control and eventually fighting the British to a successful stalemate. A politically powerful and strategically savvy IRA was succeeded by a politically wimpish and strategically idiotic Irish army. Military leaders let civilians starve the army of resources, and then let their famished flyweight organisation square up to a super heavy-weight opponent, the British army.

That a small country like Ireland should have a weak military is taken for granted. I begin this chapter by explaining why I find it puzzling. Then I go on to sketch out my answer to this puzzle, which rests on two propositions: first, that the political and strategic enfeeblement of the Irish army was the product of choices made by the army leadership – in other words, the army committed suicide; second, that this self-destructive behaviour was caused by the organisational culture of the Irish army, which led it to emulate the British army. In copying the British, the Irish army developed an inappropriate military structure and strategy, and left itself at the mercy of civilian policy makers.

The puzzle of Irish military weakness

The Irish army's political weakness is puzzling given that the new government was so indebted to it. The army had won statehood for Ireland in the War of Independence (1919–21), and had defended the new state against armed rebellion in the Civil War (1921–2). As Eunan O'Halpin noted: 'In such circumstances one might expect to find the military revered and cosseted by deferential ministers' (1994: 109). Instead, the government cut army personnel from 52,000 in 1923 to around 16,000 in 1924. At the same time, the Department of Finance decreed that army officers were not sufficiently professional to merit full pay (Duggan, 1991: 147–78). Some army officers felt so aggrieved by the government's harsh treatment of them that they mutinied in early 1924. The government used this crisis to force the established army leadership to resign (Valiulis, 1985). A decade later the situation had become so bad that army planners concluded that 'in the usual European sense the [Irish State] can hardly be said to have a Defence Force at all' (GS, 1936: 16).

Civilian control of the military appears to have been primarily exercised through the control of army expenditure. All public expenditure was placed firmly under the control of the Department of Finance by the Free State government. Departments were instructed in May 1922 to seek sanction from the Department of Finance before spending any money or making any appointments. This meant that every single item of army expenditure – from tanks to telephones – required prior approval from the Department of Finance. Since that department was run by former British civil servants who obviously did not share the army's view of a military threat from Britain or Germany (after all, Britain could 'come to the rescue'), it was content to starve the army of resources (Fanning, 1978: 36–42).

As I have already suggested, the army's political weakness stood in stark contrast to the political strength of its predecessor, the IRA. During the War of Independence, the IRA paid little heed to the civilian leadership of the republican movement, not to mention popular opinion. Members of the IRA considered themselves to be a moral elite who, by their struggle and sacrifice, had earned the right to govern Ireland. These themes of heroic struggle and blood sacrifice are traced in Irish Republican mythology back to the Easter Rising of 1916, which was launched by Irish rebels in Dublin against impossible odds in order to ignite a revolutionary impulse in the Irish people (Garvin, 1996: 37–41). The IRA was also elitist in attitude, in part because it was elitist in membership. Ireland was predominately rural, working class, and landed. IRA members were mostly young, urban, skilled, middle-class men who were unmarried, unpropertied, and socially mobile (Hart, 1999). As an elitist organisation, the IRA did not always enjoy popular support. Indeed, public support was often given reluctantly and under intimidation (Townshend, 1987: 327–9). In addition, the IRA financed and fought its war independent of political control. The first Dáil, set up in 1918 during the revolutionary struggle against Britain, and the first Irish minister of defence were largely ignored by the IRA. Indeed, IRA members resisted taking an oath of loyalty to the Dáil that the

49

minister of defence sought to impose on them and, in return, the Dáil did not take responsibility for IRA actions until 1921 (Mitchell, 1995: 65–79). Since there was only mixed support for the republican cause throughout Ireland, it is small wonder that the IRA distrusted the ordinary Irish voter (Fitzpatrick, 1978: 113–44). Equally, it is not surprising that 'the guerrillas thought of themselves as sovereign', since '[t]hey had organized and armed themselves and paid their own way' (Hart, 1998: 269). Given the IRA's political strength pre-independence, the puzzle is not government's treatment of the army so much as the fact that the army subordinated itself to civilian control and allowed the government to run it down.

The Irish army's choice of force structure and strategy is also puzzling. As a consequence of government neglect, the army was simply too poorly resourced to develop a force structure capable of repelling an invading force through sustained conventional operations. From the mid-1930s onwards such an invasion was expected to come from a Britain desperate to secure Irish ports for its naval campaign in the next great European war. Things had become so bad that the Irish army had little over 5,000 troops and an annual budget of around Ir£1.5 million throughout the 1930s (in comparison to a budget of Ir£11 million in 1924; see Duggan, 1991: 142–55; Young, 1993–4: 6–7). The intelligence branch (G-2) of the Irish general staff warned that the invading British would easily overwhelm and destroy any force that blocked their path into Ireland. G-2 recommended 'that badly armed, ill-trained Irish Brigades should [not] be permitted to sit down to be battered up to pulp by vastly superior British forces', and that the Irish army should instead deter invasion by promising a guerrilla-style campaign of organised resistance that would raise the cost of British military occupation (GS, 1934; GS, 1936). Army intelligence officers pointed to Ireland's 'guerrilla warfare tradition', and argued that 'having fought Britain on this basis before, with a certain measure of success, that it forms the obvious basis upon which we should fight them again' (GS, 1934: 89). Two years later they reiterated that 'it would be military suicide for the Defence Forces as they exist at present to make more than a show of organised resistance; they must of necessity revert to guerrilla warfare as soon as possible' (GS, 1936: 77–8).

Organising along these lines would have involved a serious effort to train and arm the populace. The Irish army view was that this would not have created an internal security problem. Indeed, as early as 1925, the Irish Chief of Staff had called for the creation of a massive reserve force to fill the gap between the 100,000 troops he needed to defend the country and the 10,000 strong force he felt the state could afford. Moreover, by 1932, the republicans who had rebelled against the state had already assumed power by being elected into government. Yet such an unconventional defence, which would have drawn on the army's guerrilla warfare heritage, was roundly rejected by the rest of the Irish general staff (Boyd, 1945). Instead, army leaders pushed ahead in 1932 with a massive programme of modernisation and expansion – imagining a 75,000 strong force well armed with tanks, artillery, and aircraft – that ultimately failed for lack of funding (Farrell, 1998: 71; O'Halpin, 1999: 132–44). In organising for conventional warfare, the Irish army emulated its old foe. But, given the lack of funds, the results were disappointing. As Irish army planners observed: 'we could only be described as a miniature and vastly inferior imitation of the British army' (GS, 1934: 90).

By 1940, the predicted threat of a British invasion seemed imminent to the Irish general staff. However, in preparing to meet this threat, officers in the plans and operations branch (G-1) dismissed the earlier recommendations of their colleagues in the intelligence branch for a guerrilla-style defence as having 'no practical application' in 1940. Instead, the main body of the Irish army plonked itself down on the inter-Irish border, and awaited the unwelcome arrival of a vastly superior British force from Northern Ireland (GS, 1940).

Even at the time, it was clear that the Irish army had no hope of repulsing a British invasion force. Army planners expected the British to invade with three divisions and an armoured brigade from Northern Ireland, and a further two divisions from Great Britain, totalling 70,000–80,000 troops with approximately 1,000 armoured fighting vehicles and up to 400 field guns. Against this, the rapidly expanded Irish army was only 40,000 strong with a mere 73 armoured fighting vehicles and 51 field guns (GS, 1940: 2). As one Irish army planner admitted: 'each forward [Irish] Battalion may encounter a force 5 to 9 times its own strength in men alone. In the nature of things unless the enemy blunders badly or we happen to be extremely lucky, the odds are against us' (Flynn, 1940: 1–2). Reports of divisional exercises carried out by the Irish army in 1942 indicate that it was the Irish who were likely to blunder, and blunder badly. These reports reveal a catalogue of basic tactical errors by Irish troops that the better trained and equipped British army would have been able to exploit with devastating effect (GS, 1943). With overwhelming British military superiority, preparing a guerrilla-style defence that avoided direct military engagement with the main British force (as suggested by G-2) was simply prudent. Indeed, such a strategy would have offered a considerable deterrent to British attack, given that Britain would not have wanted to have five army divisions bogged down in Ireland in the midst of a world war. In short, Irish security would have been better served had the Irish army modelled themselves on their revolutionary predecessors rather than their once and possible future enemy.

Was it suicide?

So there is strong evidence of the political and strategic enfeeblement of the Irish army. To what extent was this of the army's own making? In other words, did the army commit suicide? Suicide is defined here as self-destructive behaviour. I maintain that the army's enfeeblement was indeed the product of choices by army leaders. In short, the army could have chosen to exert its political influence in the early years of the Free State. Equally, it could have chosen to develop a force structure and strategy more appropriate to the resources available to it.

In focusing on the formative years of the Irish state and its army, this essay takes a 'path-dependent' (or 'history-dependent') approach. This approach explains how '[o]rganizational procedures and forms may persevere because of path-dependent patterns of development in which initial choices preclude future options, including those that would have been more effective in the long run' (Powell, 1991: 192). From this perspective, the Army's fate was sealed in 1924: four developments in that year made its political enfeeblement complete, which institutionalised civilian control over Army finances and policy. First in the passing of the Ministers and Secretaries Act, which placed in law the requirement for prior approval from the Department of Finance for all public expenditure. This Act also emasculated the office of Army Chief of Staff by designating the Minister of Defence 'commander-in-chief' of the defence forces, thereby making the general staff directly answerable to the minister instead of to the chief of staff. The second development also gave the Department of Finance further power over government expenditure by establishing that all legislation brought before the Dáil was to be first vetted by the Department of Finance. Third was the introduction of a new procedure in which 'all financial proposals concerning the army are required to be considered in the first instance by the army finance officer who will advise the minister regarding them, and who will make any necessary submissions to the Minister of Finance concerning them.' (DOF, 1924) This procedure meant that civil servants in the Department of Defence were able to offer their version of army proposals to the minister, and that this was the only version he saw. It also gave civil servants remarkably broad powers considering that just about all army policy proposals could be said to have had financial implications.

The fourth development was the army mutiny of 1924, the most serious challenge to civilian control of the military in the history of the Irish state. This mutiny occurred as a direct result of the massive demobilisation of the army. The mutiny was also caused by the army's drive to professionalise itself, leading to better qualified officers being favoured over officers with more experience in the IRA. All this was in stark contrast to what had happened during the civil war when officers were appointed on the basis of their IRA connections and ability to persuade others to side with the Free State against the republican rebels. Many of these officers faced unemployment or demotion in the new, greatly slimmed down, professional army. In reaction, a particularly disgruntled group of them, all former members of the IRA's intelligence unit, founded the Irish Republican Army Organisation (a.k.a. the Old IRA) in January 1923.

The Irish prime minister, W. T. Cosgrave, and Defence Minister General Mulcahy agreed to several meetings with the Old IRA in the summer of 1923 in order to avoid an open confrontation before the general election in August that year. Somewhat predictably, the demobilisation of some 900 army officers began shortly after the election. After months of ineffective appeals and agitation on behalf of its members, the Old IRA gave an ultimatum to the government on 6 March 1924. Dressing their personal cause up in nationalist rhetoric, they demanded that the government discuss with them its interpretation of the treaty with Britain, and that the demobilisation and reorganisation of the army be halted. Forty-nine officers around the country resigned in support of the Old IRA and another 50 deserted their posts taking weapons with them. In response, the government publicly took a hard line: Cosgrave told the Dáil that the ultimatum constituted a 'challenge to the democratic foundations of the state' and the government ordered the arrest of its two signatories. However, in private the Executive Council and the government party were keen the resolve the crises quickly, and a cabinet minister who was sympathetic to the Old IRA was dispatched to work out a deal with them. The Executive Council effectively gave in to the mutineers: on 12 March it ordered the army to stop searching for them, ordered a ministerial review of the cases of all mutineers who had resigned from the army, and agreed to set up an independent committee to investigate charges of incompetence in the Department of Defence. This, in turn, led the Old IRA to withdraw its ultimatum.

However, there were rumours in the Dáil of further action by the Old IRA, and army intelligence continued to issue reports warning that the Old IRA were plotting violent action. Acting on such intelligence, Mulcahy order a raid on a meeting of the Old IRA that was taking place in a pub (an old haunt of the IRA intelligence unit) on Parnell Street on 19 March. Eleven members of the Old IRA were arrested and some weapons seized. The Executive Council reacted harshly to what they considered to be a clear breach of government policy and, in the absence of Cosgrave who was ill, they ordered the immediate resignation of the Irish Army Council. General Mulcahy as Minister of Defence promptly resigned along with the three other most senior army generals. With the replacement of the Army Council, the Irish army lost its leadership (Valiulis, 1985).

By 1924 civilian control of the military had thus been firmly established by strengthening the Department of Finance's control over army finances, by weakening the position of the military officers in favour of civilian officials in the Department of Defence, and by removing the existing army leadership in the wake of the mutiny crisis. The army could do little about some of these developments; it could not ignore government procedure and appropriate moneys independent of control by the Department of Finance. Nor could army leaders block legislation before the Dáil which would dilute their power. They could, however, have stood up for themselves by refusing to resign when ordered to by the Executive Council. This, in turn, would have enabled the army to have been more vigorous in defending its own power within the Department of Defence.

From today's perspective, it is inconceivable that army leaders should refuse to resign their commissions when ordered to do so by the civilian government. Indeed, in his recent history of the Irish army, O'Halpin asserts that such a counterfactual is 'implausible, in the circumstances of 1924' (1999: 51). But is it really? Army leaders had both reason and ability to refuse such an order in 1924. They should have been able to hold on to their positions within the army by virtue of their stature within Irish politics and society. The Irish Free State emerged from the civil war without a major political figure to lead the country. The Irish President and Commander-in-Chief of the defence forces, Michael Collins, had been tragically killed in the closing stages the civil war. The other major figure in Irish politics, the former President of the Provisional Irish Government during the War of Independence, Eamon de Valera, had led the rebels in the civil war and had effectively disqualified himself from governing the Free State by refusing to recognise the Treaty with Britain. What was left, as O'Halpin himself notes, was 'a ragbag of obscure lightweights' (1999: 37). In such company, Mulcahy must be considered a major political figure. He had been chief of staff of the IRA, officially the most senior military officer, during the War of Independence. He emerged from the civil war as Minister of Defence and Commander-in-Chief. Collins's untimely death led to a dispute over his successor, which was resolved in favour of a compromise candidate, namely, Cosgrave. Cosgrave was not a natural leader and his style of leadership was quite low key: in Brian Farrell's characterisation, he was 'leader by accident' (Farrell, n.d.), and acted as 'chairman' rather than 'chief' of Irish government (Farrell, 1971b). In short, the Irish cabinet lacked strong leadership – moreover, the decision to remove Mulcahy and the Army Council was taken in Cosgrave's absence – and Mulcahy's cabinet colleagues were men of lesser or equal political stature.

Added to this, the Army Council had good reason to refuse to resign. They had, once again, defended the government against rebellious forces. And yet, they were harshly treated when they arrested mutineers that the Executive Council had agreed to let of the hook. This created considerable resentment among general staff officers who were loyal to the Army Council. Many of them were reportedly surprised that the Army Council 'were accepting the situation so calmly' (Valiulis, 1992: 216). Some of these officers would, in all likelihood, have supported the army leaders had they refuse to resign. As one newspaper observed at the time, they would have had good reason to do so:

> Mutiny has been condoned, and resignation has been the fate of those responsible persons who refused to condone it. Soldiers are simple men, but they can put 'two and two' together. The 'two and two' of this case are represented by the facts that the mutinous ultimatum demanded the removal of the army council and that the army council has been removed (*Irish Independent*, 1924).

The Executive Council must have been reassured by the fact that not all the press reports were favourable to the army. Moreover, nobody stood up in the Dáil to criticise the government for its treatment of the Army Council except Mulcahy himself. But against this, the Army Council made it remarkably easy for the Executive Council to get rid of them. There was considerable confusion at the time as to what was happening, confusion that even encompassed the possibility of a coup d'état. Nervously studying the Irish newspapers while abroad, my grandfather wrote to his father, John Dillon, on 22 March: 'I confess than I am extremely confused as to what is really happening, or who is trying to bring off a *coup d'état*' (Dillon, 1924). The Army Council could have used this climate of confusion and fear to their advantage. Instead, all tended their resignations immediately, except the Army Chief of Staff, General Séan MacMahon, who did so after some brief protest. Both Mulcahy and MacMahon sharply reprimanded certain officers for suggesting that they ignore the order to resign. In addition, Mulcahy publicly declared that he expected his replacement to 'get absolute and scrupulous service from every officer in the army'. According to the Adjutant-General, he and the Quartermaster-General summoned all general staff officers 'to advise them to stand loyal to the government and forget us' (Valiulis, 1992: 216).

Political enfeeblement of the army established the conditions for its strategic enfeeblement. The point is that, had the army been well resourced, then it would have made sense for it to develop a conventional strategy and organisational structure modelled on the British army. It was the army's inability to secure sufficient resources that made such a choice of strategy and organisation senseless. This point was not lost on those army intelligence officers who recommended in the early 1930s that the army be re-modelled on the IRA. Instead, army leaders also freely chose a force structure and war plan for their organisation that was wholly inappropriate given the resources available to them.

Now it could be argued that a conventional strategy and force structure was dictated by civilian intervention or indeed by the logic of army self-interest. But neither argument holds much water. For a start, civilian policy makers had little interest in how the army should organise for war. Three years after the Free State had come into existence, the government had still not formulated a policy for the country to defend itself. In the end, army leaders had to send a memorandum to the Executive Council to remind civilian policymakers of 'the urgent and absolute necessity for placing us in the possession of at least the outlines of the defence policy of the government' (DOD, 1925: 1). To the extent that some interest was shown, politicians in the Dáil and in successive governments appear to have expected that the army would simply revert to a guerrilla campaign should Ireland ever be invaded (Farrell, 1998: 76–7).

Similarly, historical evidence does not show that the army's choice of structure and strategy was dictated by organisational self-interest. Here the argument would be that army chiefs may have ignored G-2's plan because, by offering a way to defend the country within the existing limited level of resources, it threatened the army's 1932 build-up programme. However, the army had every reason to have few expectations for this programme. From its very foundation, the army's various proposals had been blocked or drastically cut by the Department of Finance. Typical on this score was the army's 1933 tank programme. In the 1930s, tanks were the badge of the modern military, and this programme was central to the army's larger modernisation plan. The army view was that 'national economic and defence policy demand that tanks should be manufactured in Ireland'. Thus, in January 1934, it proposed purchasing a completed tank from a Swedish firm and components for two additional tanks along with assembly instructions, 'with a view to gaining the practical experience which would be invaluable when the more ambitious programme is undertaken'. Needless to say, Finance officials strongly disagreed with the army's proposal. They saw 'no future for any Irish firm in the manufacture or even in the assembly of tanks'. Finance officials also warned their minister that '[t]his is the sort of thing that once started cannot be stopped and must be carried out to the bitter end, no matter what the cost'. In the end, the army obtained only two tanks in the late 1930s. Of these, one was completely destroyed in an accidental fire during tests in Sweden, while the other broke down in tests in Ireland (Farrell, 1997: 120–1). Notwithstanding Finance's uncompromising line, the army continued to press for a corps size (three division strong) field force right up to the end of 1937. The following year, however, the army proposed a field army of just two reinforced brigades. Even this extremely modest proposal was treated harshly by Finance officials who reasoned that 'provided we make it clear that we have no intention of allowing this country to be used in any way antagonistic to the security of Britain, the possibility of any attack from Britain may be ignored' (Farrell, 1998: 77). So however much they wanted a modern conventional force structure, the army leadership were not going to get it.

'Framing' the Irish army

Self-destructive behaviour by an organisation clearly cannot be explained in terms of the interaction of vested interests within that organisation. For this, we must turn to cultural accounts of organisational behaviour. In other words, it was the army's culture that ruled out military disobedience of civilian authorities and led the army to abandon its guerrilla warfare tradition in favour of a conventional warfare force structure and strategy.

Organisational culture is comprised of beliefs and norms about the ways things are and ought to be that are shared by the members of an organisation. From these, actors in organisations construct shared understandings of the social and physical environment in which they operate, and of the goals of their organisation. These shared understandings of the world and of organisational goals provide frames through which actors in organisations determine what they should and can do. As Lynn Eden explains:

> Frames are ways of knowing and doing by those in an organisation, coherent sets of organizing ideas and practices that structure how actors in organisations identify problems and find solutions. Frames incorporate assumptions and knowledge about the world, articulate or assume purpose, define problems, and shape the search for solutions (1995: 33).

Frames thus define organisational activity and capacity.

In line with the view of culture as a 'tool kit' which may offer a menu of ways of organising and doing (Swidler, 1986), Eden notes that organisational culture contains many frames, some of which may clash (1995: 36). Some frames take root and thrive in organisations, while others can wane and even die out. In this way, organisations change their forms, capacity, and activity over time.

Irish army culture contained two competing frames: a guerrilla warfare frame and a conventional warfare frame. These frames provided contradictory views of how the army should act and organise itself. The guerrilla warfare frame emphasised the IRA as a model for the army, and so prescribed a decentralised organisation that would be able to operate independently of state support and civilian control. The conventional warfare frame pointed to the British army as a model for the army, and so prescribed a centralised organisation that was highly reliant on the state for resources and political direction.

Both these frames were contained within the army's predecessor, the IRA. As it happens, the Irish rebels who rose up in 1916 wore military uniforms and acted like regular soldiers. This was their undoing: the British had little difficulty in locating the rebels and blasting them out of their static defensive positions. The War of Independence was a whole different ball game. The IRA were harder to find because many were part-timers who blended back easily into the populace, while full-timers in IRA active service units formed highly mobile 'flying columns'. Instead of directly engaging the British military, IRA units favoured assassination, sniper attacks, and hit-and-run raids. Despite this mix of unconventional units and tactics, the IRA general staff attempted to professionalise their organisation by establishing standards of dress, conduct, training, planning and operations. In so doing, it promoted military practices more closely associated with conventional than guerrilla armies, such as the 'close order drill' (GHQ, 1920). Driving this was Mulcahy as IRA chief of staff. Mulcahy was particularly concerned with developing a professional officer corps for the IRA. To this end, he ordered all IRA field divisions to set up training camps for the purpose of providing uniform training for IRA officers as laid down by GHQ (GHQ, 1921). The volume of directives flowing from IRA GHQ in Dublin out to field units lent the impression of a 'unified' and 'cohesive' fighting organisation (Bowden, 1973). In reality, the responsiveness of IRA field units to GHQ directives varied greatly from unit to unit, and from directive to directive. Certainly, nothing like a standard officer corps was achieved. In many cases units kept the incompetent and lazy officers they had elected precisely because these officers kept their units out of action. Meanwhile, the most militarily active and hard-pressed IRA field units in the South and West of Ireland were also unresponsive to GHQ direction because they resented the lack of material support from Dublin (Augusteijn, 1996; Hart, 1998; Townshend, 1983: 336–8; Townshend, 1987). Thus, while the military leadership attempted to promote the conventional warfare frame, the guerrilla warfare frame dominated IRA field practice.

Originally, the IRA was supposed to have been reformed into the Irish army in late 1921, but then came civil war. While the IRA general staff were pro-Treaty, most IRA field units were opposed to the Treaty with Britain and the Free State that resulted from it. Thus the IRA general staff, which formed the general staff of the Free State army, had to pull together urgently a new army to defend the new state against IRA rebels. The British model was adopted out of necessity, and this provided the primary mechanism through which the conventional warfare frame became institutionalised in Irish army culture. Lacking the expertise to devise their own organisational structure and routines, the general staff later explained that 'it was essential that we adopt some foreign system as a model, to train and experiment with, and as our armament and equipment was British this was as good a model to adopt as any other' (GS, 1934: 55). As this quotation suggests, the Irish general staff intended to use the British model as the basis from which to evolve a military system suitable for Irish strategic circumstances. But, as things turned out, the British model provided the blueprint for the enduring pattern of Irish military organisation and behaviour.

Army discourse in the 1930s shows an obsession with professionalising the organisation along conventional lines, combined with a complete lack of interest in guerrilla warfare. Out of around 300 substantive articles on military matters published in Irish army's professional journal *An tÓglách* between 1927 and 1933, only two were on guerrilla warfare: one was reprinted from the British army's journal, and the other was an unfinished paper originally written shortly after the Irish War of Independence. Similarly, in preparing Ireland's defences at the outbreak of the Second World War, army planners studied carefully the recent experiences of foreign armies (particularly in mechanised warfare), all the while ignoring Ireland's own experience in guerrilla warfare. This neglect of guerrilla warfare in favour of conventional warfare was institutionalised in army training. Less than one per cent of the army's command and staff course in the 1930s was devoted to guerrilla warfare. In contrast, chemical warfare took up six per cent of the course, despite the fact that the army had no ability to defend against, let alone use, chemical weapons. A similar total concentration on conventional field operations was contained in the Army's training directives in the early 1940s: guerrilla operations received a cursory three-line mention in just one three-page directive. Clearly, in the new Irish army, the conventional warfare frame predominated while the guerrilla warfare frame was removed (Farrell, 1998: 80–1).

But how does a frame come to thrive in an organisation and, equally, how does a frame come to die out? Eden gives two possible answers. The first, which she favours, draws on the sociology of technology (Bijker et al., 1987). It sees the fate of organisational frames as being tied to 'large loose networks of actors working within the assumptions and problems of each frame' (Eden, 1992: 42–3). For instance, in our case, the GHQ embodied the conventional warfare frame within the IRA, and G-2 branch embodied the guerrilla warfare frame within the army. Eden's study suggests that if the actors within a frame leave the organisation, or are marginalised within that organisation, then that frame will wane and may eventually die.

Eden's second possible answer, which she ultimately rejects, draws on new institutionalist theory of organisations. It suggests that the perception by organisational actors of a radical change in their environment can lead to a re-ordering of ideas, and hence frames, within the organisation (Eden, 1995: 42–3). New institutionalism presents the cognitive components of organisational culture as coming from the environment of an organisation, rather than from within the organisation itself. Culturally speaking, organisations are thus 'open systems' (Scott, 1992). Organisational environments are defined in functional rather than geographical terms, as organisational fields that are approximately coterminous with the boundaries of industries, professions, or national societies. It is by being institutionalised in functional organisational fields, that beliefs and norms 'come to take on a rule like status in social thought and action' within organisations (Meyer and Rowan, 1991: 42). In this way, the environment 'penetrate[s] the organisation, creating the lenses through which actors view the world and the very categories of structure, thought, and action' (DiMaggio and Powell, 1991: 13). Because they structure the thoughts and actions of organisational actors, frames are taken for granted, and so are stable and long lasting. For this reason, it is commonly assumed that institutional change occurs abruptly and only on rare occasions of sudden and massive environmental change that cause existing beliefs, norms and frames to be thrown into doubt.

Eden does not accept this explanation of cultural change within military organisations on the grounds that 'military services are buffered from external shock' in ways that, for example, 'corporations in market economies are not'; military organisations do not have to compete systematically with each other as other organisations have to, and much military work is kept secret. She concludes that 'military organisations in peacetime are relatively insulated from external shock and should be quite resistant to changes in frames' (Eden, 1995: 43). I think that Eden overstates the case here. While militaries may be less affected by radical environmental change than other types of organisations, it does not mean that they are immune to such change (Farrell and Terriff, 2002).

How then did the conventional warfare frame come to dominate the new army? Consistent with Eden's favoured explanation, we see the Irish civil war producing a large-scale turnover of army personnel with key beliefs, in that it led to the exclusion of those members of the IRA with most commitment to the guerrilla warfare frame. These were the most active fighting units of the IRA in Southern and Western Ireland who rebelled against the Irish Free State. In consequence, less than one tenth of the new 50,000-strong army were former IRA members. Furthermore, as noted already, many officers with IRA experience were demobilised following the civil war while at the same time a number of ex-British officers, who were socialised into the conventional warfare frame, were commissioned in the Irish army (Costello, 1924: 10–12).

But also critical was a major change in the institutional environment within which the IRA and Irish army operated, defining the institutional environment in terms of political norms, practices and institutions. In *The Founding of Dáil Éireann* (1971a), Brian Farrell identifies two political traditions in Irish society, namely, the revolutionary tradition and the constitutional tradition. The constitutional tradition advanced the cause of Irish nationalism by operating *within* the British political system. Thus constitutional nationalists formed the Irish Parliamentary Party to compete in the British parliament. Here Farrell sees a century's long mutually constitutive process between Irish political practice and British political institutions, with each shaping and reinforcing the other. In contrast, the revolutionary tradition advanced the cause of Irish nationalism by operating *outside* the British political system. This included the construction of uniquely Irish structures and practices. Secret societies were formed, most notably the Irish Republican Brotherhood (IRB), to generate political and military pressure to push Britain out of Ireland (Farrell, 1971a; see also Cronin, 1980; Garvin, 1996).

Before 1916, the constitutional tradition was more prominent. Indeed, the Easter Rising in 1916 was launched by the IRB without much popular support. It was two events after the Easter Rising – brutal British reprisals against the rebels and the threatened extension of conscription to Ireland for the Great War in Europe – that mobilised public support in Ireland for the revolutionary tradition and led to the War of Independence. Hence the institutional environment of the IRA was dominated by the revolutionary tradition in Irish political culture. With the end of the War of Independence, the constitutional tradition once again dominated Irish political culture. This explains the ease with which the Irish government modelled itself on the British government. For the most part, it merely took over the administrative structures and practices that had existed under the British, and even kept on many British civil servants (Fanning, 1986). It is not surprising then that the conventional warfare frame should come to dominate the organisational culture of the new army. It would have seemed 'natural' for the army leadership to model the Irish army on its British equivalents, since that was what the rest of the Irish government was doing. Structures and routines developed by the IRA were assumed to be irrelevant, not least because the IRA was essentially an amateur army. In contrast, army leaders were very concerned with acting and appearing as professionals. I would suggest that this also explains why the army submitted to harsh treatment by civilian authorities; following the British model, Irish army leaders simply believed that professional armies do not disobey their civilian masters.

Irish military weakness thus presents us with an historical puzzle. In tackling the puzzle, I have argued that the political and strategic enfeeblement of the Irish army was the product of choices by army leaders, and that these choices were determined by the organisational culture of the army. In this way the army committed suicide. I have suggested that the organisational culture of the Irish army contained two competing frames – a conventional warfare frame and a guerrilla warfare frame – each providing a contradictory view of how the army should act and organise itself. It was the dominance of the conventional warfare frame in army culture that led army leaders to forget their guerrilla tradition, to emulate the British army, and to submit themselves to harsh treatment by the government.

Bibliography

Augusteijn, Joost (1996) *From Public Defiance to Guerilla Warfare.* Dublin: Irish Academic Press.

Bijker, Wiebe, Thomas P. Hughes and Trevor J. Pinch (eds) (1987) *The Social Construction of Technological Systems.* Cambridge, MA: MIT Press.

Bowden, Tom (1973) 'The Irish underground and the War of Independence, 1919–21', *Journal of Contemporary History* 8: 3–23.

Boyd, R. (1945) 'Memorandum on "Present commitments and future policy and programme" period about 1937'. 9 February, Bryan Papers, P71/27, UCD Archives.

Costello, Colonel Michael J. (1924) 'Report to Chairman of Army Inquiry Committee', 22 April, MJC 5, Irish Military Archives.

Cronin, Seán (1980) *Irish Nationalism: A History of its Roots and Ideology.* Dublin: Academy Press.

Department of Defence (DoD) (1925) 'Memo to Executive Council Re. Defence Policy', Blythe Papers, P24/107, UCD Archives.

Department of Finance (DOF) (1924) 'Minutes of conference held in the President's room on the 22nd', 23 April, D/F S/4/80/24, NAI.

Dillon, Theo (1924) Letter to John Dillon, 22 March, Dillon Papers, P126/68, UCD Archives.

DiMaggio, Paul J. and Walter W. Powell (1991) 'Introduction', pp. 1–38 in Powell and DiMaggio (eds), *The New Institutionalism in Organizational Analysis.* Chicago: University of Chicago Press.

Duggan, John P. (1991) *A History of the Irish Army.* Dublin: Gill & Macmillan.

Eden, Lynn (1992) 'Learning and forgetting: the development of organizational knowledge about US weapons effects', paper presented at the American Political Science Association annual conference, Illinois.

Eden, Lynn (1995) Constructing Destruction: The Making of Organizational Knowledge about the Effects of Nuclear Weapons', draft ms (forthcoming as *Whole World on Fire.* Ithaca, NY: Cornell University Press).

Fanning, Ronan (1978) *The Irish Department of Finance, 1922–58.* Dublin: Institute of Public Administration.

Fanning, Ronan (1986) 'Britain's legacy', pp. 45–63 in P. J. Drudy (ed.), *Irish Studies 5: Ireland and Britain Since 1922.* Cambridge: Cambridge University Press.

Farrell, Brian (n.d.) 'W. T. Cosgrave: Leader by Accident', unpub. ms.

Farrell, Brian (1971a) *The Founding of Dáil Éireann: Parliament and Nation Building.* Dublin: Gill & Macmillan.

Farrell, Brian (1971b) *Chairman or Chief? The Role of Taoiseach in Irish Government.* Dublin: Gill & Macmillan.

Farrell, Theo (1997) '"The model army": military imitation and the enfeeblement of the Irish army', *Irish Studies in International Affairs* 8: 111–27.

Farrell, Theo (1998) 'Professionalization and suicidal defence planning by the Irish army, 1921–1941', *Journal of Strategic Studies* 21 (3): 67–85.

Farrell, Theo and Terry Terriff (eds) (2002) *The Sources of Military Change: Culture, Politics, Technology.* Boulder, CO: Lynne Rienner Press.

Fitzpatrick, David (1978) 'The Geography of Irish Nationalism, 1910–1921', *Past and Present* 78: 113–44.

Flynn, James (Major) (1940) 'Memo: General defence plan 2 – final outline', 29 November, Emergency Defence Plans (EDP) 1/2, Irish Military Archives.

G-1 (Plans and Operations Branch) (1940) 'Memorandum No. 2: Observations on general staff estimate of the situation no. 1', EDP 1, Irish Military Archives.

Garvin, Tom (1996) *1922: The Birth of Irish Democracy.* Dublin: Gill & Macmillan.

General Headquarters (GHQ) (1920) *An Introduction to Volunteer Training.* Irish Republican Army (IRA). Mulcahy Papers, P7a/22, UCD Archives.

GHQ (1921) *Training Manual.* IRA. Mulcahy Papers, P7a/22, UCD Archives.

General Staff (GS) (1934) 'Estimate of the situation that would arise in the eventuality of a war between Ireland and Great Britain', no. 1, October, DP/00020, Irish Military Archives.

GS (1936) 'Fundamental factors affecting Saorstát defence problem', May, G2/0057, Irish Military Archives.

GS (1940) 'Outline of General Defence Plan No. 2 (Final Draft)', 28 November, EDP 1/2, Irish Military Archives.

GS (1943) 'Report on Army Exercises', Parts I & II, January, Irish Military Archives.

Hart, Peter (1998) *The IRA and Its Enemies.* Oxford: Oxford University Press.

Hart, Peter (1999) 'The social structure of the Irish Republican Army, 1916–1923', *Historical Journal* 42: 207–31.

Irish Independent (1924) 'The press on the army crisis', 21 March, D/Taoiseach S3694, NAI.

Meyer, John W. and Brian Rowan (1991) 'Institutionalized organizations: formal structure as myth and ceremony', pp. 41–62 in Paul J. Powell and Walter W. DiMaggio (eds), *The New Institutionalism in Organizational Analysis.* Chicago: Chicago University Press.

Mitchell, Arthur (1995) *Revolutionary Government in Ireland.* Dublin: Gill & Macmillan.

O'Halpin, Eunan (1994) 'The army and the Dáil', pp. 107–22 in Brian Farrell (ed), *The Creation of the Dáil.* Dublin: Gill & Macmillan.

O'Halpin, Eunan (1999) *Defending Ireland: The Irish State and Its Enemies Since 1922.* Oxford: Oxford University Press.

Powell, Walter W. (1991) 'Expanding the scope of institutional analysis', pp. 183–203 in Paul J. Powell and Walter W. DiMaggio (eds), *The New Institutionalism in Organizational Analysis.* Chicago: Chicago University Press.

Scott, W. Richard (1992) *Organizations*, 3rd edn. Englewood Cliffs, NJ: Prentice Hall.

Swidler, Ann (1986) 'Culture in action', *American Sociological Review* 51 (2): 273–86.

Townshend, Charles (1983) *Political Violence in Ireland.* Oxford: Oxford University Press.

Townshend, Charles (1987) 'The Irish Republican Army and the development of guerrilla warfare, 1916–1921', *English Historical Review* 94: 318–45.

Valiulis, Maryann Gialanella (1985) *Almost a Rebellion: The Irish Army Mutiny of 1924*. Cork: Tower Books.

Valiulis, Maryann Gialanella (1992) *Portrait of a Revolutionary: General Richard Mulcahy and the Founding of the Irish State*. Dublin: Irish Academic Press.

Young, Peter (1993–4) 'Defence and the new Irish state, 1919–1939', *Irish Sword* 19: 1–10.

CHAPTER SIX

The role of Taoiseach: Chairman or chief?

GARRET FITZGERALD

—

Even for someone who has held that office, it appears almost presumptuous to write about the role of the Taoiseach in a *Festschrift* in honour of Brian Farrell. However, that does not seem sufficient reason to refuse to contribute to this volume and, in any event, there are some aspects of this subject upon which either Brian did not touch or in relation to which I feel I may be able to add some new material. However, it must be said at the outset that, whilst it is over 30 years since he wrote *Chairman or Chief?*, on re-reading it now one cannot help being struck by how relevant all of it remains today – and how sound Brian Farrell's judgements then were on so many matters about which at the time he wrote there simply did not exist archival information.

The many roles of a Taoiseach

The roles of a Taoiseach are multiple. At the outset, there is the task of appointing his Cabinet and ministers for state, and perhaps subsequently making necessary changes in these positions. Cabinet business has to be organised, and the Taoiseach has to chair and lead the government, initiating policy development and also encouraging this process amongst his Cabinet members. He has to decide on priorities for legislation; settle parliamentary business through his Chief Whip; and establish from time to time ad hoc Cabinet committees with appropriate membership to deal with issues involving more than one department.

In carrying out these tasks, he must work closely with the Minister for Finance on financial and economic policy and on the preparation of the annual budget and long-term capital programmes. He must also work with the Minister for Foreign Affairs on foreign policy and EU matters, including preparations for European Council meetings of heads of government, and also on Northern Ireland policy, in which the Taoiseach's lead role also involves close consultation with the minister for Justice and the Attorney-General. Security matters involve close liaison with the Minister for Justice and, in certain circumstances, with the Garda.

The Taoiseach also has to monitor appointments to the judiciary and to state boards. He must be in daily communication with the Government Press Office and with his political advisers about the presentation of the government's activities to the public, and must be available to journalists as a group or individually.

At the same time as leader of his political party he has to be sensitive to, and keep in close touch with, his parliamentary party both directly and through the party whip, as well as with his party headquarters, his party executive, and his party organisation in 40-odd constituencies throughout the country. Moreover, in a coalition – and save for a brief period of minority government between 1987 and 1989, all Irish governments for the past twenty years have been coalitions – he also has to work in close consultation with the leader, or leaders, of coalition partners.

He is expected to attend frequently, and almost always to address, a wide range of public bodies of one kind or another, which involves either the pre-paration of speeches, or supervision of this process if speechwriting is being undertaken by advisers or civil servants. Finally unexpected 'events' – the greatest hazard of political life – have to be handled without delay, and in a manner that will prevent them from spiralling out of control, which they all too readily do with the enthusiastic help of the ever-vigilant media. Overall, this is a quite bewildering, indeed intimidating, array of tasks for any one person to under-take, even with the assistance of able civil servants in the Cabinet Secretariat and Department of the Taoiseach, and of his political advisers.

Taoiseach and Cabinet

Each Taoiseach has his own style of cabinet leadership – both in relation to interventionism in certain departmental areas, and in relation to the manner in which the Cabinet takes decisions. On the first point, a Taoiseach may at one extreme be largely content to let ministers get on with their work, under what might by called light supervision; whilst, at the other extreme, a Taoiseach may, unwisely, try to run every department himself, or at any rate the key ones – Finance and Foreign Affairs. I believe that in recent decades we have had examples of both of these approaches.

On the second point, a Taoiseach may either allow the Cabinet to decide issues by democratic vote, offering his own view but ultimately allowing himself to be over-ridden by a Cabinet majority, or he may make it clear that on certain issues at least he intends to lead, and expects the rest of the Cabinet to accept that lead, whilst allowing, or even encouraging, ministers to raise queries on aspects of the issue in question. And, in a coalition Cabinet, he may – indeed, if he is wise, will – operate in close liaison with the other party leader(s). In such cases, neither a purely democratic decision-making system by majority vote, nor one of decision-making from the top down, will work for most issues, and a complex system of negotiation will be needed in order to secure decisions that will command a consensus of parties and ministers.

All three of these approaches were employed in the governments that I led. The issues we had to deal with included Northern Ireland, in respect of which the Cabinet knew that I intended to determine both the broad lines of policy and the detail of its application, in close liaison with the members of a small Northern Ireland committee comprising the Tanaiste, ministers for Foreign Affairs and Justice, the Attorney-General, and key officials. On this issue, my Cabinet was, however, kept regularly informed. During the Anglo-Irish negotiation of 1984–5 there were, I think, more than half-a-dozen Cabinet discussions on the negotiations, based upon information memoranda that at intervals set out the 'state of play' in the talks. Members of the cabinet who were not on the Northern Ireland committee could, and did, raise many queries on these occasions, expressing doubts and worries freely, which was often very helpful. But they did not seek to challenge the thrust of the policy being pursued.

On one other issue upon which I was known to have strong views – the maintenance of the level of development aid at a time when cuts were being imposed in almost every other area – neither the Minister for Finance nor the Cabinet expected to be able to change my mind, and did not seek to do so. All other issues were settled by agreement, sometimes by democratic vote that quite often went against my own view. But, in two areas, agreement, understandably, was hard to secure between the parties in government. One was an ideological issue: how best to stimulate industrial development through a National Development Corporation – a matter upon which the Tanaiste and leader of the Labour Party, Dick Spring, and the Minister for Industry and Commerce, John Bruton, held strongly divergent views.

The other area upon which consensus had to be secured, and which could not be dealt with either by diktat from above or by a democratic vote of ministers, was that of cuts in public spending. This is always a most difficult matter to settle, but never more difficult than in the years from 1981 onwards. For in June 1981, when I first became Taoiseach, the financial and economic situation that we inherited from our predecessors threatened a borrowing rate of almost 21 per cent of GNP in 1982, exclusive of the capital needs of state enterprises. No previous Irish government since the outbreak of the Civil War had ever faced a financial crisis of this magnitude. We had to decide both how rapidly we could wind down this borrowing rate without precipitating a collapse of the economy and also what combination of tax increases, cuts in capital spending, and reductions in current spending would best achieve the targets we had set ourselves for reduction of borrowing. In the event, by 1987 we had halved this threatened borrowing rate to just over ten per cent of GNP.

The details of how this financial and economic crisis was handled are, however, a matter of history; all that needs to be said here is that this issue necessarily imposed great strains on Cabinet decision making in that coalition, and required almost endless negotiations, in order to avoid a breakdown. It was only after more than four years that it led to a low-key and friendly departure of Labour ministers from the government, much regretted by all concerned, and then to a dissolution of the Dáil.

An earlier coalition government, in which I was Minister for Foreign Affairs, had also faced financial difficulties of a somewhat less extreme character during the first oil crisis, but these did not impose as much strain on that coalition partnership as was the case a decade later. Incidentally, in that government Liam Cosgrave felt able to adopt a fairly laid-back style of Cabinet leadership, partly because he enjoyed the respect of all his Cabinet members, including those in Fine Gael who had earlier been unhappy about aspects of his leadership in opposition, but also of the Labour ministers who appreciated the considerate and generous way in which he dealt with them. He, and the Labour leader and Tanaiste, Brendan Corish, were of course the only two members of the government with previous ministerial experience, and Liam Cosgrave was older than any other member of the government except Conor Cruise O'Brien. As I remarked in my autobiography (FitzGerald, 1991), Cosgrave had an instinct for the exercise of authority combined with a reticence and a certain remoteness that did not encourage over-familiarity, with the result that where he had a strongly held view, most ministers were reluctant to challenge him. I should perhaps add that in the three coalition governments in which I participated, a warm personal relationship existed between Fine Gael Taoiseach and Labour Tanaiste – in my case reinforced by a common social democratic commitment.

I cannot, of course, speak for other Irish governments but it seems clear that, as Brian Farrell pointed out 30 years ago, for quite different reasons de Valera and Lemass were both pre-eminent amongst their peers (Farrell, 1971). In Lemass's case, this was because, as the youngest of the founders of Fianna Fáil, he came to power at a time when his energy clearly outstripped that of his older colleagues, and also because his talents were uniquely suited to the task of reviving a stagnant Irish economy by reversing the inward-looking policies of his predecessor in office and turning Ireland's gaze outwards towards the continent of Europe. By contrast, as Brian Farrell suggested, Jack Lynch suffered from the disadvantage of feeling less authentically Fianna Fáil than some of his rivals in the leadership of that party and was thus unable to dominate his first two governments – until he was tested in, and emerged successfully from, the heat of the Arms Crisis.

Cabinet committees

In contrast to the United Kingdom, the Irish Cabinet has retained its historic role as the centre of policy making; in domestic politics, the role of Cabinet committees has remained subordinate. By contrast in Britain, especially in the past two decades, prime ministers seem to have assumed an almost presidential role, ruling through Cabinet committees whose membership they determine with a view to securing their preferred policy outcome – which seems then normally to be rubber-stamped by a once-weekly two-hour Cabinet meeting. However, Irish Governments do have a small security committee of the Cabinet that deals with issues of national security which come before the full Cabinet only in rare instances. Moreover, as mentioned earlier, Northern Ireland policy is often guided by a similar committee, which, however, reports to Cabinet.

For the rest, Irish Cabinet committees are largely ad hoc affairs. However in the 1973–7 coalition, Cabinet committees were used to advance policy in three areas: economic and social policy and the reform of higher education. As I recall, the Taoiseach was not a member of these committees; they brought their recommendations to Cabinet where they were largely adopted. The first two committees proved successful, in my view; the third, on higher education, suffered, I think, from having too many academic members, like myself, who brought to it their views and prejudices formed in earlier university merger debates, and as a result it yielded no lasting results.

The Taoiseach and the President

One role of a Taoiseach about which little seems to have been written is that of keeping the President informed about political matters. It would be interesting to know how frequently various Taoisigh have carried out this function – some perhaps more frequently than others! Where the President has been a former politician, and where the Taoiseach of the day is a member of a different party across the floor of the House, one might imagine that such briefings would be infrequent and perhaps also uninformative. But, in fact, this may not always be the case. I can speak only about what I know, namely my own relationship with President Hillery. Whilst, like other Taoisigh, I may not have visited him as frequently as I ought, I have to say that the occasions when I did so remain in my mind as very positive encounters. I always endeavoured to inform him fully about what had been happening in the political sphere, and I was very happy to be able to discuss with him some of the problems I was facing. As a result, I benefited from his wise advice and counsel. As it happens, he was a man whom I had always respected, and who I knew to be concerned for the national interest rather than for the interests of what had been his own political party, which was then in opposition. The fact is that the office of Taoiseach is necessarily a lonely one, and there are sometimes matters that one can discuss freely with no one else in the political world. To be able to talk about such matters to an experienced politician, now above politics, can be very helpful. I found it so.

Of course, not every Taoiseach may have felt this to be the case. Thus, I doubt if Liam Cosgrave as Taoiseach had much political discussion with President de Valera, if indeed the opportunity for such an encounter presented itself during the brief period of eight weeks for which their respective terms of office overlapped.

Cabinet procedure

Moving on from the 'chairman or chief' issue, there are a number of more technical matters that a Taoiseach must concern himself with. One of these is the procedure by which matters come before the Cabinet. In accordance with the principle established by Michael Collins in September 1921, any proposal involving possible expenditure must be copied to the Minister for Finance, before it is brought to government, and he must be given sufficient time to prepare his comments on the financial implications of whatever may be proposed.

The Department of Finance tends to interpret this requirement fairly tightly, with the result that even when expenditure implications are indirect, or remote, it will still wish to have its say on any matter of this kind. Other ministers may resent, or try to evade, this discipline, and there is also a marked tendency for ministers to bring proposals to government, whether or not they have financial implications, without notifying other departments which may have an interest in the matter, or whose minister may wish to comment. Attempts to 'fast-track' proposals in this way have to be tightly controlled lest decisions be taken without adequate consideration by all those who may have something to contribute.

I found that there was a lack of clarity as to whether comments submitted on proposals coming to government emanated from the minister in question, or from their department. Sometimes one had to deduce from internal evidence which of these two sources was involved. I felt it necessary to require that this issue be clarified on the face of it, so that the minister's personal comments could be distinguished from those prepared at departmental level, some of which might be rather narrowly defensive of particular interests of the department in question.

Another problem that I found with these memoranda to government was that, quite frequently, there was a conflict on fact between the memorandum and the counter-memoranda from other ministers or departments. This could waste a lot of time in government arguing about the facts, and I found it necessary to insist that memoranda should not come to government until such factual issues had been sorted out at ministerial or departmental level.

Yet another problem was that of underlapping or overlapping of responsibilities. Sometimes one faced conflicting demands by ministers or departments to control particular activities. As well as problems of overlapping – where more than one department claims responsibility – disagreements would also arise where a new activity had to be undertaken and where no department or minister wished to be responsible for it! Both of these kinds of issues can be time consuming and difficult to resolve without exacerbating ministerial or departmental tensions. Whilst the use of aide-mémoires, as a means of bypassing the strict requirements in relation to memoranda to government, posed no problem when I was Taoiseach, it has been suggested to me that in a subsequent government the orderly organisation of government business was negatively affected by the use of such aide-mémoires as a means of securing government decisions without adequate consultation.

It has to be said that genuine problems arise from time to time because of a conflict between the need for adequate consultation and a real need, in some cases, for urgent action, and it is necessary to distinguish between these cases of genuine urgency and others where there may be an attempt to bypass government procedures by a spurious claim to urgency. In all these matters the Cabinet secretariat has a crucial role to play, and orderly and effective government depends greatly upon it.

Cabinet Secretariat and Taoiseach's Department

In this connection, it is necessary to distinguish between two distinct roles – that of the Cabinet secretariat on the one hand and that of the remainder of the Department of the Taoiseach on the other. Originally, I believe, Taoisigh were served solely by a Cabinet Secretariat. The emergence of other elements which have come to make up the Department of the Taoiseach was a relatively late development in the Irish constitutional system. In part this has reflected the growth of the scale of government activity and, thus, of the needs of Taoisigh for a wider range of assistance in carrying out their functions, and for a more extensive co-ordinating role vis-à-vis the various government departments. However, it would also appear that the size of the department of the Taoiseach, as it emerged about 20 years ago, owed something to the 1979 decision to abolish the recently established Department of Economic Planning and Development, many of the staff of which were transferred to the Department of the Taoiseach at that time. The dual roles of the Cabinet Secretary and the Secretary to the Department of the Taoiseach, within the context of the Department of the Taoiseach, seemed to me problematic, and the recent decision to combine these two functions in a single official appears to make good sense.

A Taoiseach has available to him assistance from a number of different sources. Like all ministers, he has a private office; he has the Cabinet secretariat to assist him with Cabinet business; he has the staff of his department; he has programme managers/advisers; and he has the Attorney-General as a legal adviser. The private office is headed by the private secretary. In the case of the Taoiseach, the private secretary remains in office even if the government changes, providing a measure of continuity between administrations. This is not the universal practice in government. For example, in the Department of Foreign Affairs, the minister's private office is cleared when a new minister is appointed so that ministers may exercise their own choice of private secretary and private office staff. When I became Taoiseach I was unaware of the different practice in the Taoiseach's Department and, in fact, appointed a private secretary who had worked in my private office in the Department of Foreign Affairs four years earlier. That was a decision that clearly came as an unwelcome surprise to the Department of the Taoiseach!

The role of a private secretary can be a difficult one. In the Irish system the level at which this appointment is made is several rungs down in the hierarchical system and the private secretary clearly has a long-term commitment to the department as well as a primary commitment to the Taoiseach, or minister in the case of other departments. Some of the issues involved in this situation were well ventilated in the *Yes Minister* television programme in the 1980s, but it must be said that, in the Irish system, officials traditionally handle this dual loyalty with great skill.

The Cabinet Secretariat assists the Taoiseach with all matters related to Cabinet business and, more generally, the Taoiseach will normally rely very heavily on the accumulated wisdom of whoever may hold this position, not merely in relation to purely Cabinet matters but also more generally. On the other hand, the Department of the Taoiseach provides back-up assistance to the Taoiseach in regard to a wide range of issues, and has an important co-ordinating role in regard to the operation of the government system. Members of its staff also have relationships with the social partners and with other outside bodies.

A Taoiseach, like other ministers, will normally bring with him a personal secretary to handle party-political and personal matters and, depending on the scale of his constituency work, that personal secretary may be assisted by a number of civil servants in dealing with problems that emerge from his local clinics. The scale of this kind of activity varies greatly between individuals. When I became Taoiseach in 1981 I discovered that my predecessor had a 'general office' of 16 civil servants, apparently dealing with constituency matters, which on my appointment immediately evaporated, for my own requirements in this respect were met by my personal secretary without civil service assistance

Advisers to the Taoiseach

The Taoiseach may also have an economic adviser, a process initiated by Jack Lynch in 1973, with the appointment of Professor Martin O'Donoghue, who later became a politician. My economic adviser, in both the governments I led, was Dr Patrick Honahan, a very distinguished economist who was able to play a particularly valuable role because of the very high regard in which he was held within the administrative system as well as outside the public sector.

Since 1973, ministers and Taoisigh at different times have employed political advisers/chefs-de-cabinet/programme managers to assist them with their work. There has, however, been a very large variation in the extent to which this system has been used in different governments. In the National Coalition government of 1973–7, most Labour ministers appointed people with expertise who had previously been associated with their party and, halfway through my period as Minister for Foreign Affairs, I appointed as an economic adviser a distinguished economist, Brendan Dowling. Other Fine Gael ministers did not, however, follow this practice at that time.

The need for an expert adviser of this kind arises from the fact that a minister is collectively involved in the whole process of cabinet government but, in relation to many matters that come before Cabinet, his or her department will, in the nature of things, be unable to offer expert advice on issues of policy outside their own remit. I found that despite my own economics background, the pressure of work as Minister for Foreign Affairs made it increasingly difficult for me to give Cabinet memoranda from other ministers the attention they deserved so as to enable me to contribute constructively to policy decisions in Cabinet. By preparing advice for me on matters coming to Cabinet, my economic adviser enabled me to perform my Cabinet function more effectively.

I also found that even though there were only a small number of such advisers in that government, by working together they were sometimes able to resolve problems rapidly which would have taken a very long time to sort out at the normal civil service level. An example of this was a critical shortage of potatoes that occurred at one point in the life of that government. This was resolved almost instantly by a decision initiated by several of the economic advisers in conjunction with the Department of Finance. (The Department of Agriculture failed to participate as a mark of their disapproval of this procedure!) It was quickly announced that the import of potatoes would be permitted in order to bring down the astronomical level to which prices had risen. Prices were, in fact, being held at twice the necessary level by the expedient of withholding stocks from the market, and in fact only 50 tonnes of potatoes needed to be imported in order to halve the price level. If this matter had been left to normal interdepartmental procedures, I believe that the Department of Agriculture would certainly have blocked this move.

As Taoiseach I encouraged ministers to appoint advisers of this kind and endeavoured to ensure that those concerned had genuine expertise to offer, and would not simply be political friends (or relations!) of ministers. Tight control was needed in this area, however, as there is an evident danger that ministers may use this facility to appoint public relations officers, designed to promote their personal image, a procedure which can be disruptive of Cabinet unity and action. In the Rainbow Coalition government of the 1990s, programme managers were appointed by virtually all ministers, and this greatly facilitated the co-ordination of government policy and the speedy implementation of policy decisions. However, as the subsequent government largely abandoned the programme manager system, it is clear that this innovation has yet to become a clearly established feature of the Irish government system.

A Taoiseach will normally also work closely with his Attorney-General. The role of the Attorney-General in the Irish system is greatly influenced by the rigidity of the Irish constitutional system under which, to an extent which does not exist in the rest of Europe outside Germany, courts exercise an important monitoring role on legislation, with the power to strike down an Act, or part of an Act, that they regard as impinging upon one or more of the human rights that are protected by the Constitution, either explicitly or implicitly.

Because of the constant danger that legislation might inadvertently contain some provision that might impinge upon one of these rights, the Irish Attorney-General has a crucially important role in all legislative matters. He attends virtually all Cabinet meetings and clears all legislative matters that might have constitutional implications. In carrying out this role, the Attorney-General has to work closely with the Taoiseach and this can lead to the emergence of an informal advisory role that can be of great value to the incumbent Taoiseach.

It may be noted that, by virtue of his role in endeavouring to ensure that governments do not inadvertently impinge upon constitutional rights, the Attorney-General is *de facto* undertaking an important libertarian role vis-à-vis the executive and the legislature, of a kind that does not seem to have a ready parallel elsewhere.

Finally, the Taoiseach will have the assistance of a government press secretary and government information bureau. In addition to ensuring the dissemination of government decisions, the government press secretary will also advise the Taoiseach on the presentation of these decisions and will keep him in touch with trends in media and public opinion.

Parliamentary questions

Like other ministers, the Taoiseach has to answer parliamentary questions. Indeed, because Taoiseach's Question Time occurs every week, whereas that of ministers rotates over a series of weeks, he is subject to questioning on a much more extensive scale than any other member of his Cabinet. Some of the questions addressed to the Taoiseach may, more properly, relate to functions of individual ministers, and such questions may then be transferred to the minister in question. At times, however, this process has been used improperly to divert or postpone answers to questions that might embarrass the government.

In my experience, replies drafted to parliamentary questions by civil servants tend to be somewhat minimalist, as they seek to protect a Taoiseach or minister from having to disclose more to the Dáil, and the public, than the Taoiseach or minister might wish to release. It is up to the Taoiseach to expand such replies in order to avoid the accusation of being too parsimonious in his answers to questions put to him by members of the Dáil.

Appointing and reshuffling ministers

Clearly one of the most important functions of the Taoiseach is the appointment of members of his government, both at Cabinet and junior ministerial level. In the Irish system, the choice of ministers whom the Taoiseach may regard to be best qualified may be subject to modification as a result of pressures to secure a wide geographical spread of ministerial appointments. This pressure derives from the public perception, which unfortunately is all too often validated by events, that ministers and, in particular, members of the Cabinet, have the power to divert resources to their own constituencies by influencing the allocation of investments, the location of government departments, or the provision of particular grants. To an extent that does not seem to be true of most other European countries, members of the Cabinet are seen by the public not so much as being involved in an exercise in collective responsibility in the general public interest as of having the function of exercising favouritism for the constituency from which they are elected. The abuse of Cabinet membership in this way is widely tolerated within the Irish political system and has to be seen as one of its major weaknesses.

In a coalition government, the selection of ministers from small parties is primarily a matter for the leader, or leaders, of the parties concerned, although clearly the positions to which they are to be nominated in government is something that will be open to discussion between the Taoiseach and the other leader or leaders involved.

There has been very little tradition of Cabinet reshuffles in Ireland during the lifetime of a government, apart from the replacement of a minister who dies or, for one reason or another, leaves office during that period. In 1986, I sought to undertake a reshuffle of my Cabinet, and of some junior positions, with a view to rejuvenating the government and providing opportunities to promote younger people. This attempted reshuffle was not a success, partly for reasons for which I am to blame, but this experience also showed that in Ireland there is strong resistance to the reshaping of a government during its lifetime contrary to the established practice elsewhere. Reshuffling is thus largely confined to the aftermath of a general election where a government is re-elected. This tradition clearly has some negative effects upon the quality of governments in Ireland.

Over the last 80 years the number of junior ministers – originally called parliamentary secretaries, but today known as ministers of state – has been radically increased to a point where their number exceeds that of the Cabinet ministers. (It is perhaps worth remarking here that it was only in 1973 that the number of Cabinet ministers appointed used up for the first time the full constitutional quota of 15 such places. Indeed, in the early days of the state, there were only seven members of the Executive Council, as the Cabinet was then called.)

It may be questioned whether the number of tasks that can be usefully delegated by members of the Cabinet is large enough to justify so many ministers of state. My own experience is that it is difficult to find useful delegated roles for more than seven or eight ministers of state and, unless specific delegation of a coherent body of tasks occurs, government ministers tend to be reluctant to allow much latitude to their junior ministers.

Seniority in government

For protocol purposes (for example, the order in which ministers follow the Taoiseach into the Dáil chamber at the start of business), the question of seniority in Irish governments is determined by the person rather than by the office. The date of first appointment as minister is the deciding factor in terms of such precedence.

However, it is clear from the persons who have been appointed to particular posts in recent decades that the seven ministries that are regarded as most important are Finance, Foreign Affairs, Agriculture, Enterprise Trade and Development, Public Enterprise, Local Government and Environment, and Justice. Four other areas have also been singled out in particular governments for the appointment of heavyweight ministers: Social Welfare, Health, Education and Labour. Areas such as Tourism, Arts, the Marine and, disturbingly, Defence, rate low on the priority scale of most Taoisigh.

Patronage

The patronage role of the Taoiseach is clearly of considerable importance. Taoisigh and/or the government ministers appoint eleven members of the Senate, as well as European Commissioners, Judges, and Directors of State bodies, amongst others. Appointments by Taoisigh to the Senate are normally made having regard to the party or parties in power gaining seats at a subsequent election, a process that is believed to be assisted by those concerned being nominated as Senators. However, Taoisigh have occasionally appointed one or two non-party people of distinction in particular fields and, since 1982, it has also been customary to make one or two appointments of people from Northern Ireland.

Up to the late 1970s, most appointments of Judges were seen to have been influenced by political considerations, such as the fact that, at some earlier stage of their careers, they had been active in support of the government in office. This tradition was broken in 1979 by Jack Lynch, and in the two governments that I led appointments to the higher courts were made without regard to party affiliations. Since then, the practice seems to have been fairly mixed. But for some time past in nominating judges of the higher courts, governments have confined themselves to choosing one name from seven to ten put forward by an independent body. However, the fact that this body is required to submit such a large number of names has meant that the possibility of political considerations being taken into account is normally not excluded; although, of course, this system at least ensures against the appointment of people who would be seen by their peers as unsuitable for office. I believe it would be desirable to reduce such lists down to three names.

Traditionally, appointments to state bodies have been very much influenced by political considerations. They have, in fact, been widely used to 'reward' people who have supported a party in power, either financially or by political activity. Unfortunately, a number of those appointed have not been well qualified to undertake the responsibilities involved in overseeing the affairs of state enterprises or boards, and I am convinced that this has been a contributory factor in several notable failures amongst our state enterprises.

Having had some experience of how this practice operated during my first, brief period in government, in my second government I introduced a procedure under which, before nominations were brought to government by ministers, the names first had to be submitted to me and the Tanaiste and Leader of the Labour Party, Dick Spring. This was done with a view to ensuring the appointment of suitable people, and also to ensuring that not more that one political appointment would be made to each board. Only in two cases that I can recall was this rule departed from, under ministerial pressure in government. Moreover, in the appointment of a new RTÉ Authority, I accepted not merely that only one political appointment be made, but the government actually set out to devise a composition for the Authority that would produce a body that would stand up to pressure from any government, including our own.

It is not clear that these procedures survived after the end of my second government in 1987 in the case of a number of state boards, although the quality of such appointments has seemed to improve.

Resignation of Taoiseach who has lost his majority

The Irish constitution provides that the Taoiseach shall resign from office upon his ceasing to retain the support of a majority in Dáil Éireann unless, on his advice, the President dissolves the Dáil and, on its re-assembly, the outgoing Taoiseach secures the support of a majority in the new parliament. The President may, at his absolute discretion, refuse to dissolve the Dáil, on the advice of a Taoiseach who has ceased to retain the support of the majority in the house.

No request for a dissolution has, in fact, ever been refused by a President. Governments have, of course, from time to time suffered defeats in the Dáil, for example on private members' motions, but in such cases they have normally re-established their authority by means of a successful vote of confidence. Where, however, a Taoiseach has been defeated on a major issue (for example the Budget in 1982), he has sought, and been given, a dissolution of Dáil Éireann by the President. In one instance, in 1994, when Albert Reynolds lost the confidence of the Dáil, following the withdrawal of the Labour Party from his Government, he did not seek a dissolution but instead resigned, and the Dáil proceeded to elect an alternative government, led by Fine Gael. In 1989, however, when the Dáil failed to elect a Taoiseach after the general election, the Taoiseach of the day did not resign until pressed to do so in the Dáil.

A potential problem arises where, following an election, no party leader secures a majority when the Dáil meets for the first time. Clearly, however, parties feel that it is their duty in such cases to work towards the formation of a government, even if this involves an alliance of parties not previously contemplated, as occurred in 1989 and again in 1992. Awkward situations of this kind arise because of the absence in the Irish case of any role for the President in the nomination of a Taoiseach, which is a part of the Head of State's functions in most European states.

Taoiseach and party leader

In addition to his public functions, the Taoiseach is also the leader of a major political party and some part of his time has to be absorbed by party activities. He attends meetings of his party's national executive and seeks to guide that body's decisions. Through his party's national organiser he keeps in touch with the party organisation and endeavours to ensure that adequate well-qualified candidates emerge to contest the next general election. From time to time he visits constituencies and addresses members of his party and, of course, his party conferences provide him with an opportunity to rally his supporters at national level.

These party functions are quite onerous and it is not always easy for a Taoiseach to combine them successfully with his other public role. Governments in office can all too easily lose contact with the rank and file of their parties, as a result of which they are often less well prepared for elections than oppositions, whose leaders have much more time to prepare for these occasions.

Bibliography
Brian Farrell (1971) *Chairman or Chief? The Role of Taoiseach in Irish Government.* Dublin: Gill & Macmillan.
FitzGerald, Garret (1991) *All in a Life: Garret FitzGerald, an Autobiography.* Dublin: Gill & Macmillan.

CHAPTER SEVEN

Paying for government

NIAMH HARDIMAN

—

Governments need money. Modern governments need lots of money. How they get this money and whom they take it from are two of the most difficult political issues faced in any modern political economy (Steinmo, 1993: 1)

Without taxation, there can be no government. All societies need tax revenues to provide salaries for politicians and civil servants. They need taxes to pay for teachers, medical staff and police. Taxes are needed to pay for roads, water supply, and waste disposal. Without tax revenues governments could not act effectively to alleviate poverty, help people through hard times such as unemployment and illness, or support people in their old age. In short, the whole range of government functions, which we mainly take for granted, or which only come to prominence when their shortcomings are being criticised, would not be possible without an adequate, steady, and reliable supply of revenue. As the American political scientist Theda Skocpol has noted, the tax base of government can shape and constrain its spending plans in important ways: 'A state's means of raising and deploying financial resources tells us more than could any other single factor about its . . . capacities to create or strengthen state organizations, to employ personnel, to co-opt political support, to subsidize economic enterprise, and to fund social programmes' (Skocpol, 1985: 17).

The manner in which states raise these resources – who pays, how much they pay, and indeed who does not pay – is an issue of central political importance. Differences in the priorities adopted by successive governments may be less important than the continuities. One of the paradoxical features of taxation is that a good tax is generally held to be simple, easy to administer, fair – and largely invisible (Peters, 1993: ch. 1). Taxes usually make headlines when people feel they have been unfairly treated, as for example in the employee protest marches on the streets of Irish towns and cities in 1979 and 1980; or when they feel that other people have been allowed to bend the rules, as in the case of

Ansbacher accounts and other tax-evasion schemes. But any combination of taxes implemented by government is politically significant, because every tax, or tax exemption, entails a judgement about how costs and benefits are going to be distributed.

Discussion of tax policy tends to be dominated by economists; it tends to focus on more technical aspects of tax design, or on the effects of taxes on market incentives, or on the distribution of income before and after taxes and transfers. There are many aspects of tax policy making and implementation to which political scientists can usefully contribute their complementary perspective. It would be entirely consistent with Brian Farrell's longstanding and keen engagement with the evolution of public policy – both in the academic domain, and in his role as challenging television journalist – to seek to open up some of these issues for further analysis and research.

The evolution of the tax system – in three snapshots

States raise their revenues in rather different ways. There is no consensus on what constitutes the best or optimal way of raising taxes. We may see how the profile of Irish revenues has changed over recent decades, relative to an aggregated profile of other countries' experiences, by taking three snapshot views. The dates chosen here are 1965, 1985 and 2000. We will look at how the profile of the tax system changed between these three points in time, by looking in turn at trends in total taxation, the composition of taxes, and the changing significance of income tax.

Total taxation

The first of our three dates, 1965, captures the situation as Ireland was entering a new phase of economic development, with the turn towards export-led growth and greater trade openness. Total Irish tax revenues at this point were somewhat below the European average, though well above the levels typical of the southern European countries that were comparable to Ireland in terms of economic development, and about comparable with the level of taxes raised by the USA.

The second snapshot portrays the revenue system at a time when tax revenue as a proportion of GDP had reached a peak. The mid-1980s were a time of great economic and social difficulties, when governments were struggling to manage economic recession while also dealing with huge repayments on the public

Niamh Hardiman

Table 7.1 **Total taxation as a proportion of GDP**

	1965	1985	2000
Ireland	24.9	35.0	31.1
OECD average	25.8	33.9	37.4
EU 15	27.9	38.8	41.6

Source: OECD *Revenue Statistics 1965–2001* (2002), Table 3, pp. 73–4.

debt. Unemployment was rife, and emigration was running high. Total taxes at this point exceeded the OECD average; most people, especially single employees, believed they were severely over-taxed, and that income tax in particular represented a crippling burden on their incomes. In return for these taxes they saw, not an expansion of public services – in line with more highly taxed countries elsewhere in Europe – but restrictions and even retrenchments in public expenditure.

By the time of our third snapshot in 2000, Ireland had had several years of the most rapid and sustained growth it had ever experienced. Many more people were at work, and unemployment was at record low levels. Tax revenues were very buoyant, a situation that was to continue until 2001. A decade of tax reform meant that most employees were now more lightly taxed. Even though taxes had been cut, rapid economic growth nonetheless resulted in increasing tax revenues. Yet GDP was growing even more rapidly, so tax expressed as a proportion of GDP shows a marked drop in spite of the growing tax intake.

The composition of taxes

Over time, not only can we see changes in the overall level of taxies levied, but we can also see big changes in the composition of taxation. As Table 7.2 shows, between 1965 and 2000, taxes on goods and services (such as VAT, customs and excise duties) declined from providing over half to about two fifths of total revenues. This is in line with trends in a number of other countries; a widespread move to more diversified sources of taxation can be discerned.

The significance of corporation tax has varied. Recession during the 1980s depressed its significance as a revenue source. By 2000, strong growth yielded higher and rising revenues from this source. Social security contributions, on both employers and employees, show a somewhat different pattern.

Table 7.2 **The composition of Irish taxes as a proportion of total taxation**

	1965	1985	2000
Personal income tax	16.7	31.3	30.8
Corporate tax	9.1	3.2	12.1
Employee social security	3.2	5.2	4.2
Employer social security	3.3	9.4	8.6
Property	15.1	4.0	5.6
Goods and services	52.6	44.4	37.2
Total tax revenue, €m.	317	8,586	32,153
GDP, €bn.	1.3	24.5	103.5
Tax as per cent of GDP	24.9	35.0	31.1

Source: OECD *Revenue Statistics 1965–2001* (2002), various tables.

Having risen until the mid-1980s, their contribution to overall revenues had fallen back by 2000.

The most striking trend, though, is the doubling in the significance of income tax between 1965 (that is, just five years after the adoption of the Pay-As-You-Earn or PAYE system of income taxation) and 1985. Between 1985 and 2000, despite the cuts in tax rates, income tax retained its importance as a source of taxation. Moreover, while income tax had been a good deal less important in Ireland than elsewhere in the OECD area in the 1960s, this situation had changed by 1985. And once again, despite the tax reforms – especially in employee income tax – during the 1990s, income tax was still relied on more heavily in Ireland than was typical elsewhere (though we must allow for the fact that there are considerable variations in the patterns in evidence across a range of countries – see Hardiman, 2002a).

Table 7.3 **Personal income tax as a proportion of total taxation**

	1965	1985	2000
Ireland	16.7	31.3	30.8
OECD average	26.1	29.7	26.0
EU 15	23.9	28.0	25.6

Source: OECD *Revenue Statistics 1965–2001* (2001), Table 11, p. 78

The distribution of income tax

What is striking about the changing profile of taxation is not only that income tax came to be so much more important as a revenue source, but also that the distribution of the burden has varied considerably over time. This is the main reason that it became a highly contentious issue during the 1970s and 1980s. Table 7.4 shows that single people earning the average industrial wage paid about 15 per cent of their earnings in tax and social insurance in 1965, and married people just over four per cent. Single people on somewhat higher earnings – double the average industrial wage came close to the pay of middle-ranking civil servants or middle managers in private enterprise – were paying a little higher, at just over 19 per cent, and married people about 14 per cent. People on very low earnings, half average industrial earnings, were not in the tax net at all at this point, and were liable only to social insurance contributions on their earnings.

Table 7.4 **Income tax and employee social security contributions as a proportion of direct earnings in Ireland in 1965, 1985, and 2000, for three income levels and two family types**

	1965	*1985*	*2000*
½ average industrial earnings, single	5.6	22.1	7.5
½ average industrial earnings, married + 2	5.6	8.5	—
Average industrial earnings, single	15.0	34.5	20.4
Average industrial earnings, married + 2	4.3	25.1	14.0
2 x average industrial earnings, single	18.6	49.4	34.4
2 x average industrial earnings, married + 2	14.0	35.8	24.4

Source: Author's own calculations. Earnings data are taken from *Statistical Abstracts* and *Statistical Bulletins*, Central Statistics Office, various years. Tax rates are calculated from Revenue Commissioners' Annual Reports, various years. Social Insurance liabilities are calculated from Department of Social Welfare Annual Reports, various years and Budget Books, various years. 'Married + 2' refers to a single-income married couple with two children. Tax treatment of married couples changed from the early 1980s; and the move to tax individualisation of two-earner married couples changed again from 2001; but these considerations do not affect the calculations shown here. Only statutory allowances are taken into account. See Hardiman (2002a).

By the mid-1980s, this situation had changed greatly. People earning the average industrial wage were now paying over one third of their earnings in tax and social insurance if single, a quarter if married. Those on twice the average industrial earnings were paying over one third if married, and just about half their earnings if single. Those on very low incomes now found themselves inside the tax net and liable to pay over one fifth of their earnings in tax and social insurance if single, and almost eight per cent if married. Between income tax and social insurance, revenue liability had at least doubled for most, and for some categories had grown fourfold.

What was even more striking was the growth in marginal tax rates. Table 7.5 shows that all categories of employees faced significantly higher tax and social insurance charges on each additional pound of earned income between 1965 and 1985.

Table 7.5 **Marginal rate of combined tax and social insurance for three income levels and two family types, 1965, 1985, 2000**

	1965	*1985*	*2000*
½ average industrial earnings, single	—	43.5	22
½ average industrial earnings, married + 2	—	8.5	—
Average industrial earnings, single	31.7	56.3	28.5
Average industrial earnings, married + 2	31.7	43.5	28.5
2 x average industrial earnings, single	31.7	62	46
2 x average industrial earnings, married + 2	31.7	50	46

Source: As for Table 7.4.

By 2000, however, we see that all income categories were being taxed much more lightly. Single people on very low incomes still found themselves in the tax net, and most of the improvements in their situation – until after 2000 at any rate – had come through reductions in social insurance liability; married people at this income level were now completely outside the tax net. Single employees on average and on twice-average industrial earnings had seen something like a 15-point drop in their liability, and married people a drop of a little over ten points.

Understanding tax changes

What accounts for these dramatic shifts in the profile of the Irish tax system, firstly between the mid-1960s and the mid-1980s, and secondly between the mid-1980s and the present day? We might think of our explanation as featuring three different elements. None of them works entirely separately, so the distinction can be somewhat artificial. But attempting to distinguish between them might nevertheless help to illuminate why things happened as they did.

The first element might be thought of as the inheritance of policy provisions which every government encounters when it assumes office. The revenue system needs stability and can be difficult to change quickly; moreover, governments are generally reluctant to modify taxes that are seen as reliable and that yield a good flow of income. This element of the explanation might be thought of as the 'inertia' of the system – more of the same (see Rose and Karan, 1987). For long periods there might be very little demand in a society for changes to the tax system, as long as most people think it is both efficient and fair. But even in the face of taxpayer discontent, governments may be unwilling to consider fundamental changes to any tax that has proven to be a reliable and sizeable source of revenue.

The second element, in contrast, might be thought of as featuring innovation, that is, deliberate decisions taken by government to introduce initiatives that alter the existing profile of the tax system. This might mean introducing new taxes, or it might mean a decision to change the effects of existing taxes. This would have to amount to something more than the year-on-year marginal adjustments of tax bands and allowances that are a normal part of the inertia of the tax system. There might be good reasons to expect that different political parties might evince different priorities, on issues such as who pays, and how much they pay, in the innovative decisions they take. But from time to time we may also expect to see a sea change in the fundamental principles that governments believe should underpin their tax strategy. As we shall see, a wave of new thinking about taxation spread widely and rapidly across the countries of the developed world during the latter half of the 1980s and into the 1990s, and Ireland was no exception.

The third element concerns the wider circumstances in which governments make decisions about continuing with existing tax instruments or changing the thrust of tax policy. Governments are of course sovereign when it comes to making tax policy. But they do not make it in circumstances of their own choosing, or not entirely at any rate. The economic environment in which the tax system is embedded may constrain governments' freedom of choice at some times, or permit greater freedom of manoeuvre at others. A set of tax measures might work quite well for a time. When economic circumstances change, continuing to run tax policy the same way may produce perverse incentives. In a buoyant economic environment, government may have more scope for initiative and innovation than in the middle of a recession. And finally, of course, membership of the EU may shape government's options and preferences in distinctive ways.

We have three elements of explanation to draw on: inertia, innovation and economic environment. We now turn to explore the relative importance of each over the two timespans in which we are interested.

Phase one: the rise and rise of income tax

The story of the tax system in our first time-frame – from the mid-1960s to the mid-1980s – is largely one of 'taxation by inertia', compounded by a narrowing in governments' options in the worsening economic environment that set in towards the end of the period, during the 1980s.

Taxation by inertia

At the start of the period in which we are interested, the Irish welfare state was not well developed by European standards, and spending on income maintenance and social services lagged developments in most continental countries. During the 1960s and 1970s, new spending commitments meant that Irish governments developed a growing need for steady revenue flows. We see some government interest in tapping new sources of revenue; this diversification may be thought of as a modernising trend in tax policy. For example, during the 1960s, Fianna Fáil governments introduced new forms of indirect taxation, which were consolidated in 1972 into the Value Added Tax.

But we have also noted that governments increased their dependence on income tax relative to other tax sources, as it was reliable, relatively easy to administer, and yielded a good revenue flow. As Gladstone once famously remarked, income tax provides government with 'a colossal engine of finance' (in 1853; cited in Réamonn, 1981: 37).

What is remarkable about this phase is how narrowly based the tax system remained, notwithstanding the need for a greater revenue yield. The story of who did not pay is just as interesting as the story of who did. In some cases, a relatively light tax burden was a matter of policy. From the 1950s, Ireland had been committed to tax-based incentives for industrial investment, initially targeted at exporting companies, then extended to all manufacturing industry. Low corporation tax rates were recognised as providing the foundation for the increased inflow of American and other foreign investments, especially once Ireland joined the European Economic Community (as it then was) in 1973.

But apart from the deliberate policy decisions to implement some preferential corporation tax rates, the distribution of the tax burden became increasingly skewed during the time period we are looking at here. People who were not inside the Pay-As-You-Earn net encountered relatively few efficient tax-gathering mechanisms. Farm income was not targeted effectively. And while farmers' earnings were still quite low during the 1960s, Ireland's accession to the EEC brought improvements for many. Income from self-employment and income from property were similarly subject to a fairly lax regime of self-assessment, and weak monitoring by the tax authorities made full compliance less than mandatory.

In these circumstances, governments depended ever more heavily on the 'colossal engine' of direct income tax, and indeed they relied increasingly on 'fiscal drag' to raise revenues from this source. Inflation started to become more pronounced from the late 1960s – well before the oil-price crisis that drove inflation spiralling upwards after 1973 – but governments failed to index allowances or to adjust tax bands accordingly. The result was that more and more people were drawn into the tax net – and found that more and more of their income was subject to tax and social insurance contributions. Between 1960 and 1975, while the numbers at work had grown by about 55,300, the number of individual taxpayers had expanded by more than ten times that number, from 220,000 to 740,000 (Byrne, 1989: 42). Indirect taxation was also perceived as inequitably distributed, adding to the grievances of many employees. With essentials such as food and clothing liable to VAT, the Household Budget Survey of 1980 reported that lower income households paid some 21 per cent of their incomes on indirect taxes, compared with 14 per cent among higher income households. Ireland is not the only country to have experienced tax revolt in such circumstances. Massive public discontent spilled out into street demonstrations; something had to be done.

Thwarted initiatives

Governments faced real political difficulties in any attempt to remedy the skewed tax system – any extension of the tax base was likely to encounter resistance from the groups affected. Significant initiatives had to await the advent to power of a coalition government of Fine Gael and Labour (1973–7). In an attempt to broaden the tax base, Fine Gael Minister for Finance, Richie Ryan, introduced three new taxes on different types of resources – a Capital Gains Tax, a Capital Acquisitions Tax, and a Wealth Tax. Sandford and Morrissey

(1985) document the extraordinary lobbying and opposition encountered by the government over these taxes. Quite independently of the merits of the taxes, the relatively privileged groups who would be affected by them mounted a sustained campaign of opposition. Fianna Fáil won power in 1977 amid promises not only to abolish the Wealth Tax, but also to remove other targeted sources of revenue, particularly domestic property rates and car tax, thereby throwing an even greater burden on the central exchequer and its existing revenue base. Electorally, this proved a winner. From the point of view of broadening and diversifying the tax base, however, it was a backward step.

Taxing farm incomes proved equally politically difficult. Fianna Fáil attempted to introduce a resource tax in 1979, but met with vociferous resistance from farmers, to which government acceded. The farmers' capacity to resist further encroachment by the tax authorities was strengthened by a Supreme Court decision in 1982 which deemed agricultural rates, hitherto the principal kind of tax paid by farmers, to be unconstitutional in virtue of their design and implementation (O'Connor, 1993).

During the latter half of the 1970s, both coalition and Fianna Fáil governments made a number of adjustments to the tax rates and tax bands applying to employees. But they could not forestall the tax protests of the end of the decade. A Commission on Taxation was set up in 1980, and produced a series of reports over the following years, including a number of acute analyses of the shortcomings of the existing system. Its recommendations for reform were radical: it proposed that the existing income tax system should be scrapped in favour of a much lower tax on income at source, combined with a greater reliance on expenditure taxes. This anticipated some aspects of the tax reform movement that gained currency later in the 1980s, in prioritising a comprehensive definition of income, implying a broad tax base with few exemptions, low basic rates, and transparent application.

Crisis in the economic environment

The reports of the Commission on Taxation played only a very slight political role in shaping tax policy, although they increasingly worked their way into the broader debate about tax reform through commentary by expert analysts (see, for example, O'Toole, 1996). Two of our three explanatory factors may be drawn upon to explain why this was so.

The first is the economic environment. Just when discontent with the tax system reached a crescendo, governments were beginning to acknowledge the enormity of the fiscal problem they faced. The Fianna Fáil fiscal boost of the late 1970s had resulted in high and rising borrowing requirements – but international recession after 1979 made subsequent correction difficult. Public spending was still surging ahead. Servicing the public debt alone consumed a growing share of revenues. Debt service charges amounted to about two thirds of the revenues generated by income tax in 1977, but 94 per cent in 1985 (Budget Books, various years). Government instability in the early 1980s also made a consistent tax stance very difficult to adopt. Once the Fine Gael–Labour government of 1982–7 established itself, the severity of the recession made deep cuts undesirable. Tax-based fiscal adjustment seemed the most prudent strategy (Honohan, 1999).

This sets the scene for our second explanatory variable, the reliance on the force of taxation by inertia. Existing revenue instruments had proved their worth; the middle of a recession was no time for innovation. Therefore, bad as the tax burden had seemed to employees in 1980, it became even more onerous by 1985.

These factors help us to understand the seeming paradoxes of Irish tax policy at this time. A country in which nearly one in five workers was unemployed was adding to the 'tax wedge' each year, that is, the gap between total employer payroll costs and employee take-home pay, thus further reducing the incentives to create jobs. A country in which about two thirds of the unemployed were classed as long-term unemployed made it additionally difficult for many of these to escape welfare dependency because of the tax and social insurance liabilities they faced once they took paid work.

Phase two: tax reform and its limits

In contrast with the first phase in the development of the tax system, the second phase, from the mid-1980s to the present, displays a considerably greater measure of innovation. But the economic environment also proved crucial to the scope afforded to governments to engage in new directions in tax policy.

The innovations of tax reform

There was no major departure from the lineaments of the existing system during our second phase, from the mid-1980s to the present, notwithstanding the recommendations of the Commission on Taxation. But the stance of governments changed. It would appear that the main political parties in Ireland all became committed to the principal tenets of the international tax reform movement. These ideas were widely disseminated by the OECD. They accorded priority to improving supply-side policy through broad-based taxation with fewer exemptions, fewer and simpler tax bands, and lower tax rates. Tax shelters were to be dismantled, and similar tax rates were to apply to income from diverse sources, to provide a 'level playing field' for all economic actors. Tax policy was no longer seen as an appropriate means of shaping people's economic behaviour, or indeed of altering distributive outcomes (e.g. Steinmo, 1993: 160).

The essential features of this new approach run through the policies adopted by all the governments that have held power since 1987. The demon-stration effect of Britain's early and radical adoption of these principles was undoubtedly an important influence. In 1983–4, employee income tax in Ireland was structured into five rates, ranging from a low rate of 25 per cent and a standard rate of 35 per cent to the highest rate of 65 per cent. By 2002 there were only two rates, set at 20 per cent and 42 per cent. Tax expenditures and write-offs had been severely curtailed, and most remaining allowances could only be taken up at the standard rate. The tax base had thereby been broadened and the structure of the tax system flattened out. The principle of progressive taxation had given way to the primacy of efficiency. This represents what we might think of as a 'Gestalt shift' in tax principles – a far-reaching change in the basic assumptions according to which the efficiency, effectiveness and equity of taxes are evaluated.

Complementing this shift in the visible face of tax, especially income tax, was a major reform in tax administration. The tax amnesty of 1988 signalled a move towards a more effective tax-gathering system. This opened what was widely expected to be a once-only window to those in the black economy, or whose tax affairs were not in order, after which the full rigours of prosecution were promised. Reforms to the self-reporting system for self-employed workers and for farmers increased the incentives for voluntary compliance, while the sanctions available to the Revenue Commissioners were strengthened (Cassells and Thornhill, 1993). These reforms to tax administration were an integral part of the tax reform movement that characterised the 1990s.

This is not to deny the pivotal role of key individuals at various moments in this process. For example, the role of Fianna Fáil Finance Minister Ray MacSharry was certainly important in setting the minority government of 1987–9 firmly on the track of implementing both tax cuts and spending cuts. So too was the role of Fine Gael leader Alan Dukes in the 'Tallaght strategy' of providing parliamentary support for these measures. A little later, Sandford (1994) identifies a distinctive contribution by the Progressive Democrats to the market-oriented priorities adopted by the coalition government that they formed with Fianna Fáil between 1989 and 1992.

Nor should we overlook the possibility of differences in emphasis between parties, within the broadly accepted shift to a tax reform strategy. For example, the governments in which the Labour Party participated (with Fianna Fáil between 1992 and 1994, and with Fine Gael and Democratic Left between 1994 and 1997) displayed a somewhat greater interest in orienting the distributive outcomes of tax cuts towards the lower paid, by placing greater emphasis on widening allowances and bands rather than cutting tax rates (Hardiman, 2000).

Yet differences in distributive emphases are also very much in evidence within a single administration. The Fianna Fáil–Progressive Democrat government of 1997–2002 swung between measures favouring the wealthy, such as cutting top rates and halving the Capital Gains Tax rate, and measures favouring the less well off, such as widening bands and increasing tax-free allowances, and raising the eligibility threshold for social insurance payments. On the whole, the tax measures of the latter half of the 1990s were more favourable to wealthier people (see Hardiman, 2002a). To some extent this is an inevitable corollary of the move away from progressive taxation towards fewer and lower rates. But a number of initiatives sought to change the thrust of the tax system in important new ways that did not lend themselves to easy summary in terms of conventional partisan politics.

For example, this government introduced two major initiatives with divergent distributive consequences for households. In Budget 1999 (December 1998), tax-free allowances began to be replaced by a system of tax credits, which were most beneficial to those paying tax at the standard rather than the higher rate. In Budget 2000 (December 1999) the basis on which married couples' tax liability was calculated was altered. Since a Supreme Court decision in 1979, they had been accorded two full allowances, to be shared as they pleased, implicitly favouring single-earner married couples and supporting the home-making role of the non-earner. Now the signal was given that the system would move, over a period of time, to fully individualised tax allowances. This was defended on grounds of efficiency, as it increased the incentives to spouses to take paid work at a time of labour shortages. While moving away from progressivity in total household taxation, it represented an increase in distributive equity for individuals (see Callan et al., 2001: ch. 5).

By the early 2000s, therefore, we can see that a major change had been wrought in the thrust of tax policy and in the design of the tax system. Within the framework of existing tax instruments, significant innovation had occurred on a number of fronts.

The determinants of innovation

Changes in the effects of some taxes were driven by debates taking place at EU level, for example in the case of VAT (O'Toole, 1996). The most striking of these is undoubtedly the case of corporation tax. Ireland's preferential rate of ten per cent for manufacturing was later extended to internationally traded financial services and to areas such as computer software. These provisions came under growing EU scrutiny in the late 1990s. Irish government representatives strongly resisted proposals for EU-wide tax harmonisation, as the capacity to control corporation tax incentives was perceived as central to the country's successes in attracting foreign direct investment. Intensive lobbying secured agreement that all Irish corporation tax rates could converge upon a single low rate, set at 12.5 per cent, by 2003 (although firms in the international financial services sector would continue to benefit from the ten per cent rate until 2005, and some manufacturing firms until 2010). The standard Irish corporation tax rate for most firms had been set at 50 per cent for most of the 1980s; this was brought down progressively and stood at 24 per cent by 2000. This already placed Ireland second in an international survey of tax competitiveness undertaken in that year (Forfás, 2001: Table 7, col. 10). The extension of an even lower and uniform rate to all firms can only be explained by the EU context.

However, other changes in tax policy cannot be so easily explained. The overall design of tax reform does not display the coherence of an overarching vision. Alongside the tax reform priorities of base-broadening, a range of new allowances and tax incentives was allowed to develop. While each was defended with reference to its desirable social purposes, the trend nevertheless ran counter to the central tenets of the tax reform movement.

Where major innovations have occurred, they have relied on the energy and vision of particular individuals to drive them through. They have not, in the main, entailed much of a consultative process – notwithstanding the well-established consultative mechanisms that have developed out of social partnership processes (see O'Donnell, 2001). In this, tax policy making in Ireland is more like that of Britain than that of, for example, Sweden (see Steinmo, 1993).

The two major income tax initiatives of the late 1990s – the move to tax credits, and the individualisation of tax assessment of married people – illuminate both the strengths and the weaknesses of tax policy-making processes in Ireland. Radical choices could be made and implemented fairly quickly by strong-minded ministers (in this case, Fianna Fáil Finance Minister Charlie McCreevy). On the other hand, the consultative process was so limited that the interests and concerns of many affected groups were not taken into account. For example, cuts in personal income taxes were central to the pay-tax deals negotiated by the main social partners during the 1990s (Hardiman, 2002b). The minister acknowledged no obligation to respond to the tax priorities identified through the National Economic and Social Council (NESC), the consultative social partnership body, whether in the adjustment of allowances and bands, or in the far more radical shift to tax credits. Similarly, the move towards individualisation disappointed the many lobbyists, inside as well as outside the social partnership structures, who had hoped for more systematic fiscal supports for families, particularly those with child-rearing responsibilities. The minister's innovations cut through potentially crippling political opposition. But the extent of the opposition could nevertheless prove politically embarrassing at times. Widespread criticism greeted the minister's announcement of individualisation, notwithstanding the complementary increases in direct family support through increases in child benefit. His response was to hastily introduce a new non-employed spouse allowance. This was an example of what NESC has described as a 'proliferation of new tax reliefs without any obvious guiding principle', which it called 'a cause for concern' (NESC, 1999: 202).

Constraints on innovation: the power of vested interests

Tax innovation has not been firmly and consistently grounded in a clearly articulated set of widely shared principles. It would be a mistake to believe that tax reform priorities extended quickly to all areas of policy making or indeed of tax administration. This opens the question as to how governments' priorities have in fact been shaped.

Some privileged groups continued to be able to pay disproportionately low levels of tax, finding means of sheltering much of their income in quite legitimate ways. Early in 1998, for example, the Department of Finance released a summary of the findings of the Revenue Commissioners concerning the income tax paid by very high earners. This stated that in 1994–5, 8.5 per cent of those earning over a quarter of a million pounds had paid no income tax at all, and a further one fifth paid at an effective rate of less than 25 per cent.

Privileged groups were clearly adept at protecting their interests, often through direct influence over the policy process. In one notable instance, that of Residential Property Tax (1983–97), open opposition caused governments to change their mind. This tax was originally intended not only to generate extra revenues but also to widen the tax base at a time when it was well known that incomes were already too heavily taxed. Kevin Rafter concluded that the whole experience 'indicated a responsiveness to middle class voters to the detriment of the wider community' (Rafter, 2000: 63).

But less overt lobbying, while harder to trace, may be even more successful in shaping government decisions. Former Finance Minister Ray MacSharry noted that the lobbying power of vested interests was 'a threat which every tax reforming minister for Finance has to deal with', and that 'lobbies operate much more effectively in secret' (MacSharry, 1994).

A number of decisions on tax policy remain unexplained, among them the reasons for the extraordinary second tax amnesty of May 1993. The Fianna Fáil–Labour government was deeply divided about it, and while it was perceived as the brainchild of Taoiseach Albert Reynolds, Fianna Fáil Minister for Finance Bertie Ahern is reported to have opposed it vehemently until the day of the Cabinet meeting (see Finlay, 1998).

This was signalled as the very last opportunity for tax evaders to become fully tax compliant before the full rigours of the law finally fell upon them. Yet it became clear throughout the 1990s that numerous schemes facilitating tax evasion continued to thrive – and numbered among their beneficiaries former Taoiseach Charles J. Haughey (Keena, 2001). Other schemes included collusion between banks and their customers to evade tax on deposit interest, and ingenious arrangements such as the Ansbacher offshore bank accounts. These were the subjects of only two of a number of official investigations in the early 2000s. It was not until the Finance Act of 1999 that the Revenue Commissioners finally obtained the legal powers, and began to acquire the personnel resources, that they claimed they needed in order to do their job properly.[1] Yet as the American political scientist Margaret Levi has pointed out, where tax evasion can be practised with impunity this tends to erode the general legitimacy of the tax system even further: 'widespread compliance cannot thrive if people think they are suckers' (Levi, 1988: 177).

The changing economic environment

Notwithstanding the ongoing problems of tax evasion and incomplete tax reform, the logic of the tax-reform movement held sway over all governments during the 1990s. Indeed, there seemed little reason to question it. Governments were able to cut taxes and increase spending simultaneously. The remarkable spell of economic growth between 1994 and 2001 resulted in average annual growth in GNP of 7.9 per cent (Department of Finance, 2002: Table 12); it also resulted in a growth in numbers at work of almost half a million, or some 40 per cent (Central Statistics Office, Labour Force Surveys). These buoyant

Niamh Hardiman

economic conditions ensured a steady and rising flow of revenues to government. Yet, as Table 7.6 shows, people on average industrial earnings were paying a little less in tax and social security than the OECD average, and a good deal less than the EU average.

Table 7.6 **Income tax and employee social insurance**
as a proportion of average industrial earnings, 1998

	Single, no children	Married, single earner two children
Ireland	24.9	18.1
OECD – total	25.5	19.9
EU 15	29.9	23.9

Source: OECD, Taxing Wages 1998–9. Paris: OECD, 1999, Table 3, p. 46

On the face of it, the relative size of the government tax take declined during the 1990s, making Ireland appear to be a model case of implementing tax reform objectives. But this was mainly an artefact of the statistics. As Table 7.7 shows, GNP was rising rapidly, and GDP more rapidly still. The role of the multi-national sector in the Irish economy makes GNP a more accurate measurement of domestic growth. Whichever denominator is chosen, the trend indicates a fall in the percentage of the government's tax share, a trend shared in a number of other OECD countries over this period time too. But the volume of taxation was itself rising rapidly, fuelled by the continuing boom.

Table 7.7 **Tax revenues as a proportion of GDP and GNP**

	Tax+SI,[1] €bn	GDP €bn	GNP €bn	Tax+SI as %GDP	Tax+SI as %GNP
1980	3.9	12.0	11.5	32.6	33.9
1985	8.4	22.8	20.3	35.4	39.6
1990	11.8	34.5	30.5	34.2	38.7
1995	16.9	52.7	46.7	32.0	36.1
1996	18.4	58.1	51.5	31.8	35.8
1997	20.9	67.0	59.0	31.1	35.4
1998	23.5	77.1	67.7	30.5	34.7
1999	26.8	89.0	75.8	30.1	35.4
2000	30.8	103.5	87.1	29.8	35.4
2001	32.8	115.2	95.8	28.6	34.3

1   Exchequer Tax Revenue plus PRSI plus Health Contribution
Source: Dept of Finance Budgetary and Economic Statistics, March 2002, Tables 4 and 11.

A similar trend is in evidence when one looks at government spending, which fell from 45.4 per cent of GDP in 1994 to 39 per cent in 2002 (Department of Finance, 2002: Table 1). But in nominal terms, total government expenditure grew from €18.9 bn in 1994 to €40.3 bn in 2002, and the rate of annual increase stepped up sharply in the early 2000s.

The 1990s, then, seemed to be a decade in which government could have it all. It could engage in extensive tax-cutting strategies while also increasing public spending commitments, yet benefit from revenues so buoyant that not only could Exchequer surpluses be run by the end of the decade, but an annual investment could be made into a national pensions fund. Rapid growth deferred the moment when any hard choices would have to be made.

But the fiscal miracle could not last indefinitely. Events largely beyond the control of Irish governments began to alter the economic environment. A slowdown in the US economy began to ripple outwards in 2001–2, and Ireland was more sensitive than most other European countries to changes in the flow of investment. GNP growth was estimated at about five per cent in 2001, and a projected 3–4 per cent in 2002, still respectable in comparative European terms, but a big drop on previous years' performance. Furthermore, the strengthening of the Euro began to change the terms of trade with the sterling and dollar areas. A decline in revenue buoyancy was already in evidence in 2001, when the Exchequer balance was barely in the black, after three years of surpluses (Department of Finance, 2002: Table 5). A shortfall was widely expected for 2002 – a result due in part to the cost of tax individualisation for married dual-earner couples, in part to changes in the timing of revenue flows with the move in 2002 to calendar-year tax accounting, and in part to the general economic slowdown.

Yet that other inexorable fiscal engine, that of public spending commitments, continued to gather pace in Ireland throughout this phase. Moreover, the results of the Public Sector Pay Benchmarking Body, set up under the terms of the social partnership agreement, the Programme for Prosperity and Fairness, reported in July 2002, recommending sizeable new increases for many public sector employees.

Furthermore, public expectations still ran high for an improvement in the quality of public services. While funding levels cannot be the sole measure of the quality of provision, Ireland in the late 1990s still ranked fourth lowest among the European 15 in the total volume of spending on social protection per capita, including both public and private sources of spending (European Commission, 2002: 12). In areas such as health care and social services, many began to wonder what of lasting value remained after the years of plenty.

Only a short time before, the Fianna Fáil and Progressive Democrat government had anticipated cutting the top rate of tax from 42 per cent to 40 per cent. Following its re-election in May 2002, the issue seemed to be how to manage the public finances without having to revert to tax increases – but without having to make politically unpopular spending cuts either. How this could be done remained unclear. But what was amply clear was that the phase of policy innovation based on tax cuts had finally come to an end.

Conclusion

Issues of taxation typically elicit two types of reaction among people. The first is boredom, an all but complete indifference to broad patterns and trends, and incredulity that anyone apart from economists or accountants who were paid to do so could find tax issues interesting. The second is an impassioned engagement with the implications of the annual budget for their own personal finances, often coloured by a deeply rooted cynicism about the justice of the system in general.

We have seen that political science can offer a different perspective which accords full weight to the deeply and inextricably political aspects of revenue policy. The profile of the dramatic changes in who pays, how they pay, and how much they pay, raises fascinating questions about how the crucial decisions are made. While we cannot shed any new light on the private deliberations of policy makers here, we have shown that three perspectives can be brought to bear which help at least to frame the right questions. These have been termed inertia, innovation and environment. It should now be clear that in each of the two phases we have examined, all three elements are needed to provide an adequate explanation. Perhaps at least by setting out the issues in this way, the ground can be cleared for others to provide more detailed examinations of the tangled issues involved in paying for government.

Note

1   See 'Revenue powers and penalties', Department of Finance Tax Strategy Group, report 01/09, 2001; also 'Tax Compliance', Office of the Revenue Commissioners, August 2001, Department of Finance Tax Strategy Group, report 01/10, 2001.

Bibliography

Byrne, Seán (1989) *Wealth and the Wealthy in Ireland.* Dublin: Combat Poverty Agency.

Callan, Tim, M. Keeney, B. Nolan and J. Walsh (2001) *Reforming Tax and Welfare.* Policy Research Series no. 42. Dublin: ESRI.

Cassells, Frank and Don Thornhill (1993) 'Self-assessment and administrative reform in Ireland', pp. 152–78 in Cedric Sandford (ed.), *Key Issues in Tax Reform.* Bath: Fiscal Publications.

Department of Finance (2002) *Budgetary and Economic Statistics.* March.

European Commission (2002) *Eurostat Yearbook.* Luxembourg.

Finlay, Fergus (1998). *Snakes and Ladders.* Dublin: New Island.

Forfás/National Competitiveness Council (2001) *Annual Competitiveness Report.* Dublin: Stationery Office.

Hardiman, Niamh (2000) 'Taxing the poor: the politics of income taxation in Ireland', *Policy Studies Journal* 28: 799–826.

Hardiman, Niamh (2002a) 'The development of the Irish tax state', *Irish Political Studies* 17: 29–58.

Hardiman, Niamh (2002b) 'From conflict to coordination: economic governance and political innovation in Ireland', *West European Politics* 25: 1–24.

Honohan, Patrick (1999) 'Fiscal adjustment and disinflation in Ireland: setting the macro basis of economic recovery and expansion', in Frank Barry (ed.), *Understanding Ireland's Economic Growth.* Basingstoke: Macmillan: 75–98.

Keena, Colm (2001) *Haughey's Millions.* Dublin: Gill & Macmillan.

Levi, Margaret (1988) *Of Rule and Revenue.* Berkeley, CA: University of California Press.

MacSharry, Ray (1994) 'Tax reform in Ireland: the way forward', in *The Irish Dilemma: How to Achieve Fiscal Reform.* Proceedings of the Annual Conference of the Foundation for Fiscal Studies, TCD, September.

NESC (1999) *Opportunities, Challenges and Capacities for Choice.* Dublin: Stationery Office. Report no. 105.

O'Connor, Tom (1993) 'The farm tax – a political casualty', *Seirbhís Phoiblí.* April: 21–31.

O'Donnell, Rory (2001) *The Future of Social Partnership in Ireland.* Discussion Paper prepared for the National Competitiveness Council, *www.forfas.ie/ncc/index.htm*

O'Toole, Francis (1996) 'Tax reform since the Commission on Taxation', *Journal of the Social and Statistical Inquiry Society of Ireland*: 85–123.

Peters, B. Guy (1993) *The Politics of Taxation.* Cambridge: Basil Blackwell.

Rafter, Kevin (2000) 'Making it up as they went along: Residential Property Tax and the process of policy change', *Irish Political Studies* 15: 63–82.

Réamonn, Seán (1981) *History of the Revenue Commissioners.* Dublin: IPA.

Rose, Richard and T. Karan (1987) *Taxation by Political Inertia.* London: Allen & Unwin.

Sandford, Cedric (1994) *Successful Tax Reform.* Bath: Fiscal Publications.

Sandford, Cedric and Oliver Morrissey (1985) *The Irish Wealth Tax: a Case Study in Economics and Politics.* Dublin: ESRI Paper no.123.

Skocpol, Theda (1985) 'Bringing the state back in: current research', pp. 3–37 in Peter Evans, Dietrich Rueschemeyer and Theda Skocpol (eds.), *Bringing the State Back In*. Cambridge: Cambridge University Press.

Steinmo, Sven (1993) *Taxation and Democracy: Swedish, British and American Approaches to Financing the Modern State*. New Haven, CT: Yale University Press.

CHAPTER EIGHT

The Office of the Ombudsman in Ireland

MICHAEL MILLS

—

The setting up of the Office of Ombudsman in Ireland was the result of a lengthy process of debate that began in the 1960s and culminated in the passing of the Ombudsman Act in 1980. It took a further three years for the legislation to be brought into effect and for the first Ombudsman to be appointed.

In 1969, a Public Services Organisation review group, under the chairmanship of the then Chief Justice, the late Cearbhall O'Dalaigh, reported on the steady growth in the functions of government and the extent to which they impinged on the citizen. The need for the provision of adequate institutions and procedures of appeal to ensure fairness for the citizen was highlighted. The review group put forward a number of proposals for the creation of a new system of administrative justice, including the appointment of a commissioner for administrative justice who would have the powers of an Ombudsman.

While these were radical proposals in the context of the existing public administrative system in Ireland, they also reflected happenings outside Ireland in this area. Ombudsman offices or their equivalent were established in other countries that had close social, cultural and economic associations with Ireland, as is shown by trends in the UK around this time. In 1967, a parliamentary commissioner for administration was appointed in Britain. In Northern Ireland, a commissioner for complaints and a parliamentary commissioner for administration were appointed in 1969. These appointments were followed, in 1973, by the establishment of the health services commissioner in Britain. Commissioners for local administration in England, Scotland and Wales were appointed in 1974–5.

With the establishment of the Department of the Public Service – another of the recommendations of the Public Service Organisation review group – the task of examining the proposal of the group with regard to the appointment of a commissioner for administrative justice began in earnest. This examination was given added impetus with the passing of a private member's motion from a government backbencher, Mr Fergus O'Brien, that 'Dáil Éireann favours the appointment of an ombudsman.'

The debate on the motion in the Dáil indicated that, while there was a shared view that the general idea of the establishment of an ombudsman office was good in principle, there were varying views on the extent of the powers and the role of such an office. Doubts were expressed with regard to what was perceived as the overlapping of the roles of the ombudsman and the elected public representative. As a means of providing full parliamentary involvement in the assessment of the merits of the case and to allay fears among elected representatives of any diminution of their roles, the Minister for the Public Service proposed the establishment of an all-party informal committee of the Oireachtas to consider all aspects of administrative justice.

The committee, which met from July 1976, examined existing arrangements for administrative justice within the Irish public service, and found that while there were wide-ranging facilities for administrative justice, the greater part of the public service, including areas with a high incidence of direct dealings with the public, were not provided for. The committee concluded that what was required was an institution which could, through the examination of complaints, review the operation and execution of the legislative provisions enacted by the Oireachtas, and which would guard against or eliminate maladministration in any form. It concluded that the institution best suited to undertake this work was an ombudsman's office.

In May 1977 the government indicated that it had accepted the recommendations of the committee in principle and that it proposed to legislate to give effect to these recommendations. Following a change in government in June and the subsequent response to a Dáil question in October from Richie Ryan TD, asking when the proposed legislation would be introduced, an advertisement was placed in the national newspapers in January 1978 drawing attention to the report of the committee and inviting comments from interested persons and bodies. At the same time, work on the drafting of a Bill translating the recommendations of the all-party committee report into legislation was undertaken by the Department of the Public Service. The Office of the Ombudsman was established under the Ombudsman Act 1980, which was brought into effect three years later in July 1983.

The early years

My nomination as Ireland's first Ombudsman was announced on 17 October 1983 by the Minister for the Public Service, Mr John Boland. The appointment, which followed consultation with all the political parties, was made with effect from 3 January 1984.

The Ombudsman Office was initially located in temporary accommodation at Harcourt Road, Dublin. It was staffed by civil servants on loan from a variety of government departments pending the recruitment of permanent investigative staff through open competition conducted by the Civil Service Commission. Following the recruitment of four investigators, one senior investigator and a director, the Office of the Ombudsman moved to its permanent address at 52 St Stephens Green. The budget for the Office in 1984 was Ir£275,000.

In 1983 the Department of the Public Service issued a circular to all government departments and offices announcing the appointment and setting out the legislative background to the establishment of the office, and outlining initial instructions to departments with regard to their contacts with the office. Each department was requested to nominate a liaison officer of at least principal officer level to act as first point of contact between the Ombudsman Office and the department and to ensure that all responses to enquiries, requests for reports and files were dealt with in a satisfactory manner.

Even before I took up my appointment, a steady stream of complaints were received in the office that had been established late in 1983 to put in place the administrative infrastructure to enable the functions of the Ombudsman to be carried out. At this stage the Ombudsman's remit extended to all government departments and offices, and in the first year I received a total of 2,267 complaints of which 1,544 were within jurisdiction. Of these social welfare accounted for almost half (at 744) with the revenue commissioners next (at 295).

On receipt of a complaint that falls within his remit, the Ombudsman carries out a preliminary examination, which involves the gathering of relevant information and facts from the body concerned through a designated liaison officer. The Ombudsman may also seek additional information from the complainant. The main purpose of the preliminary examination is to establish in a quick and informal way whether there is a prima facie case for a formal investigation. It has a second and equally important function in that it provides a mechanism whereby a complaint can be resolved with the minimum amount of formality, especially where the circumstances of the case point to a straightforward resolution of the matter.

Investigations are carried out in private. If I decided to carry out a formal investigation I wrote to the head of the body concerned enclosing a written summary of the complaint and requesting a written report. In the course of an investigation I could require any person to provide evidence that I considered relevant to the investigation and where necessary to attend before me as a witness.[1]

If, having completed an investigation, the Ombudsman upholds the complaint made to him he can request the body against whom the complaint was made to reconsider the matter, take specific measures to remedy, mitigate or alter the adverse effect of the action, or to specify the reasons for taking the action. In keeping with similar offices throughout the world, Ireland's Ombudsman has no authority to change an administrative decision or action, and the body against whom the complaint is made is not under any obligation to comply with his recommendation. If the Ombudsman is not satisfied with the body's response to his recommendation he may make a special report on the case to the Oireachtas.[2]

My first year in office saw the adoption of procedures for carrying out examinations of complaints. A procedure whereby particular decisions could be reviewed was outlined in my first annual report, in which I explained that I had adopted a system of seeking to find a solution to many complaints by way of request for a review to the department involved. These requests for a review were made in the context of having carried out a fairly detailed preliminary examination and having reached certain tentative conclusions as to the outcome.

At the stage where I had established the nature of the likely recommendation, I would ask the department concerned if they would like to respond favourably along certain lines. The purpose of this procedure was to enable a department to alter a decision on its own initiative rather than await a formal recommendation from the Ombudsman.

In my annual report for 1984 I commented that I had received the fullest co-operation at all times from government departments and officials but pointed out that some civil servants had a difficulty in accepting the role of my office in investigating complaints in certain areas. This had led to legal challenges to prevent the office carrying out or continuing its investigations. The first such challenge to the office came from the Department of Posts and Telegraphs. The department informed me that, on the basis of legal advice, they considered that I had no authority to investigate telephone accounts. I informed the department that I intended to investigate telephone accounts for the period from July 1983 (when the Ombudsman Act came into force) to the end of that year when Bord Telecom Éireann was officially established. While Telecom Éireann was initially reluctant to accept that I had authority to investigate such accounts, after various discussions they accepted my position and a formula was agreed upon for the examination of telephone bills.

A challenge came also from the Department of Social Welfare in relation to the authority of the Ombudsman to investigate the decisions of appeals officers. I found the legal advice given to the Department of Social Welfare unacceptable in the context of the Act, which specifically provided that the actions of appeals officers were subject to investigation. The legal advice I received confirmed this position and left no doubt about the intention of the Oireachtas in the passing of the Act or about the clear provisions of the Act itself in regard to the decisions of appeals officers.

In the course of these early years, specific complaints highlighted the need for review of legislation. In the area of social insurance, for instance, I highlighted the anomaly in the law that prevented people who had many years of social insurance contributions receiving a contributory old age pension. I felt that it was inequitable that persons who had paid more for social insurance stamps should get fewer benefits than those who paid less because the deciding factor was the number of years from their first contribution after 1953. I received numerous complaints from pensioners who found on reaching 66 years of age that they were not entitled to a contributory old age pension. I called for amending legislation to help resolve the problem. Many other bodies also made representations to the government on the matter. Amending legislation to provide pro-rata pensions for many of these pensioners was subsequently introduced. It did not completely resolve the problem, but it was a significant step forward.

Another anomaly which I found most disturbing was in relation to a person who was deemed ineligible for a deserted wife's allowance when her husband left her, and who also failed to obtain a widow's pension when he died. I pointed out that the case exemplified the need for examination of the law of 'domicile' under which the woman was regarded as having the same domicile as her husband even though he may have left the country years ago, divorced her and remarried. I suggested that pending legislation in this area the Oireachtas might look at the possibility of allowing a discretionary power to the Department of Social Welfare to ensure that the very small number of widows affected by the existing situation could be helped. The law of 'domicile' was subsequently amended. A further anomaly related to the position of the deserted husband. Under existing legislation, a husband who had been granted custody of the children by the courts after the mother had deserted the family could receive considerably less by way of social welfare assistance than would a deserted wife in similar circumstances. Some welcome changes have since taken place.

The question of delayed payments was another area that I felt was in need of resolution. It seemed to me inequitable that interest could be charged by the state on money due from citizens while no similar facility existed for reciprocal payments. Particular concern was expressed in respect of persons who failed to receive their entitlements under the social welfare acts because of mistakes in deciding their claims. I cited the example of a widow who was refused a pension in 1977 because of a mistake in the Department of Social Welfare and was paid her pension in 1984 with arrears over the seven years. Instead of receiving the payment at current value, she was paid the actual amount set out in the 1977 legislation and similar amounts in the subsequent years in accordance with the social welfare legislation for the particular year. There was no provision in law to meet this kind of situation. While ex-gratia payment could be made with the sanction of the Department of Finance, there was no provision in law to ensure that persons will receive their entitlements in accordance with the current value of the money. An arrangement was made with the Departments of Finance and Social Welfare after I had written to a number of ministers indicating my intention to report the issue to the Dáil unless the Department of Social Welfare was prepared to pay the real value of the money due.

As a result, in a number of later complaints of mistakes by the department in paying social welfare benefits at the due time, substantial compensation was made to restore the real value of the money.

Extension of the Ombudsman's remit

The extension of the remit of the Ombudsman Office in 1985 resulted in an increase in the office's budget to Ir£655,000. Staffing in the office was augmented and the appointment of a total of 15 new investigators was approved by the Department of the Public Service. These appointments were made following open competition carried out by the Civil Service Commission, and they brought to the office a complement of staff whose range of experience extended from the civil service, to local government and the public health sector as well as the private sector.

The expanded remit also represented a substantial increase in the areas under the authority of the Ombudsman. Prior to April 1985 the number of persons employed in the bodies subject to investigations totalled 30,000. After 1 April this swelled to an excess of 130,000.

The new arrangement required the establishment of a good working relationship between the Ombudsman Office and the new bodies. To this end, early in the year, officials from the Ombudsman Office met with the chief executive officers of the health boards to discuss the practical arrangements necessary to give effect to the new jurisdiction of the Ombudsman. While the response of the health boards was generally favourable, I received a number of challenges from medical officers regarding my right to examine medical records. The medical officers expressed concern at the effect that this would have on their relationship with their patients and, in particular, with the confidential nature of that relationship.

Under the Ombudsman Act, the Ombudsman is empowered to require that any information or document considered relevant to an examination be given to him. The issue was discussed with representatives from the Irish Medical Council and the Irish Medical Organisation. Both bodies recognised the right of the Ombudsman to examine all records, medical and otherwise. They were assured that medical records would be requested only when it was considered absolutely necessary and that, in all such cases, the Ombudsman would obtain the permission of complainants before examining these records.

In the case of local authorities, when staff from the office entered into discussions with the County and City Manager's Association, with a view to establishing procedures for dealing with complaints against local authorities, a number of difficulties were encountered. This was basically the result of a perceived view of some managers that the role of the Ombudsman was one of making representations: they felt that locally elected public representatives might look on the Ombudsman's involvement as interfering with their traditional role. It was brought home to them that the Ombudsman Office was not involved in making representations and that the Ombudsman had been charged by the Oireachtas with the statutory function of investigating complaints concerning the administrative actions of public bodies and, where appropriate, securing redress for those adversely affected. Following further discussions with a subcommittee of the County and City Managers' Association, satisfactory procedures for processing complaints were established.

The year 1985 saw a large increase in the number of complaints received. The number of complaints, including those carried forward, was 5,277. Of these, 3,411 were completed leaving 1,866 to be carried forward to 1986. The increase in the number of complaints resulted from the extensive publicity campaign carried out by the office following the extension of the remit and the introduction of a programme of visits by staff to local centres.

The reason for the introduction of regional visits was explained in my annual report for 1985. I pointed out that since my appointment as Ombudsman I had been acutely aware of the need for the office to operate in close proximity to the public. This need, I believe, had assumed greater importance from April 1985 when my remit was extended. When recruitment of the extra investigative staff was completed in mid-1985, I decided that my staff should visit local areas for the purpose of dealing directly with complaints from the public at local level.

Up to the end of 1985, ten centres were visited where more than 750 members of the public called to have their complaints examined. From the outset the value of the regional visits was evident. Many of those who came to the temporary offices explained that, because of the complexity or nature of their complaint, they would have had difficulty in communicating the details by letter or telephone and consequently would not have found it possible to have their complaint examined. The process had a second and equally important knock-on effect. The publicity associated with the visit increased public awareness of the existence and role of the Ombudsman. This was reflected in the increased volume of written complaints received from each area after a visit had been made.

The years 1986 and 1987 witnessed a growing backlog of complaints in the office. In 1986 the number of complaints within jurisdiction received in the year and those carried forward from the previous year amounted to 6,862. Of these 5,382 were completed with 1,480 carried forward to 1987. The corresponding figures for 1987 were 6,203 with 4,155 finalised and 2,048 carried forward to 1989. The estimate for expenditure for the office for 1987 remained the same as that sanctioned for 1986 at Ir£775,000.

In 1986 there were two significant developments affecting the office. Early in the year the appeals officers of the Department of Social Welfare accepted that I had the power to recommend changes in their decisions (as in the decisions of all public servants within my remit). Towards the end of the year the principle of compensation for loss of purchasing power was established. The effect of this was to benefit people deprived of their entitlements by public bodies over lengthy periods.

There were instances where recommendations from the Ombudsman were resisted by a number of public servants. I was obliged to inform them that while recommendations could not be enforced, I had been given considerable authority by the Oireachtas to ensure that any recommendation was acted upon and that I would have no alternative but to present a special report to the Oireachtas setting out the full facts of the case and the nature of the response received.

In my 1987 report I described that year as the most difficult since the office was set up. In April 1987 the government announced that the budget for the office would be reduced by Ir£100,000. This resulted in the removal of four investigative staff and some support staff as their salaries could no longer be paid. In addition a senior investigator who had left the office was not replaced. In July 1987 I was informed that the office would receive a further reduction in funding in 1988 totalling Ir£125,000, which would result in a further loss of staff.

The combination of financial cutbacks and an increasing backlog of unresolved complaints forced me to conclude that unless remedial action was taken, the backlog by the end of 1988 could be out of control, which would have serious long-term effects on the credibility of the office. Complainants were informed that considerable delay was likely because of the cutbacks. When efforts to secure a change of heart on the financial cutbacks failed, I decided that it was necessary to place a special report on the matter before the Oireachtas. I was acting in accordance with my obligations under the Ombudsman Act to inform the Oireachtas of my ability to carry out my statutory functions. It was the only special report laid before the Oireachtas during my term of office.

The report produced an immediate reaction in the media. Editorials in national and provincial newspapers criticised the government decision to reduce the financial allocation to the office. Letters to the newspaper editors indicated that there was growing public unrest about the decision to reduce the funding. This was also reflected in the activities of political parties: motions were put down in the Dáil order papers condemning the decision; the Labour and Fine Gael parties combined in a motion of no confidence against the government; and the Workers Party tabled a bill to allow the Ombudsman to determine the number of staff he needed. The Irish Congress of Trade Unions also became involved in the controversy.

In the light of this, in June 1988 the Minister for Finance announced a government decision to review the staffing in the office. This review was carried out by officials from the Department of Finance. When the estimates for 1989 were announced by the Minister for Finance in October 1988, additional funding was provided to enable the Ombudsman to take on an additional seven members of staff. By the end of June 1989 the staff of the office had been restored to 35 and it was announced that regional visits would resume on a limited basis. At the height of the financial cutbacks the staff of the office had been reduced to nine investigators, one senior investigator and an acting director, from a total before the cutbacks of 16 investigators, four senior investigators and a director.

My second term of office

I was reappointed Ombudsman for a second term in December 1989. By 1990 a pattern of change regarding some of the anomalies to which I had drawn attention in my first six years in office began to emerge.

Old age pensions

A series of complaints from 1984 onwards related to the unfairness which many older people experienced in the system of 'averaging' of social contributions, and which precluded an estimated 2,000 people aged 66 or over from obtaining contributory old age pensions because they did not meet the required minimum 'average' of 20 contributions per year. This anomaly has now been removed for many of these elderly persons by the introduction in 1988 by the Department of Social Welfare of pro-rata pensions for persons who had an average of five contributions and upwards and who came back into full insurance in 1974. While I welcomed the improvement, I pointed out that I still continued to receive complaints from a number of older people who were unaffected by the change because they did not meet the requirement of coming back into full insurance in 1974.

Compensation for late payments

An issue that had led to serious difficulty before it was eventually resolved was the question of restoration of the true value of money to persons who had been incorrectly refused benefits by the Department of Social Welfare over lengthy periods. The practice had been to pay the arrears of benefit at the rate provided for in the legislation of the particular year. I contended that account should be taken of inflation in the interim. The issue was eventually resolved as I was preparing to submit a special report to the Oireachtas on the issue outlining the inherent unfairness of paying people benefits to which they were legally entitled at a rate which took no account of the decline in the value of money since the original failure to pay arose. A system for paying such compensation for delayed payments has since been put into operation by the Department of Social Welfare.

Discrimination against husbands and widowers

This issue had been raised in my annual reports of 1984 and 1986, in which I described the unfair way in which widowers and deserted husbands were treated by the state in so far as they were entitled to claim much less state assistance than would their wives in similar circumstances. This appeared to be a distinct discrimination against men. Subsequent changes in social welfare legislation have brought improvements in this area.

Dependent domicile

In 1984 I drew attention to the unfairness of the concept of dependent domicile under which a wife could be deprived of certain benefits because she was regarded as having the same domicile as her husband even though he might have deserted her and have been living abroad for a number of years while she continued to reside in Ireland. The concept of dependent domicile was abolished in 1986.

Benefits for trade unionists

Following complaints by a number of trade unionists, I suggested that changes be made in the social welfare legislation to permit workers not directly involved in a trade dispute at their place of employment to be paid benefits. The necessary changes were made in the 1987 Social Welfare Act.

Higher education grants

The Department of Education decided to revise its interpretation of a provision of the higher education grants scheme after a number of complaints from affected students. The department issued a circular to local authorities permitting them to pay a higher rate of grant to students whose homes were near a university but who were refused entry to that university (or that university did not provide the course of studies which the student wished to pursue).

Disabled Persons Maintenance Allowance (DPMA) payments

Following a number of complaints, I found that persons who applied for the payment of DPMA were being paid by some health boards only from the date of approval of their application. I pointed out to these boards that their procedure was not in accordance with the law and that applicants for DPMA who were found eligible were entitled to payment from the date of receipt of their applications. The Department of Health accepted that this was the correct interpretation of the law and new procedures were brought into operation to effect this.

Public service widows

A surprising fact brought to my attention was that some widows of former civil servants were unaware of their right to claim social welfare pensions on the death of their husbands and that some departments did not automatically inform them of this right. Following my intervention, it was agreed that in future all departments of state would inform widows of former civil servants of their rights in this regard. In one instance a widow had failed to claim her pension for 14 years because she was unaware of her rights.

The tone for my second term of office was set in my annual report for 1990. Commenting on my re-appointment I said that I was happy to be given the opportunity to continue in office for a second term and that it was a great privilege to be associated with an institution that had the power to resolve people's problems. I added that it was desirable that the first holder of the Office of Ombudsman should have sufficient time to ensure that the office was established on very firm foundations, that its future was secure and that the philosophy governing its operations was clearly defined.

The number of complaints levelled off at about 3,000 per annum and was within the compass of my staff of 33 to handle competently.

At the end of 1993, the Office of the Ombudsman completed its first ten years of work. In that time, a total of 37,122 complaints were received, of which 5,269 were outside jurisdiction. Of the 31,853 complaints examined, 6,705 were resolved in favour of the complainants; assistance was provided in 8,525 cases, and 11,684 complaints were not upheld. A further 4,303 were discontinued or withdrawn, and some 640 cases were carried forward into 1994.

Battles of the early years are mainly a memory now, but from time to time major difficulties are still encountered because some public bodies cannot accept that they have been guilty of maladministration. Eventually, and only after detailed correspondence and contacts, they are faced with the possibility of a special report being made to the Oireachtas unless they are prepared to respond reasonably to the Ombudsman's recommendation. This provision in the Ombudsman's Act is also a very powerful weapon that has been given to the office. I am very glad that, over the years, despite my being compelled on a number of occasions to inform public bodies and public servants of the possibility of my using this power, I never had occasion to use it.

The implementation by public bodies of the recommendations made by the Ombudsman over the past years has effectively demonstrated the fallacy of the criticism at the time the office was being set up that it would be 'a mouse that roared'. The path of the office is now set firmly for the future. The office is accepted and recognised by the public as an independent agency that will impartially examine complaints and will take every possible step to have cases of genuine grievance resolved.

For me, personally, the experience of the early years of the Ombudsman's Office provided a unique opportunity for which I am extremely grateful. It has been a rare privilege to have the opportunity to work from its foundation with an organisation that is capable of achieving widespread benefit for people and to know that the office has succeeded in resolving thousands of complaints that in most cases would never have been resolved without its existence.

Notes

1   The Ombudsman may be requested in writing by a minister of the government not to investigate a particular complaint. In such instances the Ombudsman must terminate his investigation. Such a request has never been made since the Office was established, and I do not anticipate such a request being made.

2   To date, this has not been necessary.

CHAPTER NINE

Irish government and European governance

BRIGID LAFFAN

—

In 1975 Brian Farrell published an article entitled 'Irish government re-observed', in the *Economic and Social Review* (Farrell, 1975). In that piece, Brian revisited some of the issues raised by Basil Chubb[1]and David Thornley in a 1964 *Irish Times* article on the same theme. Brian Farrell had an enduring interest in the structures, processes and personalities of Irish government and politics, as highlighted by his work on the role of the Taoiseach, cabinet government in Ireland, the appointment of ministers and government formation. His focus in his 1975 analysis was on the interface between politics and administration, the pervasive secrecy of the Irish political elite, the 'hereditary' aspect of Irish governmental recruitment and the subservience of the two houses of the Oireachtas to the executive. For Farrell what was 'remarkable about the Irish political system – in personnel, procedures, and structures – is the degree of continuity'. However, he suggested that 'Entry into the EEC has created a totally new context for public policy discussion and decision-making' (1975: 406). The decision to join was a decision to embed the Irish state, political system, economy and society in a wider European frame.

The objectives of this chapter are, first, to trace the impact of membership of the EU on governance in Ireland in the thirty years since the Irish electorate voted by a majority of 83 per cent to join what was then the EEC, and second, to assess the impact of the rejection of the Nice Treaty on Ireland's relations with the EU. Four major impacts are identified in this chapter: the significance of an additional arena of public policy making, the need to live with the Brussels system, the EU in the domestic arena, and EU framing of national choices. The chapter ends with an analysis of the crisis in Ireland's relations with the EU in the light of the debacle over the efforts to pass the Nice treaty reform. Before engaging in an analysis of Ireland and the EU, it is necessary to ask just what does EU membership demand of its member states.

The EU demands

The EU is an unsettled and unsettling political system. Scholars of integration continue to grapple with the nature of the beast. This challenge was high-lighted early on in the literature on integration by Donald Puchala in a paper entitled 'Of blind men, elephants and international integration' (Puchala, 1972). In this piece, Puchala used the analogy of blind men examining an elephant to illustrate the difficulty scholars face in categorising the EU. He suggested that if a number of blind men touched the elephant to discover what the beast looked like, because they touched different parts they would come to very different conclusions. The man who touched the trunk would conclude that the elephant was tall and slender, the one who touched the ear would conclude that the elephant was oblong and flat, and so on. In a nutshell, no one would have an accurate picture of the elephant. The EU is unsettled along five important dimensions: constitutional order, institutional format, decision rules, policy scope and membership. Member states and candidate countries are thus confronted with the need to adjust and adapt to a system of public policy making that is inherently dynamic. They need to develop and defend their preferences not only on particular policy regimes, but also on the future of the EU itself. The latter requires them to develop preferences on the big constitutional issues, decision rules, institutional roles and the minutiae of EU committees. EU membership requires more not less of national governments.

While acknowledging the dynamic and fluid nature of the EU, it is necessary to explore what the member states must adjust to in order to partici-pate in the Union's systems of public policy making. What does organising for Brussels mean? Broadly speaking, the member states are adjusting to the internationalisation and multilateralisation of public policy making within a regional frame. The Union's system of public policy making has the following four characteristics.

1   The EU is characterised by a high level of *institutionalisation*, far higher than found in any other multilateral framework in the international system. All policy fields that become the common concern of the member states go through a process of institutionalisation. Administrative responsibility is assigned to a unit in the Commission; the Council infrastructure establishes a working party and ministerial responsibility; the EP (European Parliament) institutionalises the area in one of its committees. Institutionalisation at an EU level usually takes the form of committees – expert and advisory committees in the Commission,

working parties and high level committees in the Council, and parliamentary committees in the EP. Institutionalisation is underpinned by treaty provisions and budgetary instruments. Once an area is institutionalised the member states must service the relevant Commission and Council committees, the European Council and ministerial councils. Institutionalisation may follow different pathways – pillars, decision rules – and may be characterised by institutional rivalry and conflict, but the underlying pattern is remarkably similar. Apart from the month of August when Brussels is in holiday mode, the Commission and Council rooms are in constant demand for meetings, many of which go well into the night. In the 1990s, three additional policy areas have been characterised by extensive institutionalisation. These are the common foreign and security policy/European security and defence policy, co-operation in Justice and Home Affairs (JHA), and economic and social governance as a result of the Euro. In addition to government by committee, the EU has seen the growth of a significant number of regulatory agencies.

2 The policy regimes of the EU demonstrate a high degree of *functional differentiation* and ambition. There are major differences between the level of co-operation and collaboration sought in different policy areas, which in turn affect the degree of adjustment required at national level. The EU deploys various modes of governance, most notably regulation, common policies, complementary policies, intensive transgovernmentalism, benchmarking and co-ordination. Different modes of governance make distinct demands on the member states. It is important not to exaggerate the policy reach of the EU because large areas of public policy remain predominantly national, such as social welfare provision, taxation, education policy, health, cultural policy and most areas of criminal and civil law. That said, since the mid-1980s the policy reach of the EU has expanded into controversial areas of public policy that touch on sovereignty.

3 The *acquis communautaire* – the body of rules, laws, norms and practices – must be transposed, implemented and observed by the member states because the EU system is a system based on law. States will be brought to the European Court of Justice (ECJ) if they fail in their obligations to the Union's legal system. In addition, the *acquis* brings with it additional *principles of governance* such as partnership, mutual recognition, home country control, additionality and so on, that have an impact on domestic paradigms.

4   The EU's system of public policy making is characterised by a rhythm of activity that is beyond the control of any one member state. The *calendar technique* and pre-determined *time frames* are deployed extensively in the EU. These range from the six monthly presidencies to seven-year budgetary frames. All EC laws and major policy regimes contain a pre-determined commitment to review and evaluation. These time frames interact with and are affected by national calendars, notably by national elections, but they also have a dynamic of their own.

The national meets the European in a complex ecology of processes that differs across time and policy area. It functions not by creating a strong governance capacity at EU level but by co-opting the member states into the European. National prime ministers, ministers, senior officials and those at the operating core are drawn into the Brussels arena. Nor is involvement restricted to those in government and central administration. Government agencies, interest groups and cause groups are drawn into the EU web as politics and public policy making are no longer restricted to the domestic arena.

Policy making in the Union has a multilevelled character that stretches from Brussels to sub-national governments in the member states. Decision making involves nested games within each member state and connected games in Brussels. National and EU institutions form an integrated if loosely coupled system of joint policy making based on policy networks in all of the policy fields with an EU competence. With more member states, a widening co-operative agenda and the advance of communications technology, there is discernible increase in bilateral interaction among the member states at all levels – prime-ministerial, ministerial, senior official and desk official. Specialists are forging and maintaining links with their counterparts in the other member states on a continuous basis. Deliberations are no longer left primarily to meetings at working-party level in Brussels. Sophisticated networking is part and parcel of the Brussels game.

Impact on Ireland

An additional arena of public policy making
The most significant impact of EU membership on public policy making is the fact that policy making may begin at home but no longer ends there. Part and parcel of being a member of the Union is interaction on a bilateral and

multilateral basis with counterparts from the other member states in the Council of Ministers. The role of the Taoiseach is increasingly internationalised with at least four meetings of the European Council each year (see also chapter 6). The Council is best described as a club of heads of government with its own rhythm, norms and hierarchy. Before each Council meeting, the Taoiseach must be briefed on all items that may be raised on the agenda, and in informal meetings with his counterparts. As the representative of a small state, the Irish Taoiseach must use his opportunities for engagement and influence carefully.

Attendance at European Councils is augmented by a continuous series of bilateral visits in and out of Dublin. Managing the demands of internationalisation is a necessary skill for a head of government in contemporary Europe. It has added to the visibility of the Taoiseach as bilateral visits and European Councils are major media events. The enhanced international role of the head of government is particularly evident when a country holds the Presidency of the Union. During the six month Presidency, the national capital becomes a magnet for those wishing to influence the EU.

Government ministers are drawn into the Brussels web in their own sectors to attend formal and informal meetings of the Council and they must also maintain good bilateral relations with the Commission and their counterparts in other member states. Engagement with Brussels forms a core part of the work of Irish ministers for Foreign Affairs, Agriculture, Finance, Justice, Enterprise, the Marine and Public Enterprise. All of these ministers attend between three and six Councils each year. Increasingly ministers for Health, Education, Sport, Culture and Defence participate in one or two Councils each year.

EU business is part of the routine business of the Irish cabinet. Ministers will always keep the cabinet informed of major EU developments that are likely to have an impact on the exchequer finances, require national legislation and have constitutional implications. Traditionally, the Irish cabinet dealt with EU business much as it dealt with national business. Unlike the German cabinet, the Irish cabinet does not hold routine discussion of EU business at its weekly meeting. Ad hoc EU Cabinet sub-committees were established from time to time to deal with specific agenda items but during the 1997–2002 Ahern government a decision was taken to establish a permanent cabinet committee that meets on a monthly basis to review EU business. The shock of the Nice 'no' in June 2001 has augmented the importance of this committee.

Living with the Brussels system

The proliferation of Councils, high-level committees and working parties in Brussels demand an active Irish involvement. Meetings must be attended, reports written, negotiating tactics worked out, and interests consulted. And as noted above, the system works to a calendar and rhythm beyond the control of any one member state. The projection of national interests and preferences in the EU imposes tight deadlines on the Irish administrative system in terms of consultation and homework. Tracking what is happening in the Commission and in other national capitals is part of the necessary intelligence of domestic government. Building up personal relationships with Commission officials and administrators from partner governments is essential to the projection of Irish interests. All member states, including Ireland, must have their cadre of 'Brussels insiders' who know the treaties, how the EU does business, and how to find coalition partners. These Brussels insiders are at ease in a multi-national, multi-cultural and multi-lingual working environment. The Irish system does not have large numbers of boundary managers but those that it has are well used to burning the midnight oil for Ireland Inc.

One of the main strengths of the Irish system for managing EU business is its flexibility. The pragmatic and adaptive nature of Irish political and administrative culture enables the Irish to track the ebb and flow of EU negotiations and to develop tactics for different stages of the negotiations. The informality, ease of personal contact and collegiality among the EU cadre in central government leads to a culture of sharing information, consultation and 'singing from the same hymn sheet' in Brussels. The size of the Irish system and the small number of people working on any EU dossier ensure that lines of communication are short. This is a distinguishing feature of EU governance in Ireland. Ministers can be and are briefed quickly and informally. Each official tends to have a broader range of EU responsibilities than counterparts in other administrations, which militates against the dangers of over-specialisation. Good networking skills and a culture of pragmatism are beneficial in the informal politics characteristic of Brussels and Strasbourg (Laffan, 2001).

The weaknesses reflect the weaknesses of the system of Irish public policy making more generally. The system is too informal and ad hoc given the growing complexities of integration and the changing pattern of EU policies. Because the Irish system is driven by the agenda, important developments might be missed. The Irish system appears barely conscious of the growing importance of the European Parliament. The dominance of the departmental line leads to insufficient questioning of departmental orthodoxy. For example, the

Department of Agriculture's policy on the CAP (Common Agricultural Policy) or the Department of Finance policy on taxation would not be challenged. The system of interdepartmental co-ordination is much too weakly institutionalised to be effective in a strategic sense. It may be effective in relation to particular tasks but not in a strategic sense. Within departments, the EU co-ordination units are not central to getting the department to address European issues or to 'think European'. Individual officials working in specific sectoral areas have considerable autonomy in the development of national positions and are subject to fewer procedural constraints than their counterparts in other member states.

The high level of delegation, a consequence of the paucity of human resources, means that the calibre of individual officials matters more than it would in a more tightly controlled and better-resourced public administration. It also means that the level of detailed expertise that can be brought to bear on any one dossier is limited. Individual officials have developed strategies for dealing with the lack of resources by focusing on a limited number of areas that they have identified as significant for Ireland. Many officials when interviewed for a study of Ireland's EU management suggested that they were on some occasions 'flying by the seat of their pants', or in the game 'just to stay alive' (Interviews in Laffan, 2001). In many areas Ireland is a taker rather than shaper of EU policy, and responds in a defensive rather than a proactive manner. The change in Ireland's position in the EU arising from economic catch-up and the 'no' to Nice in 2001 will require a more strategic approach to Ireland's engagement with the EU in future.

The EU in the domestic

Membership of the EU is not just about projecting Ireland's interests in the Brussels arena. The tentacles of the EU have extended into the Irish economy, society and polity. The influence of the EU is manifest in different sectors, in approaches to governance, in law and in relation to different social groups. The Union is a system based on law, produces law that must implemented in the member states, and offers judicial review to individual Irish citizens if the Government is in breach of its obligations under Community law. We are now governed within a dual constitutional framework – the national and the European. Non-implementation of Community law is met with reasoned opinions from the EU Commission and ultimately with cases in the Luxembourg Court of Justice.

Irish interest groups are no longer confined to politics within the state. They engage in multi-levelled politics in Brussels. While the farmers, employers and trade unions were in Brussels from the outset, they have been joined by environmental groups, women's groups, groups representing the unemployed, single parent families, local communities and consumer interests. The battle for 'who gets what, where and how' is fought out at home and in the Brussels arena. National politics is complemented by a layer of transnational politics. Interests engage actively in EU politics to influence Community law, to get a slice of the Brussels budget, and to get external validation of what they are doing. The vibrancy of Irish associations in the Brussels arena is in stark contrast to the weak impact of the EU on Irish political parties and parliament.

Engagement with the EU has introduced new principles of governance and enhanced others in the Irish system. The insistence of the Commission on the principle of partnership in the deployment of EU structural fund monies loosened the grip of central administration on territorial politics in Ireland. Although Ireland remains one of the most centralised states in Europe, partnership and consultation opened up political space for local community and regional initiatives. Programmes, such as Leader for rural areas and integrated community initiatives in towns and cities, allowed for public policy experimentation rather than control from Dublin. Ireland's civic fabric was thereby strengthened following the deep social and political problems of the 1980s. The emphasis in the EU on balanced regional development did not foster sensible spatial policies in Ireland. The weakness of the regional tier of government and the intense competition between Irish towns has stymied efforts to promote regional development around a number of growth poles in Ireland. The enduring effects of localism in Irish politics are evident in the manner in which the decentralisation programme was carried out.

The impact of EU governance is clearly felt in the regulatory area because regulation is one of the main instruments of public power in the EU. In addition, modernisation of national regulation was necessary as the economy and society modernised. One of the striking developments of Irish government since Farrell observed it in 1975 is the rise of the regulatory state. A large number of regulatory agencies have been established, notably the Employment Equality Agency (now the Equality Agency), the Health and Safety Authority, the Food Safety Authority, the Environmental Protection Agency, the telecommunications regulator and the company law enforcer. Most of these agencies are part of a wider network of European regulatory networks and they interact on a continuous basis with the EU level agencies and the Commission. They are independent of government with a role in regulating and monitoring the behaviour of public and private actors. There is a very live EU debate on regulatory reform, which is mirrored in Ireland by the publication of a consultative document on better regulation.

Framing domestic policy choices

As the range of EU public policy expanded, its cumulative impact on policy choices at domestic level increased. Three areas are particularly noteworthy. First, EU public procurement and state aid policy limit the ability of the Irish state to show preference to local producers or to prop up ailing companies. In the mid-1990s, the Irish authorities ran into difficulties for the non-notification to the Commission of a number of urban renewal schemes including the Dublin Dock lands designation and non-airport enterprise zones. These required prior approval by the Commission as tax relief falls under the Union's state aid rule. The government was forced to introduce a number of amendments at the committee stage of the Urban Renewal Bill in June 1998 and had further lengthy negotiations with the Commission on all of these schemes. Although the constraints have been apparent, on balance it is in Ireland's interest that there are limits to what richer member states can do to support local producers. Moreover, given the localism of Irish political culture, constraint on the actions of governments in these fields is no bad thing.

The second area where the impact of the EU on national policy choices is evident is in relation to national budgetary policy. With participation in the European Monetary System from 1979, followed by the preparations for meeting the Euro convergence criteria, life in Euroland has meant that national budgetary policy is now framed by a set of collective EU processes. The Stability and Growth Pact and the Broad Economic Guidelines form part of the framework of national budgetary policy. National economic policies are a matter of common concern to all of the member states. In 2001, the ECO–FIN Council, on the recommendation of the Commission, issued a non-binding recommendation on Irish budgetary policy because the Commission felt that the Irish budget had deviated from already agreed guidelines. The Minister for Finance did not change the Irish budget nor did he have to because it was only a recommendation, but the 'spat' with the Commission and the other member states fed negatively into the debate on the Nice Treaty in June 2001.

Even in policy areas where there is minimal EU competence, the EU engages in thin policy co-ordination in what is known as the 'open method of co-ordination'. The open method is based on the development at EU level of a theory about what needs to be done in a particular field. Member states prepare a National Action Plan (NAP) setting out what current practice is and how they might achieve the objectives set at EU level. The NAPs are evaluated in a system of benchmarking, monitoring and peer review. The results of each evaluation are then filtered into a process of analysis to evaluate best practice and to support the diffusion of best practice throughout the system. In this manner, Irish employment policy, measures to foster social inclusion, and pensions policy are part of a wider transnational process of policy deliberation. Members of the Irish government and their officials are taken out of the domestic to participate in collective EU processes and the EU is taken into the domestic.

Nice: a critical juncture in Ireland's engagement with the EU

Until mid-2000, Ireland's profile in the EU and the tone and substance of European policy was largely consensual. Successive Irish governments portrayed Ireland as a constructive player in the system with a disposition to be as *communautaire* as possible within the limits of national preference. Rather than attempting to shape the broad outline of EU developments, the Irish concentrated on the details of key policy areas and the protection of a number of key interests. The objective was to ensure that there was a good fit between EU developments and domestic policies, that Ireland could afford the level of regulation that was emerging from Brussels, that maximum receipts were garnered from the EU budget, and that domestic space was protected particularly in relation to taxation. The success of the Agenda 2000 negotiations from an Irish perspective in March 1999 illustrates just how the Irish play the EU system. A small group of officials in Foreign Affairs, Agriculture, Finance, and Enterprise and Employment developed the Irish strategy and tactics over two years and the Taoiseach, Bertie Ahern, engaged in bilaterals with his counterparts, kept in touch with the Commission and managed to persuade the other member states that Ireland should be given a smooth landing in relation to receipts from the budget between 2000 and 2006. It was the Irish system at its most effective in dealing with Brussels.

Having succeeded in this important and complex set of negotiations, the Irish government then began to lose its coherence in relation to the EU and Ireland's engagement with it. The changing governmental discourse on the EU was brought sharply into focus in a number of speeches and articles written by the Minister for the Arts, Culture and the Gaeltacht, Síle de Valera, and the Tánaiste, Mary Harney, in summer 2000. These speeches were important because of what they contained and the audience to which they were delivered.

The Tánaiste's address was delivered in July 2000 to a meeting of the American Bar Association in Dublin. In it she asserted that 'Geographically we are closer to Berlin than Boston. Spiritually we are probably a lot closer to Boston than Berlin.' She went on to say that 'There are some who want to create a more centralised Europe, a federal Europe, with key political economic decisions being taken at Brussels level. I don't think that that would be in Ireland's interests and I don't think it would be in Europe's interests either.' She ended by saying that she believed in a 'Europe of independent states, not a United States of Europe' (Harney, 2000a).

The July speech was followed by an opinion piece in *The Irish Times* in September 2000 in which she posed a number of questions about the prospect of a European government, a United States of Europe, and of all major social and economic decisions taken by qualified majority voting. Again the tone of the article was that of support for an enlarged and liberal Europe but rejection of excessive integration. In sum, the minister said, 'we believe the future of the EU lies not in a United States of Europe, but in a Union of independent sovereign states' (Harney, 2000b). The latter statement was reminiscent of De Gaulle's 'L'Europe des patries' or Margaret Thatcher's celebrated Bruges speech in 1988. The discourse deployed in both pieces was a discourse that placed considerable emphasis on 'sovereignty' and 'independence' with no discussion of what these contested terms mean at the beginning of the twenty-first century. The political content reflected a concern about EU regulation and a clear preference for Anglo-American capitalism rather than the continental model. Progressive Democrat preferences about political economy were translated into preferences about the future architecture of the EU. Clearly the Tánaiste was happy with market Europe but uneasy about political Europe.

Another address by Síle de Valera in Boston College in September 2000 raised additional issues about the EU and Ireland. In this speech she asserted that 'Participation in the European Union has been good for Ireland. The Union has worked well. But it is not the cornerstone of what our nation is or should be.' She went on to say that 'we have found that directives and regulations agreed in Brussels can often seriously impinge on our identity, culture and traditions', and she looked 'forward to a future in which Ireland will exercise a more vigilant, a more questioning attitude to the European Union' (de Valera, 2000). Again the discourse was that of protecting national identity and vigilance about guarding the national interest. These speeches were in marked contrast to the tone adopted by Bertie Ahern and the Minister for Foreign Affairs, Brian Cowan, in this period.

The 'soft Euroscepticism' evident in the Harney and de Valera speeches was fuelled in early 2001 during the spat between Commission and the Minister for Finance, Charlie McCreevy, about the Irish budget and the EU's broad economic guidelines discussed above. Preoccupied with foot and mouth disease, the government decided to hold the referendum on the Nice Treaty in June 2001 after a very short campaign of just three weeks. The government clearly felt that the issue was not contentious and that a majority could be secured with relative ease. As the short campaign progressed, it became evident that the government was in trouble. This was the fifth referendum in Ireland on the EU since 1972. All of the others had been passed by a comfortable, albeit declining, majority. On 7 June 2001, the Irish electorate voted 'no' to the Nice Treaty by 53.87 per cent to 46.13 per cent, in an extremely low turn out of just 34.8 per cent. The outcome of the referendum was a major reversal for the government that had negotiated the treaty, for the main opposition parties that had advocated a 'yes' vote, and for the peak groups in civil society, notably the main business associations, farming organisations and the trade union congress.

There is no doubt that the 'no' side, not only won the referendum, but conducted the most effective campaign. There were far more 'no' posters than 'yes' posters throughout the country. The 'no' forces consisted of a myriad of groups who were opposed to different aspects of the EU. They shared little in common but their desire to defeat the government and to secure a 'no' to an EU treaty. The 'no' forces included on the right conservative Catholic forces and Sinn Féin, and on the left the Green Party, pacifists and third world activists. The two political parties with representation in the Irish parliament, the Green Party and Sinn Féin, who opposed the Nice Treaty had three deputies from a total of 166. The 'no' campaign had simple clear messages such as 'You will lose: power, money and freedom' and 'No to Nice: No to NATO'. Unlike previous referendums, the 'no' campaign was supported by highly respectable establishment figures including a former Attorney-General, who was concerned with the lack of parliamentary scrutiny of Ireland's EU policy and with the growing legislative role of the Union.

The rejection of Nice altered the context and agenda of Ireland's European policy. A relatively stable institutional and policy relationship – as analysed above – was cut loose from its moorings. The government was faced with the challenge of re-establishing a stable European policy domestically, mending relations with EU institutions, the member states and candidate countries. The referendum result represented a critical juncture in Ireland's relationship with the EU and 2002 was a very significant year in determining just how Ireland's European engagement would proceed.

The government had to manage two arenas – the domestic and the EU – as it sought to re-establish a stable European policy. Domestically, the government was faced with an electorate, most of whom did not vote on the Nice Treaty, and the majority of those that did voting 'no'. The campaign and analysis of why people voted 'no' highlighted considerable uncertainty among the 'electorate' about the EU. Three main concerns were identified in post-referendum research. (Sinnott, 2001) These were that:

1 Voters felt that they did not have sufficient time or information to understand the issues.
2 Some voters felt that Ireland did not have sufficient control or input into EU decisions.
3 Some voters felt that Irish neutrality was threatened by the Nice Treaty.

Given the importance of the Nice Treaty for enlargement, the government held a second referendum in autumn 2002. The response to the Nice 'no' was to set up a National Forum on Europe in October 2001, which met in Dublin Castle in plenary session and in mini fora around the country. The Forum, chaired by Maurice Hayes, was based on representation from the political parties, although Fine Gael refused to participate until after the May 2002 election. The Forum was augmented by an observer pillar consisting of both the anti EU and pro EU forces. Unlike the situation following the Danish 'no' to the Treaty on European Union in 1992, there was no evidence that a national consensus on how to proceed following Nice1 could emerge. All sides essentially retained their positions on the Treaty of Nice.

The second pillar of the Government's response related to parliamentary scrutiny of EU business. Notwithstanding the establishment of a Committee for Foreign Affairs and a European Affairs Committee, parliamentary scrutiny of what the Irish executive did in Brussels and how it implemented EC law was one of the weakest in Europe. Governments were largely unfettered in the development of European policy. The Oireachtas did not have a European cadre of deputies and senators well versed in the complexities of EU policies or policy making. The localism of Irish politics militated against the emergence of parliamentary expertise on Europe. Moreover, parliamentary committees lacked the research back up and administrative capacity to keep track of the flow of EU business.

In response to concerns about parliamentary scrutiny, the government sought and obtained all-party agreement on proposals to enhance the scrutiny of EC proposals before they become law. Departments will be obliged to prepare 'notes' on all developments for the relevant committees, and ministers and officials will attend meetings if required. This may lead to the development of a cadre of Europeanised parliamentarians in the Oireachtas, but the committee will need additional administrative and research capacity if parliamentary scrutiny is to be enhanced.

The third pillar in the government's strategy was to get a political declaration from the European Council in Seville at the end of June 2002 on the Union's Common Foreign and Security Policy (CFSP) and the European Security and Defence Policy (ESDP). Such a declaration was unlikely to influence the neutrality lobby in Ireland, which aims to remove Ireland from the ESDP and the CFSP, but it was designed to have an influence on the wider electorate rather than on foreign policy activists. Armed with a declaration, enhanced parliamentary scrutiny, and a renewed electoral mandate, the Government opted for a second Nice referendum on 19 October 2002.

Nice2 was very different from the first both in its conduct and outcome. The vote in the second Nice referendum was a decisive 'yes' of 62.89 per cent to 37.11 per cent against. The turnout of 49 per cent was significantly up on the previous referendum and the vast majority of the additional voters voted 'yes'. The 'no' vote increased by some 5,000 votes whereas the 'yes' vote increased by just under 500,000. The preparations for the second Nice campaign were much more thorough because the Taoiseach was acutely aware of what was at stake for Ireland and for his own political position. The second campaign was characterised by far higher mobilisation on the part of the government parties, the pro-EU opposition parties and civil society groups. Public meetings were organised by the National Forum, the European Movement, the 'No to Nice' campaign, the Fine Gael party, student debating societies and many others. Garret FitzGerald, a former Taoiseach, came out of retirement to campaign actively on the 'yes' side. The country was festooned with pro and anti posters. The print and electronic media ran the Nice story throughout the summer and intensively for the four weeks of the campaign, although it rarely hit the front pages. There was a very high level of international interest in the referendum with television and radio crews and print journalists from all over the world travelling throughout the country in search of the Irish voter.

The mobilisation of civil society on the 'yes' side was a distinctive feature of the second Nice referendum. The employers' organisations, the trade unions and the farming groups ran far more intensive campaigns. A group of young students and professionals established the 'Ireland for Europe' group that added energy to the campaign. In addition, the 'Irish Alliance for Europe' an umbrella group was set up. The Alliance was a 'coalition of the willing' involving organised civil society (the employers, chambers of commerce, farmers and trade unionists) and a series of additional nodes, such as 'Women for Europe', 'Greens for Europe', 'Lawyers for Europe' and the 'Disability Alliance'. Although the Alliance began without any material or human resources, it managed to attract sufficient resources to organise a campaign that involved intensive on-the-ground campaigning, participation in public meetings through-out the country and an extensive media campaign using television, radio, and print both at national and local levels. The Alliance provided an arena for all those who wanted to contribute to the campaign to do so.

On the face of it, the decisive 'yes' to Nice suggests that Ireland's European policy is back on track within a stable framework. This may be overly optimistic, however, as difficult choices must be made on Europe in the context of the Convention on the Future of Europe.

The post Nice agenda

The Nice referendums in Ireland have lessons for those who mediate Ireland's European policy. The key lesson is that communicating Europe cannot be left to three or four short weeks before a referendum is held. If complex European issues must be submitted to the Irish electorate, a continuous process of communication and engagement between the political class and the citizens is essential. Governments cannot take the electorate for granted or think that it will blindly follow their lead. This is a challenge given the nature of EU pro-cesses and the technical character of policy making in the Union. It is also a challenge because interest in European issues is low, and knowledge about the EU limited. The public space in Ireland, as for all of the member states, is dominated by domestic issues. European issues tend to be treated only when contentious, and then from a national perspective. Nice exposed the fact that Ireland does not have many politicians comfortable with explaining and advo-cating the benefits of the Union. Most share a sense that that the EU has been good to Ireland but find it difficult to go beyond this. The limited cadre of knowledgeable politicians is drawn from those who have served as ministers or ministers of state in the Council or had experience in the European Parliament.

Nice exposed a disjuncture between Ireland's highly internationalised economy and localised politics.

Nice also exposed a deep uncertainty among the Irish political and administrative class about just what kind of EU they want. Ireland's image as a constructive player in the Union has been replaced by 'minimalism' and defensiveness. In the past, support for further integration was usually portrayed as congruent with Ireland's interests. The benchmark was to be at least more supportive than the United Kingdom. The Blair government, however, has changed the tone and substance of British policy (apart from over the Euro). The UK is no longer perceived as the awkward partner and is a leader in relation to defence, the Lisbon agenda and anti-terrorism measures. Irish governments, on the other hand, appear uncertain about the constitutional and institutional development of the Union. Following the shock of Nice, the Irish position appears hesitant and overly concerned with a limited number of policy areas, particularly taxation. What Ireland does not want is far clearer than what Ireland wants. There is a certain nostalgia for an EU that is no longer feasible given the continental enlargement of the Union.

Conclusions

Brian Farrell was correct in suggesting in 1975 that the European Union created a new context for public policy discussion and decision making. This chapter identifies the impact of membership of the Union on the structures, processes and content of Irish public policy. What was not quite so evident in those early years of membership was the inherent dynamism of the Union. Since then the EU has broadened its policy reach, deepened its institutional and constitutional fabric, and expanded its membership. The Union that Ireland is now a member of at the beginning of the twenty-first century is very different from the Union that Ireland joined in 1973. The processes of economic, political and legal integration have deepened as Western Europe responded to changes in the international political economy and international politics. Further change is in prospect arising from the collapse of communism and the enlargement of the Union to Central and Eastern Europe.

The impact of integration on statehood in Europe was less evident in 1975. To be a member state is now to become locked into a highly institutionalised constitutional framework with other states. Neighbours are transformed into partners. The ties that bind go well beyond traditional international organisations. The EU reaches into the tentacles of the member states, and domestic actors operate at national and European level. The Union influences state identity and the individual identities of some of its citizens.

Irish politicians and civil servants have managed to navigate the Union's institutional and decision-making processes with relative ease. Concentrating on a number of key policy areas has allowed them to survive with limited human resources. An enlarged Union will be more challenging as it heralds the arrival of many more states all seeking voice and influence. In addition, future Irish governments are likely to face difficult dilemmas regarding the institutional and constitutional fabric of the Union. Successive governments have been conservative and cautious on the 'polity' dimensions of European integration. This is partly to do with political culture, and it partly arises from Ireland's size and geographical position. There is a disjuncture between Ireland's highly globalised economy, localised political culture, and a society that is both internationalised and local.

Note

1   This is being written just after Basil's death in May 2002. As Basil's last PhD student, I recall my personal debt to him as mentor and good friend. Basil Chubb and Brian Farrell were pioneers in mapping the Irish political system.

Bibliography

De Valera, S. (2000) Address to Boston College, 18 September.

Farrell B. (1975) 'Irish government re-observed', *Economic and Social Review* 6: 405–14.

Harney M. (2000a) Address to a Meeting of the American Bar Association, Dublin, 21 July.

Harney M. (2000b) Opinion piece in *The Irish Times*, 20 September.

Laffan B. (2001) *Organising for a Changing Europe: Irish Central Government and the European Union*, Dublin: Trinity Blue paper.

Puchala D. (1972) 'Of blind men, elephants and international integration', *Journal of Common Market Studies*, 267–84.

Sinnott R. (2001) 'Attitudes and Behaviour of the Irish Electorate in the Referendum on the Treaty of Nice', Institute for the Study of Social Change Working Papers, University College Dublin.

CHAPTER TEN

Critical elections and the prehistory of the Irish party system

JOHN COAKLEY

—

Introduction

It is now more than three decades since Brian Farrell drew attention to the formative influence of the general election of 1918 on the Irish party system. This election constituted, in his words, 'the real foundation of contemporary Irish politics' (Farrell, 1970: 488), and had a determining effect on the shape of the party system that developed subsequently. But foundations, to follow the metaphor, do not tell the whole story. The present contribution argues that in accounting for the earliest phases in the development of the Irish party system we need to consider also two other critical junctures. In addition to the crucial election of 1918, we need to look back at the general election of 1885, which cleared the site and allowed the foundations to be excavated, and forward to the general election of 1922, in the course of which the present party political edifice was constructed.

A vigorous tradition in historical research has done much to explain particular aspects of the evolution of Irish party politics in the pre-modern period. The pre-union Irish parliament has been extensively studied (for example, Johnston, 1963; McCracken, 1971; Hayton, 2001), and its political activities have been comprehensively documented (Johnston-Liik, 2002). In addition to the analyses of particular parties and movements referred to later in this chapter, three researchers have produced path-breaking studies of particular aspects of nineteenth-century Irish politics: Peter Jupp (1967; 1969; 1973; 1986) on the two immediately post-union decades, Theodore Hoppen (1984) in his definitive work on Irish political organisation from the 1830s to the 1880s, and Brian Mercer Walker (1973; 1978; 1981; 1989; 1996) on the latter part of the century, especially in Ulster. Specific themes have also been explored in depth;

these include the link between electoral politics and the revolutionary under-ground (Garvin, 1981; 1987), the tension between parliamentary and agrarian politics (Bew, 1978; 1987) and the influence of two crucial groups on electoral behaviour in the nineteenth century: priests (Whyte, 1960) and landlords (Whyte, 1965).

Yet attempts to generalise about the relationship between party system development and Irish social and institutional transformation before 1922 have been surprisingly rare. The leading interpretations of the post-1922 party system (Mair, 1987: 12–29; Sinnott, 1995: 277–97) rightly trace its roots to the Sinn Féin victory at the 1918 general election, and do not probe further into the political soil in which these were embedded. A major exception to this approach is R. K. Carty's (1993) original and insightful account of party building from 1832 to 1918, which relates episodes in the evolution of the party system to phases of more intense electoral competition, with 1832, 1852, 1872–92 and 1918–32 as the high points.

The Irish party system of the pre-1922 period is of exceptional comparative interest. First, in its early stages it offers further evidence of the powerful tendency towards political dualism that has been so characteristic of the early stages of party organisation, especially in conditions of limited democracy. Second, it draws attention to the striking importance of social mobilisation – in addition to the more obvious pressure of institutional reform and franchise extension that has so prominent a place in the comparative literature – as the motive force of party political evolution in its early stages. Third, it illustrates the remarkable capacity of social structure to determine the shape of the party system, unusual though this shape was by European standards. Fourth, however, it also shows the extent to which the 'normal' pattern of organic evolution of the party system may be utterly disrupted, and it highlights the manner in which a securely established mass-based system may be replaced almost overnight by a radically different alternative; indeed, this occurred, in very different forms, on three occasions – in 1885, 1918 and 1922. The rest of this chapter develops these points in turn.

The origins of the party system

The tendency towards dualism in party systems has been acknowledged for more than half a century. One classic summary identified this not just in party political contexts but in others too:

Throughout history all the great factional conflicts have been dualist: Armagnacs and Burgundians, Guelphs and Ghibellines, Catholics and Protestants, Girondins and Jacobins, Conservatives and Liberals, Bourgeois and Socialists, 'Western' and Communists . . . whenever public opinion is squarely faced with great fundamental problems it tends to crystallise round two opposed poles. The natural movement of societies tends towards the two-party system (Duverger, 1964: 216).

There is much evidence that the initial stages of party system development have been rooted in dichotomous differences over specific political issues, with dynastic succession a common source of disagreement. The eighteenth century division between Whigs and Tories in the British parliament and between Hats and Caps in the Swedish Riksdag are examples.[1] But the dual character of party politics that has been apparent from an early stage in the evolution of representative parliaments has a more obvious explanation than policy disagreement. To the extent that parliaments had a voice in the process of government, it was in the interest of the governing authorities (typically, the king and his advisers) to ensure its systematic acquiescence. The most obvious mechanism for doing this was to form a durable alliance with a parliamentary majority. It was thus natural for the ruling group to recruit a body of dependable supporters, and for a 'government' and an 'opposition' party to emerge, however unstable their membership. As is well known, this tendency was reinforced by traditional electoral systems, which, whether plurality or majority based, promoted a dualism at constituency level that was at least neutral in respect of such alliances as were to emerge at parliamentary level but that more typically promoted a two-party system (see Duverger, 1964: 217). This tendency was not, of course, confined to pre-democratic Europe; it is commonly found to the present in semi-authoritarian states in many parts of the world.

The vague concepts 'Whig' and 'Tory' were to emerge in the Irish parliament in the eighteenth century, as they did in Britain, but as the century ended the more obvious dividing line was that which separated members of the 'Government' party led by the Lord Lieutenant from the 'Patriot' opposition, a disparate group the motivation of whose members ranged from thwarted self-interest to long-standing commitment to an independent outlook (see Johnston, 1963: 272–82). Yet however embryonic, it is clear that the notion of party in the modern sense already existed. One observer in 1790 described this as a 'union of honourable and independent men, connected by a conformity of sentiment', and went on with a prescient description of the twin motors that would animate Irish party politics for many decades – divisions between classes and between nations:

> Mr Hume has well remarked that besides the general tendency of a free state to produce political dissensions, there exists in our mixed monarchy, a particular source of controversy: It is the diversity of opinions men may form as to the degree of power to which each order is entitled. In the peculiar circumstances of this country we may extend still further the observation, and point out, in our connection with England, an additional cause of distrust and disunion (Anon, 1790: 4, 12–13).

After the Act of Union of 1800, the last speaker of the Irish House of Commons, John Foster, tried to form an Irish party in the new United Kingdom House of Commons, but most Irish MPs eventually aligned themselves with the two loose groupings already in existence in Great Britain (Jupp, 1969). The number of non-aligned Irish MPs declined from 50 (exactly half of the Irish representation in the House of Commons) in 1801 to five in 1818. Over the first ten post-Union elections (1801–31), 51 per cent of Irish MPs could be classified as Tories, 35 per cent as Whigs and 14 per cent as non-aligned.[2]

In the second phase in the development of the Irish party system the tendency towards dualism was confirmed, though it was already beginning to come under strain towards the end of this period. In the course of the 12 elections between 1832 and 1880, 36 per cent of Irish seats were won by Tories and the remainder by their opponents. The latter group consisted almost entirely of Whigs (later transformed into Liberals) and their Irish allies, groups not easily distinguishable from each other. Whigs or Liberals in the narrow sense made up the largest number (35 per cent of the total); the remainder comprised O'Connell's Repeal Party (13 per cent, 1832–47), the Independent Irish Party (five per cent, 1852–59) and the Home Rule Party led by Butt and Parnell (ten per cent, 1874–80).[3]

Up to this point, there are striking similarities with the pattern of party development in other parts of Europe. The closest parallels will be found in some of Europe's smaller emerging democracies.[4] As in Ireland, the early stage in the emergence of the Scandinavian party systems was characterised by the growth of a strong but internally diverse Liberal Party that was capable of overshadowing its Conservative opponents. This was the case in Norway (where Liberals and their allies won 69 per cent of seats, 1882–97), Sweden (52 per cent, 1882–97) and Denmark (72 per cent, 1887–98). In Belgium during the corresponding formative period, the Catholic and Liberal parties were almost equal in strength (51 per cent and 49 per cent of seats respectively, 1848–92). In The Netherlands, Liberal dominance (52 per cent of seats, 1888–94) was challenged by the Catholic party (25 per cent) and the (Calvinist) Anti-Revolutionary Party (21 per cent).[5]

The roots of party organisation

If Irish Conservative–Liberal (or, more accurately, Tory versus anti-Tory) dualism resembled the pattern elsewhere in Europe, the shape that the party system was to acquire as political reform and franchise extension proceeded diverged increasingly from the more 'normal' model. In the countries mentioned above, it was the liberal opposition that tended to organise formally first, especially in Scandinavia. Thus, we find the Swedish liberals originating in the 1860s and forming a parliamentary organisation in the 1890s; their Danish counterparts organising as *Venstre* ('the Left') in 1870; and their Norwegian equivalent (also known as *Venstre*) organising at around the same time. In each of these cases, conservative organisation tended to be later and looser, relying on its links with the political establishment. In Belgium, similarly, it was the Liberals who organised first (1846), followed much later by their Catholic rivals (1888), since the latter had been able to rely on the infrastructure of the Catholic church. In The Netherlands, by contrast, it was the conservative Calvinist Anti-Revolutionary Party that organised first (1879), to be followed by the Catholics and the Liberals in the 1880s. In each of these countries a socialist party appeared at a relatively early stage, even if its electoral base was insufficient to ensure it a significant parliamentary presence: in Denmark (1871), The Netherlands (1882), Belgium (1885), Norway (1887) and Sweden (1889).[6]

The evolution of Irish party organisation was sharply different. On the one hand, parties organised earlier; on the other, their development illustrated strikingly the impact of social mobilisation in modifying the effects of electoral reform. This point may best be appreciated if we look at Irish party evolution in the context of the broader European pattern as described by Lipset and Rokkan (1967), Rokkan (1970) and Sartori (1976). These classic works recognised the centrality of institutional reform as a driver of party organisation. As summarised by Sartori (1976: 20–3), there were three stages in party evolution. In the first, the emergence of the *parliamentary party* was intimately linked to the process by which the notion of responsible government (with its central component, ministerial answerability to parliament) emerged. Responsible government led to the first wave of electoral enfranchisement, and promoted the creation of the second type, the *electoral party*, a kind of organisation that was geared to fighting for votes and whose advent marked the solidification of the party system and the beginnings of party government. This was followed, in turn, by large-scale franchise extension; at the point where involvement of the community in the electoral process reached a critical mass (a point that might fall well short of universal suffrage, or even of universal male suffrage), the process was completed, with the appearance of the *mass party*. These types correspond closely to the micro-organisational patterns described in the earlier standard work (Duverger, 1964: 17–27): in the first, the absence of any local organisation; in the second, the existence of a constituency-level *caucus*; and in the third, the creation of a network of *branches* within each constituency.

In terms of its internal logic, Sartori's model is a compelling description of the path of party evolution, and it is compatible with the thrust of Rokkan's (1970: 87) argument to the effect that the introduction of mass suffrage ushered in the era of mass electioneering and mass organisation. But its capacity to account for the *actual* pattern by which European party systems emerged in the nineteenth century is much less obvious. There is, indeed, a good deal of counter-evidence. Thus, in Denmark, France and Germany, where effective male suffrage was introduced in the middle of the nineteenth century, the party system appeared at a much later stage, and appears to have been a response to social and political stimuli rather than to later institutional reforms. In Belgium, The Netherlands and Norway, the modern party system began to emerge even before the introduction of mass suffrage. In Great Britain itself, which Sartori uses as his main example, alternative interpretations of the sequence of development are commonly accepted; instead of the sequence he describes (responsible government – parliamentary party – franchise extension – electoral party), it is at least arguable that the order of the first three of these should be altered (parliamentary party – franchise extension – responsible government – electoral party).

In Ireland, the absence of fit between party organisation and institutional reform on the Sartori model was even more striking. Franchise reform proceeded at a very uneven pace (it should be noted that even after the Union of 1800, Irish electoral law continued to be separate from English and Scottish law; common UK-level provisions date only from 1884). The electorate was concentrated overwhelmingly in rural areas, where it had traditionally been based on the 'forty-shilling freehold' – occupation of a freehold premises with a minimum valuation of £2. Before the union, there were essentially two types of urban electorate. First, in eight 'counties of cities' and 'counties of towns' (equivalent to today's county boroughs), franchise provisions were similar to those in the countryside; and in a number of smaller boroughs there was a similarly extended electorate, under a variety of legal and de facto arrangements. Second, however, in about half of the boroughs the right to vote was confined to the members of the corporation – typically, 13 people. The system was even more exclusive, in that after 1692 only Protestants were permitted to sit in parliament, and after 1716, only Protestants were allowed to vote. This system was reformed in a number of phases.

- The Roman Catholic Relief Act, 1793, extended the right of voting to Catholics, causing a huge increase in the size of the electorate; the county electorate rose from about 46,000 in 1784 to about 160,000 in 1803 (Jupp, 1986: 101).
- The Act of Union, 1800, did not affect the franchise directly, but it brought about a reduction in the number of Irish MPs from 300 to 100 by abolishing 84 smaller and particularly unrepresentative boroughs and reducing the level of representation of others (Jupp, 1973: 152).
- The Parliamentary Elections (Ireland) Act, 1829, enacted at the same time as the Catholic Emancipation Act that permitted Catholics to take seats in parliament, was designed to counteract the effects of the latter: it raised the qualification for county voters by a factor of five, to £10, thus reducing the electorate from about 216,000 in 1828 to about 37,000 (Evans, 2000: 123).[7]
- The Representation of the People (Ireland) Act, 1832, extended the county and borough electorate to include leaseholders of property with a value of at least £10, more than doubling the electorate, to 93,000 in 1832 (Gash, 1953: 90).
- The Representation of the People (Ireland) Act, 1850, a response in part to a collapse in the size of the electorate following the famine, introduced rateable valuation as the criterion for voting in the counties, setting the limit at £12; the electorate expanded from 61,000 in 1850 to 164,000 in 1851 (Lampson, 1907: 300).
- The Representation of the People (Ireland) Act, 1868, reduced the qualification in urban areas to £4 and introduced a new lodger franchise; the urban electorate increased by about 50 per cent, but the total electorate increased only slightly, from 206,000 in 1862 to 224,000 in 1871 (Walker, 1973).
- The Representation of the People Act, 1884, introduced a uniform householder and lodger franchise and greatly extended the electorate; it increased from 226,000 in 1884 to 738,000 in 1885 (Walker, 1973).

- The Representation of the People Act, 1918, extended the suffrage to all adult males and to qualified women aged at least 30; the electorate increased from 697,000 in 1915 to 1,926,000 in 1918 (Walker, 1973; Coakley, 1994).[8]

Aside from the 1829 act, the pattern here is of steady or occasionally dramatic increase; but developments in party organisation were only in part a response to these reforms, as the history of its gradual evolution shows.

In view of its geopolitically marginal location and relatively low level of socio-economic development, the Ireland of the 1820s is one of the more improbable parts of Europe in which to seek out the vanguard of modern party political development. Yet the evidence of such development seems incontrovertible, and has for long been well documented in Irish historiography, though not acknowledged in the comparative literature. Studies of the Catholic Association (1823–9) led by Daniel O'Connell have paid tribute to that body as 'a colossus of democratic power unprecedented in the annals of political organisation in the British Isles', or indeed elsewhere (Reynolds, 1954: 13), or have described it as 'the first Irish mass political party which focused primarily on parliamentary and constitutional objectives', while noting its great European significance (O'Ferrall, 1985: 145, 279–80). In addition to the role of this form of political organisation as a model for English radicals (Reynolds, 1954: 173–5), it also had an impact on radicals in continental Europe, as in Italy, France and among the Czechs and other Slavs (Williams, 1984), and it became a model for German Catholic political organisation between 1830 and 1850 (Grogan, 1991).

The significance of the Catholic Association was not just that it developed a blueprint that resembled the structure of a modern mass party (this was adopted in 1828); this blueprint was partly translated into reality, with a network of Liberal clubs at county (constituency) level co-ordinating the activities of parochial or baronial clubs. The extent to which the organisational structure of the Catholic Association penetrated the countryside may be seen from its large membership (about 14,000), the number of local reading rooms that it sponsored with a view to promoting political education, the large sums that its local organisers were able to collect as 'Catholic rent' to fund the association's activities, and the enormous numbers of people (hundreds of thousands) that turned out at its meetings. Of course, much of this participation was of an essentially extra-parliamentary form (many of those attending the association's 'monster' meetings were not eligible to vote); and organisational capacity depended also on the structure of the Catholic Church.

Although the vigour of O'Connell's organisation was later to wane, it had a lasting impact on Irish Catholic electoral organisation. At local level, many Liberal clubs survived into the 1830s, 1840s and beyond, commonly reconstituted as 'Independent' clubs and establishing relationships with later O'Connellite and other Dublin-based organisations. The Catholic Association was banned by the government in 1829, but between then and 1840 O'Connell established about a dozen similar societies in succession, several of them also banned (McDowell, 1952). These included the National Political Union (1831), the Anti-Tory Association (1834), the General Association (1836) and the Precursor Society (1838). But the most important was the Repeal Association (1840–8), committed to re-establishing Irish independence by repeal of the Act of Union, which emulated the remarkable popular movement of the 1820s, with its local reading rooms, 'monster meetings' and 'repeal rent', a system for collecting financial support from all classes that stretched to the remotest parts of the island (MacIntyre, 1965: 77–98, 266–98).

The next three initiatives in this tradition were more modest organisationally. In 1850 there appeared the Irish Tenant League, a federation of local agrarian-oriented societies that succeeded briefly in linking Catholics and Presbyterians and that functioned as the electoral arm of an 'Independent Irish Party' in 1852–9 (Whyte, 1958). Following a lapse in 'independent' organisation, there appeared in 1864 the National Association, a clerically inspired attempt to defend the interests of the Catholic Church, but one which attracted little support from Liberal MPs and which faded out in 1873 (Corish, 1962; Norman, 1965: 135–89). The last years of the National Association overlapped with the first years of the Home Government Association, an organisation founded in 1870 by a Tory lawyer, Isaac Butt, with the object of achieving a modest measure of devolution ('home rule') for Ireland. This was replaced in 1873 by a more vigorous body, the Home Rule League, one that had a major impact in the general election of 1874 and that was to pave the way for the country's first modern mass party, as we will see below (Thornley, 1964: 83–175).

This pattern had no counterpart among Irish Whigs or Liberals, who lacked any kind of central organisation in Ireland but instead depended on the leadership of Liberal politicians in Dublin Castle when a Liberal administration was in office in London; it was only at a very late stage that a modest level of regional organisation was attained, with the Ulster Liberal Society, founded in 1865, as the outstanding example (Walker, 1989: 58; Harbinson, 1973: 7). But the great enemies of the Whigs and Liberals, the Tories, were better organised. For more than two centuries, the Orange Order (founded in 1795) has functioned as a mechanism for providing a forum for interdenominational religious, social and political activism among Protestants, though its electoral role has been limited and its organisational activity has been uneven over time. However, the activities of the Catholic Association sparked the formation of a Protestant counterpart. First in this category was a network of 'Brunswick clubs' in 1828–9; these were followed by other electoral organisations, including the Irish Protestant Conservative Society (1831–3) (McDowell, 1952). The Tory electoral baton was later taken up by the Irish Protestant Metropolitan Society (1836) and by other electoral organisations, but the foundation in 1853 of a more permanent Central Conservative Society of Ireland provided an ongoing organisational base (Hoppen, 1984: 278–332). As in the case of Catholic mobilisation, then, Protestant electoral mobilisation took off before the early stages of franchise extension, to which it seems to have had at best a weak relationship.

Voters and parties under the restricted franchise

The third general theme in the prehistory of the Irish party system is the relationship between party support and social structure. The dualism of the party system and the motive force for electoral organisation stemmed from the outstanding characteristic of Irish society: the significance of the Catholic–Protestant division. This separated not merely two religious groups, but two communities that were becoming increasingly differentiated in terms of national identity. It is true that the Catholic emancipation and repeal movements had received support from some Protestants, and that the Tenant League brought northern Presbyterians into a shaky, temporary alliance with southern Catholics; but the long-term trend was towards increased coincidence between the religious division and the party political one. This may be seen at three levels: the composition of the parliamentary parties, voting tendencies in the constituencies, and the pattern of individual voting behaviour.

The characteristics of political elites such as parliamentarians are, of course, no more than that: they will not necessarily tell us very much about the characteristics of the people who support them. The phenomena of the 'working class' party led by intellectuals and the middle class, and of the 'peasant' party led by teachers and shopkeepers, are well known: marginalised groups commonly rely on articulate defectors from more privileged groups to provide the leadership cadres that political organisations require. In the Irish case, similarly, there is nothing surprising in the notion of a Catholic, peasant movement being led by members from outside this group – or even by Protestant land-lords, that central component in the country's ruling class. This was not just a survival from a period in which this class was seen as the sole repository of 'natural' leaders, but reflected the reality that unpaid MPs required either an independent income or a party stipend.

On the one hand, then, it is not surprising that the Irish Tory party, one of whose organs described it in 1832 as serving 'the English interest, the Protestant interest, the conservative interest' (McDowell, 1952) should have been made up overwhelmingly of Protestant landlords. Over the whole period 1832–85, indeed, only one of its MPs was a Catholic; and in 1832–59 81 per cent of its MPs were landlords (with 12 per cent professionals, 5 per cent merchants and 2 per cent other) (Hoppen, 1984: 264, 336). On the other hand, most non-Tory MPs in the 1830s were also Protestant, though by the 1870s and 1880s Catholics outnumbered Protestant MPs in this group by about two to one; and this group also relied heavily on landlords as its principal members (65 per cent of all non-Tory MPs, 1832–59) (Hoppen, 1984: 264, 336). Catholic dominance among anti-Tory MPs adhering to 'independent' Irish parties was more pronounced: Catholics accounted for 26 of 39 Repeal Party MPs (67 per cent) in 1832, 38 of 48 Independent Irish Party MPs (79 per cent) in 1852 and 46 of 59 Home Rule Party MPs (78 per cent) in 1874 (calculated from MacIntyre, 1965: 74; Whyte, 1958: 180–1; Thornley, 1964: 210).

When we look at the characteristics of voters, we are confronted with two basic kinds of data, similar to those available to us for the study of contem-porary elections: aggregate data (about the collective behaviour of voters in constituencies) and individual data (about the choices of individual voters). Figure 10.1 gives some indication of the pattern of the former. It breaks down party support at each election from 1832 to 1880 within two main zones: the counties that now constitute Northern Ireland, and the rest of the island. The extent to which the Protestant areas that now form Northern Ireland were dominated by the Tory Party (indeed, 'independent' Irish parties failed to win a single seat there at any election over the period 1832–80) emerges very clearly. So, too, does the very weak position of the Tories in the Catholic south.

But we may examine the position in the south more carefully. The 50 southern constituencies that existed over the period 1832–80 fall into three clearly defined groups: first, nine solid Tory constituencies, where that party won at least two thirds of the seats over the period; second, 37 anti-Tory constituencies, where Whigs, Liberals or independent Irish MPs were almost always returned (in 13 of these, no Tory was *ever* returned); and, third, four

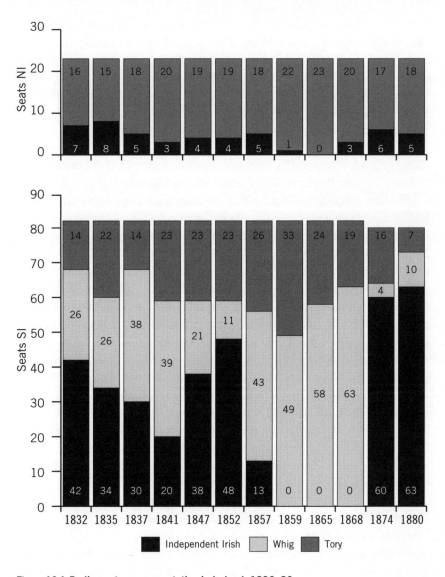

Figure 10.1 **Parliamentary representation in Ireland, 1832–80**

Note: The top set of bars refers to northern Ireland as conventionally defined, the bottom to southern Ireland. The total number of seats was 23 in northern Ireland; in southern Ireland it dropped from 82 to 80 with the disfranchisement of the boroughs of Cashel and Sligo in 1870. 'Independent Irish' includes two Irish Confederates in the South in 1847; 'Tories' include three Peelites in the South and eight in the North in 1847, and two Peelites in the North in 1952.
Source: calculated from Walker, 1978.

marginal constituencies, where Tories won more than a quarter but no more than half of the seats. It is striking that the solid Tory constituencies all had large Protestant populations, and presumably proportionally larger Protestants electorates (these were the three border counties of Cavan, Donegal and Monaghan; the counties of Dublin, Sligo and Carlow; the boroughs of Bandon and Portarlington; and Dublin University).[9] From the scattered information that we have on the composition of the electorate, we know that the proportion of Protestants was highest in the south precisely in the two solid Tory boroughs (Bandon, with a 70 per cent Protestant electorate in 1863, and Portarlington, with a 61 per cent Protestant electorate in 1835) (Hoppen, 1984: 37).

We have a yet more solid body of evidence regarding nineteenth-century Irish electoral behaviour. Prior to the Ballot Act of 1872, voting was open and public, and interested parties (including local newspapers) commonly published 'poll books': lists of all persons who had voted, indicating which candidates each had supported. Though seen as a form of electoral intimidation by many, this practice could be justified by, say, a county Independent club on the grounds that it was a form of counter-intimidation: it exposed publicly those who refused to rebel against landlords hostile to the popular interest. Of course, poll books commonly amounted to little more than a record of how the local gentry were lining up in respect of the candidates, since the pressure on a voter to follow the guidance of his landlord was typically very strong (Whyte, 1965). As the nineteenth century progressed, it is true, the influence of the Catholic clergy became a major counterweight (Whyte, 1960). Taking account of these caveats, it is still possible to draw interesting inferences from poll books, which illustrate the very powerful role that religion played in structuring electoral behaviour. The extent of denominational polarisation is clear in particular from many borough elections. Thus, in Tralee in 1835, 78 per cent of Catholics voted Liberal, while 98 per cent of Protestants voted Tory; in Newry in 1868, 97 per cent of Catholics voted Liberal, while 89 per cent of Protestants voted Tory; and in Derry City in 1870, 97 per cent of Catholics voted Liberal while 77 per cent of Protestants voted Tory. There is similar evidence, though not based on poll books, from counties Carlow and Wexford in 1880 showing that the Tory vote was virtually confined to Protestants (based on Hoppen, 1984: 38, 329).

Mass mobilisation: the general election of 1885

The imperfect relationship between stages in party system development and franchise extension in Ireland described in the last section was characteristic also of the period in which mass suffrage was introduced. Elsewhere, the introduction of mass suffrage transformed the party system by facilitating the introduction of a new, radical political force – the socialist party. Thus, the position of the Belgian Workers' Party was transformed by the introduction of universal male suffrage in 1893: in 1894 it made a dramatic entry to parliament, pushing the Liberals into third position. In The Netherlands, the franchise extensions of 1887 and 1896 allowed the Social Democratic League to establish a small but significant presence in parliament even before the introduction of universal male suffrage in 1917. In Norway the introduction of universal male suffrage in 1898 permitted the steady growth of the Labour Party from 1903 onwards. In Sweden the Social Democrats established a presence in parliament even before the introduction of universal male suffrage in 1907, and that measure transformed them into a significant parliamentary force. In Denmark, with its wider franchise, the Socialists grew slowly but steadily from their first entry to parliament in 1887.

In Ireland, the position was rather different. To start with, notwithstanding its social structural similarity with some of the societies just mentioned – commonly overlooked in conventional explanations of the weakness of Irish socialism – no parliamentary socialist party appeared. The Irish Socialist Republican Party (1896) and its successor, the Socialist Party of Ireland (1904), were electorally marginal, even at local level (Mitchell, 1974: 20–1). There was a good deal of independent labour activism from 1899 onwards, but the organised left was essentially a post-war phenomenon. Instead, the radical position was occupied by an agrarian, nationalist movement, one that bore some – though not close – similarities to Venstre in Norway, but that resembled more obviously the anti-landlord peasant parties that were to emerge in the early twentieth century in central and eastern Europe. The second contrast with the pattern in other smaller west European countries was the timing of the radical upsurge and the thoroughgoing nature of its victory: it took off *before* the introduction of mass suffrage, and it wiped out all other electoral forces in the present territory of the Republic of Ireland.

The origins of Ireland's first mass party lay in agrarian combination rather than in party organisation. The decisive development was the creation in 1879 of the Irish National Land League – an improbable source, at first sight, for a new, catch-all nationalist party. The league was concerned, at least on the surface, overwhelmingly with the issue of land; and it did not evoke especially negative reactions among Ulster Protestants (Bew, 1978: 217–8). But, with about 1,000 branches at the height of its organisational influence, it was a formidable machine for popular mobilisation, and played a significant role in supporting the Home Rule Party in the general election of 1880. The link between the league and the party was symbolised in the fact that Charles Stewart Parnell became president of the league in 1879, and he was elected chairman of the party in 1880.

The suppression of the Land League by the government in 1881 opened up a new possibility: it was replaced in 1882 by a new organisation headed by Parnell, the Irish National League – but this was much more an instrument of the party rather than an independent ally. Indeed, the new movement became the country's first mass political party, with a structure similar to that of its conventional contemporary counterparts: tens of thousands of members (161,000 in 1889); a large network of branches (almost 1,300 by mid-1886); county conventions for the selection of candidates; a central council; and a smaller organising committee. If oligarchic control is, as Michels (1915) reminds us, the hallmark of the modern party, then the Irish National League and its parliamentary group fell into this category. The organising committee was controlled by members of the parliamentary party, who were also able to use a whole range of now familiar ruses to control selection conventions; and the parliamentary party was in turn dominated by its leader, Parnell (O'Brien, 1957: 126–33).

On the unionist side, modern party organisation followed the Representation of the People Act, 1884, rather than anticipating it. Here, there was a considerable difference between Ulster and the South. In the South, conservatives and liberal unionists united in 1885 in the Irish Loyal and Patriotic Union (renamed the Irish Unionist Alliance in 1891) (Buckland, 1972: 1–28). Its organisational structure resembled that of the Irish National League, but it was necessarily smaller in scale. Ulster evolved differently (Walker, 1981; 1989). Although an Ulster Loyalist Anti-Repeal Union was established in 1886, it did not survive; indeed, a range of other political organisations aiming to defend the union appeared in the years that followed, and it was not until 1905 that the Ulster Unionist Council, the body that still constitutes the base of the Ulster Unionist Party, was created (Buckland, 1973: 8–21).

The link between these developments and denominational divisions was obvious from the outset. The constitution of the Irish National League provided for the automatic attendance of Catholic clergy at county candidate selection conventions; the Ulster Loyalist Anti-Repeal Union made all Protestant clergy in Ulster honorary members; and the Ulster Unionist Council has always had significant *de jure* representation from the (exclusively Protestant) Orange Order. But the coincidence between party politics and the denominational division is clear not merely in the case of the parliamentary parties and among middle-level activists; ecological data from 1885 and subsequently illustrate the near-perfect correlation between unionism and Protestantism, and between nationalism and Catholicism (Coakley, 2002). The ultimate reflection of this was the disappearance of the Liberals and the near-disappearance of Tories or Unionists from southern Ireland; after 1885 there was only one secure unionist constituency (Dublin University), and only one other (Dublin South) where unionists had a realistic chance of winning a seat.[10]

Yet, as has been suggested here, it was not just the franchise extension of 1884 that was responsible for the wave of electoral mobilisation. It has been argued convincingly that even before the advent of mass politics the pattern of Irish politics had already been transformed by the twin forces of the Home Rule movement and the secret ballot, between 1868 and 1874 (Hanham, 1959: 179–87). The mass mobilisation itself can also be seen vividly at local level: in the late 1870s and early 1880s a remarkable revolution took place in the membership of the boards of 'guardians' of Ireland's poor law unions, the main elected local authorities – and it took place in the context of a restricted, traditional franchise that had existed for several decades. This is to be seen in the manner in which, beginning in the late 1870s, control of these boards shifted from landlord to tenant hands, so that by 1886 most boards outside Ulster were in the hands of tenant farmers (Feingold, 1975: 227–30).

Mass rebellion: the general election of 1918

The results of the 1885 general election set a pattern that was to last until the First World War, one that saw Ireland depart radically from the path in the other smaller European countries with which it has been compared above. If we measure electoral support for social radicalism in terms of the overall proportion of seats won by the socialist, social democratic or labour party in the period after the introduction of mass suffrage, then Sweden heads the list (32.5 per cent, 1900–15), followed by Belgium (19.7 per cent, 1894–1914), Denmark (19.6 per cent, 1901–13), Norway (11.8 per cent, 1900–15) and The Netherlands (7.8 per cent, 1897–1913). But if we are to compare these parties with the Irish

Nationalist Party (whose radicalism, admittedly, was agrarian rather than working-class oriented), the contrast is staggering. On the island of Ireland over the period 1885–1910, the official party won 59.5 per cent of all seats, to 17.2 per cent for unionists; but an additional 17.1 per cent went to anti-Parnellite nationalists (who won the great bulk of nationalist seats in the two elections that followed the split in the Nationalist Party in 1890) and 1.9 per cent to independent nationalist supporters of William O'Brien in 1910, leaving only 4.3 per cent for others. In the present territory of the Republic of Ireland nationalist domination was overwhelming: the official party won 71.8 per cent of all seats, with 20.5 per cent going to anti-Parnellites and 2.6 per cent to O'Brienites.

Organisationally, too, the dominant position of the Nationalist Party seemed secure in the long term. Its unity had been ripped apart in 1890 in the bitter division over the leadership of Parnell following the celebrated divorce scandal in which he was involved. His supporters retained control of the party organisation, but most MPs broke with the party and established a rival organisation, the Irish National Federation, in 1891 (Lyons, 1951). Based on a similar structure to the league, the broader appeal of the anti-Parnellite position was reflected in the fact that by the end of 1891 it had 83,000 members, while the league had shrunk to 13,000 (O'Brien, 1976: 98). But a combination of factionalism and political circumstances led to a reduction in the vigour of these bodies, and they were overshadowed by a new organisation with a strong agrarian dimension, the United Irish League (UIL), founded in 1898. In 1900, indeed, the two main wings of the party came together again, this time adopting the UIL as their organisational foundation. This did not altogether end factionalism; ironically, in 1909 the architect of party unity, William O'Brien, who had founded the UIL, seceded to form his own All-for-Ireland League, which performed creditably in the two elections of 1910, though its successes were mainly confined to the southern county of Cork (O'Brien, 1976).

Right on the eve of the 1918 election, there were indications that the Nationalist Party might not fare badly. Membership of the UIL, though showing signs of decline, was holding up (Coakley, 1986: 42), and the party was entering the campaign with 73 seats, to six for the new Sinn Féin party. But these hopeful signs were overshadowed by others more ominous for the party. Sinn Féin, founded in 1905, had been no match for the Nationalist Party before the war. It built up its branch network to reach a total of 128 in 1909, but many of these existed in name only, and active membership in that year was probably not much greater than 500 (Davis, 1974: 83). The party was re-invigorated through its perceived association with the 1916 rebels, whose leaders moved in

1917 to take it over as their own political vehicle. Following a major organi-sational drive, it was increasingly challenging the UIL as an organisational force; by October 1917 it had an estimated 1,200–1,300 branches and about 120–130,000 members (Laffan, 1999: 185), and by November 1918 it had more than 1,800 branches (Mitchell, 1995: 120–1). It had youth, enthusiasm and novelty on its side, and was well poised to compete for the support of first-time voters. Indeed, we can estimate that in 1918 about 82 per cent of the electorate had never voted previously in a parliamentary election. Quite apart from the enormous expansion in the electorate brought about by the Representation of the People Act, 1918, such was the dominance of the Nationalist Party that many Irish constituencies had not been contested for decades (in Donegal West, for example, nobody had voted in a general election since 1880; see Coakley, 1994).

The results of the election are well known. Notwithstanding the fact that the All-for-Ireland League and the infant Labour Party stood aside, the Nationalist Party was reduced to six seats, Sinn Féin won two and Unionists 23. Sinn Féin's victory in the present territory of the Republic was yet more striking: it won 69 of the 72 territorial seats (96 per cent). It is true that, elec-torally, Sinn Féin's victory was a little less striking. In contested constituencies in the south it won 65.3 per cent, to 28.6 per cent for the Nationalist Party and 5.4 per cent for Unionists. But this understates its strength, since it secured unopposed returns in 25 constituencies.

What made the 1918 result so decisive in the evolution of the Irish party system was not just the extent of Sinn Féin's victory over the Nationalist Party, but the complete collapse of the latter after the election. Although the party survived in Northern Ireland and remnants were resuscitated in the South in the 1920s, its organisational arm, the UIL, simply faded away or was absorbed by Sinn Féin. The Sinn Féin victory of 1918, a consequence not only of its own electoral power but of the plurality electoral system, was seen, by the Nationalist Party and others, as having inflicted a devastating blow. That the blow might have been critical rather than mortal seems not to have occurred to the Nationalist elite; under proportional representation, the electoral system of the future, their 175,000 votes in Southern Ireland should have given them a parlia-mentary party of about 35 members after 1921, rather than the two with which they ended up in 1918. Their long-term prospects were not, then, as wholly negative as party leaders seemed to believe; but this perception became a self-fulfilling prophecy.

Mass dissent: the general election of 1922

The third critical election in the emergence of the Irish party system took place not in the context of any further extension of the franchise (universal suffrage was introduced only in 1923) but in the wake of significant constitutional and institutional change. It would determine, for the first time in Irish electoral history, the composition of a government; and it would do so on the basis of a parliament elected by proportional representation. For both of these reasons, some level of fragmentation in the party system was likely: unity against an external 'enemy' was no longer necessary in the context of independence, and it would in any case be hindered by the new electoral system, which was likely to encourage the representation of diverse interests.

Like the election of 1918, that of 1922 took place following a period of apparent electoral unanimity. This pattern had been confirmed in 1921, when, once again, other parties stood aside in the election to the proposed new House of Commons of Southern Ireland: Sinn Féin won all 120 of the seats in territorial constituencies without a contest, together with four of the eight university seats (the remaining four, in Dublin University, were won by unionists). In Northern Ireland, Sinn Féin won only six seats, to the Nationalists' six and Unionists' 40. It is not clear that this appearance of uniformity in the South reflected the reality of public opinion. Sandwiched between the 1918 and 1921 results were the local elections of 1920, conducted by proportional representation, which showed the survival of support for Nationalist candidates, a strong performance by Labour and extensive support for independent candidates; but the elections also gave Sinn Féin virtually complete control of local authorities outside Northern Ireland, either alone or in alliance with sympathisers (Mitchell, 1995: 120–6).

The 1922 election showed not just the full maturing of these tendencies, but a new development: the final stage in the long-running split in Sinn Féin over the terms of the 1921 Treaty. The election set the tone for the party system of the new Irish state – a party system that survived for most of the 1920s, and, with some modification, ever since. Measured in terms of parliamentary representation, the two wings of Sinn Féin won 94 seats between them, with 17 for Labour, seven for the new Farmers' Party and ten for independents and others (see Gallagher, 1979). In the 80 years that followed, the Irish party system was not to deviate greatly from this pattern; the big difference arose from competition within the Sinn Féin tradition. In 1922 the pro-Treaty side had a decisive majority over the anti-Treaty group (58 to 36), and it continued to beat the latter into second position for the rest of the 1920s; but in 1932 this relationship was reversed, and the lead of the anti-Treaty side (now Fianna Fáil) over its opponents was subsequently consolidated.

If continuity between the 1922 and later elections is obvious, the challenge in this chapter is to establish the relationship between this election and earlier ones. In this, we are facilitated by one technical circumstance: the constituencies adopted in 1922 were those defined in the Government of Ireland Act, 1920, and used in the 1921 election. These multi-member constituencies were, in turn, produced by grouping single-member constituencies used in Westminster elections – most of them unchanged since 1885. While comparison of the 1922 results with those of elections extending back to 1885 is thus possible, the results of analysis at constituency level over time are not especially revealing. First, the tendency towards electoral unanimity before 1918 provides us with little evidence of divergence of opinions within the electorate. Second, the number of unopposed returns in 1918 (25 out of 71 territorial constituencies) is not helpful in indicating the state of local opinion. Third, the no-contest rate in 1922 was also high; Sinn Féin had sought by means of a 'pact' between its two wings to avoid contests entirely, but intervention by other parties forced contests in all but seven of the 26 new constituencies.

We are thus left with 12 constituencies that were contested in 1922, all parts of which were also contested in 1918; and we can add a further four 1922 constituencies where at least one part was contested in 1918, giving us some idea of local patterns of party support. Because of the greatly varying ranges of options open to voters, comparison is hazardous; but we may make the following generalisation. First, in certain constituencies support for Sinn Féin appeared to have consolidated in 1922 beyond its 1918 level: Monaghan, Sligo–Mayo East, Dublin Northwest and Galway, for instance. Second, in others Sinn Féin support was significantly reduced, but this can be explained in part by a very strong showing by the Labour Party: Cork Borough, Laois-Offaly, Waterford-Tipperary East, Wexford, Kildare–Wicklow and Carlow–Kilkenny. Third, in the other constituencies support for Sinn Féin seemed substantially unchanged, but in one case (Dublin Mid) it dropped dramatically, shifting mainly to independents.

Conclusion

The prehistory of the Irish party system, then, offers interesting evidence on the process of political mobilisation. The most obvious general conclusion is that if we measure party organisation over time we end up not with a characteristic growth graph, rising from bottom left to top right over the nineteenth century in the manner of other European party systems, but with a U-curve: a high level of organisation in the 1820s and 1830s fading gradually before building up again in the 1870s and 1880s. But the right-hand side of this 'U' also diverges from the European norm: instead of organic evolution, we get a pattern of striking electoral rebellion, most notably in 1885 and 1918, of a kind not to be found elsewhere, and a party political explosion in 1922.

But if the form of the Irish party system departed from that of its counterparts elsewhere, so too did its content. It is true that religion was an issue; but this separated Irish Catholics from a ruling Protestant group that was seen increasingly not just as foreign from a theological perspective but also as alien in an ethnonational sense. It is also true that agrarian unrest was a crucial factor; but from the perspective of Irish peasants the enemy was not vested urban interests but another rural class, their own landlords. Furthermore, it is true that constitutional questions were to the foreground; but here the issue was not electoral, parliamentary or governmental reform, but a redefinition of the territorial relationship between Ireland and its larger neighbouring island. Thus, the crucial ingredients in the emerging Irish party system had little, if anything, in common with the party systems of the other small west European countries with which it has been compared above, instead sharing much with patterns of party political evolution in early twentieth century central and eastern Europe.

The level of intensity of political mobilisation in Ireland was, then, very high – so high, indeed, that it is appropriate to conclude with some speculation on the boundary between party political and other kinds of political organisational activity. The menacing forms of political organisation that arose in Ireland over the century before independence – from the Catholic Association to Sinn Féin – indeed threatened the political establishment, and evoked support from marginal groups and committed opposition from defenders of the status quo. But there is an important sense in which all but one of these (Sinn Féin being the obvious exception) also contributed to political stability: their leaders sought to channel grassroots activism away from support of secret agrarian or nationalist paramilitary societies and into an alternative form of political activity. Fear of 'Ribbonism' (a form of agrarian activism) was a recurring concern of O'Connell's, for example; Isaac Butt and his conservative colleagues founded the Home Government Association because of a fear of the thrust towards Irish independence that was being propagated by the Fenians; and later Nationalist leaders, from Parnell to Dillon, walked a difficult tightrope between electoral activism and the more robust methods of the countryside. In this respect, once again, the Irish experience gives us pause for thought, and begs the question whether our most appropriate base for comparison indeed lies in the eastern rather than the western periphery of the European continent.

Notes

1   For the seventeenth-century roots of the English Tory–Whig dichotomy in attitudes towards the monarchy and the church, see Bulmer-Thomas, 1967: 3–9. For the rise of the Swedish Hats and Caps, with their less definite origins in dynastic preferences, see Roberts, 1986: 111–54.

2   Given the fluid nature of party allegiances at the time, these figures are approximations; they have been calculated from Smith, 1973. Jupp (1986: 107–8) provides estimates of the numerical strength of pro- and anti-government Irish MPs, 1802–18.

3   In addition to these, there were a few 'Peelite' supporters of Sir Robert Peel, whose support for free trade divided the Tory Party (one per cent, 1847–52), and two Confederates (radical nationalists) in 1847; calculated from Walker, 1978.

4   It is difficult to make a comparison with countries where until the early twentieth century representation was estate-based (such as Austria and Finland), or where parties were largely regionally based (such as Germany and Switzerland). It is also difficult to make comparisons with Italy (where parliament was dominated by various Liberal factions until the First World War). There are some similarities with France (with its Republican–Conservative dualism, 1876–89) and Bulgaria (with its Liberal–Conservative dualism, 1879–99). Outside Europe, the Conservative–Liberal dualism in Canada (1878–1921) and New Zealand (1890–1911) and the pattern of Democratic–Republican competition in the USA that began in 1856 and that has survived until the present are similar examples.

5   Calculated from Mackie and Rose, 1991 (for more detailed results, see Caramani, 1999). In arriving at these figures, in Norway the Moderate Venstre has been grouped with Venstre ('the Left', i.e. the Liberals); in Sweden the Freetraders and Moderate Freetraders have been grouped with the Liberals; and in Denmark, the Liberals, Moderate Liberals and Liberal Reform Party have been grouped.

6   For the early history of these party systems, see the relevant parts of Cook and Paxton, 1978; Jacobs, 1989; McHale and Skowronksi, 1983; and Wende, 1981.

7   Reynolds (1954: 168) argues that the various estimates that place the electorate at more than 200,00, including the figure of 213,000 officially reported for 1829, are unreliable, and that the actual size of the electorate was a little over 100,000.

8   The statutes referred to above were as follows: the Roman Catholic Relief Act, 1793 (33 George III c.21); the Union with Ireland Act, 1800 (39 & 40 George III c. 67); the Parliamentary Elections (Ireland) Act, 1829 (10 George IV c. 8); the Representation of the People (Ireland) Act, 1832 (2 & 3 William IV c. 88); the Representation of the People (Ireland) Act, 1850 (13 & 14 Victoria c. 69); the Representation of the People (Ireland) Act, 1868 (31 & 32

Victoria c. 49); the Representation of the People Act, 1884 (47 & 48 Victoria c. 3); and the Representation of the People Act, 1918 (7 & 8 George V c 64). The first of these was an act of the Irish parliament. Universal suffrage was introduced in the Irish Free State by the Electoral Act, 1923 (no. 12 of 1923).

9   Calculated from Walker, 1978. Official information on the religious composition of the constituencies refers only to the population, not to the electorate; but the higher social position of Protestants is likely to have ensured them a significantly larger proportion of the electorate than of the population. Such evidence as is available supports this; for example, in 1859 the proportions of Protestants among the voters of Dundalk and Sligo boroughs were respectively 35.5 per cent and 52.6 per cent, but in 1861 the proportions of Protestants among the population of these boroughs were respectively 17.5 per cent and 21.7 per cent (Hoppen, 1984: 37).

10   Unionists won Dublin South (38.2 per cent Protestant in 1891) in four of the eight general elections from 1885 to 1910; but from 1885 onwards they never again won a seat in Donegal East (39.5 per cent Protestant), Monaghan North (35.2 per cent) or the Dublin St Stephen's Green constituency (31.4 per cent). The only other southern seat to fall to unionists after 1885 was Galway city (8.7 per cent Protestant) in 1900.

Bibliography

Anon (1790) *The Utility of Party in a Free State Considered, Particularly with Regard to the Present State of Parties in Ireland*. Dublin: J. Jones.

Bew, Paul (1978) *Land and the National Question in Ireland 1858–82*. Dublin: Gill & Macmillan.

Bew, Paul (1987) *Conflict and Conciliation in Ireland, 1890–1910: Parnellites and Radical Agrarians*. Oxford: Clarendon.

Blake, Robert (1970) *The Conservative Party from Peel to Churchill*. London: Eyre & Spottiswoode.

Buckland, Patrick (1972) *Irish Unionism: One: The Anglo-Irish and the New Ireland 1885–1922*. Dublin: Gill & Macmillan.

Buckland, Patrick (1973) *Irish Unionism: Two: Ulster Unionism and the Origins of Northern Ireland 1886–1922*. Dublin: Gill & Macmillan.

Bulmer-Thomas, Ivor (1967) *The Growth of the British Party System, Vol. 1 1640–1932*, 2nd edn. London: John Baker.

Caramani, Daniele (1999) *Elections in Western Europe Since 1815: Election Results by Constituencies*. London: Macmillan [with CD-rom supplement].

Carty, R. K. (1993) 'From tradition to modernity, and back again: party building in Ireland', pp. 24–43 in Ronald J Hill and Michael Marsh (eds), *Modern Irish Democracy: Essays in Honour of Basil Chubb*. Dublin: Irish Academic Press.

Coakley, John (1986) 'The evolution of Irish party politics', pp. 29–54 in Brian Girvin and Roland Sturm (eds), *Politics and Society in Contemporary Ireland*. London: Gower.

Coakley, John (1994) 'The election that made the First Dáil', pp. 31–46 in Brian Farrell (ed.), *The Creation of the Dáil*. Dublin: Blackwater Press.

Coakley, John (2002) 'Religion, national identity and political change in modern Ireland', *Irish Political Studies* 17 (1): 4–28.

Cook, Chris, and John Paxton (1978) *European Political Facts 1848–1918*. London: Macmillan.

Corish, Patrick J. (1962) 'Cardinal Cullen and the National Association of Ireland', *Reportorium Novum* 3: 13–61.

Davis, Richard P. (1974) *Arthur Griffith and Non-Violent Sinn Fein*. Dublin: Anvil.

Duverger, Maurice (1964) *Political Parties: Their Organization and Activity in the Modern State*, 3rd edn. London: Methuen [first published in French, 1951].

Evans, Eric J. (2000) *Parliamentary Reform in Britain, c.1770–1918*. Harlow: Longman.

Farrell, Brian (1970) 'Labour and the Irish party system: a suggested approach to analysis', *Economic and Social Review* 1 (4): 477–502.

Feingold, William L. (1975) 'The tenants' movement to capture the Irish poor law boards, 1877–1886', *Albion* 7: 216–31.

Gallagher, Michael (1979) 'The pact general election of 1922', *Irish Historical Studies* 21 (84): 404–21.

Garvin, Tom (1981) *The Evolution of Irish Nationalist Politics*. Dublin: Gill & Macmillan.

Garvin, Tom (1987) *Nationalist Revolutionaries in Ireland 1858–1928*. Oxford: Clarendon.

Gash, Norman (1953) *Politics in the Age of Peel: A Study in the Technique of Parliamentary Representation 1830–1850*. London: Longmans.

Grogan, Geraldine (1991) 'O'Connell's impact on the organisation and development of German political catholicism', pp. 119–27 in Maurice R. O'Connell (ed.), *Daniel O'Connell: Political Pioneer*. Dublin: Institute of Public Administration.

Hanham, H. J. (1959) *Elections and Party Management: Politics in the Time of Disraeli and Gladstone*. London: Longman.

Harbinson, John F. (1973) *The Ulster Unionist Party 1882–1973: Its Development and Organisation*. Belfast: Blackstaff.

Hayton, D. W. (ed.) (2001) *The Irish Parliament in the Eighteenth Century: The Long Apprenticeship*. Edinburgh: Edinburgh University Press for the Parliamentary History Yearbook Trust [special issue of *Parliamentary History*].

Hoppen, K. Theodore (1984) *Elections, Politics, and Society in Ireland 1832–1885*. Oxford: Clarendon.

Jacobs, Francis, ed. (1989) *Western European Political Parties: A Comprehensive Guide*. London: Longman.

Johnston, Edith M. (1963) *Great Britain and Ireland 1760–1800: A Study in Political Administration*. Edinburgh: Oliver & Boyd.

Johnston-Liik, Edith Mary (2002) *History of the Irish Parliament 1692–1800: Commons, Constituencies and Statutes*. 6 vols. Belfast: Ulster Historical Foundation.

Jupp, P. J. (1967) 'Irish parliamentary elections of 1801–20', *Historical Journal* 10 (2): 183–96.

Jupp, P. J. (1969) 'Irish MPs at Westminster in the early nineteenth century', pp. 65–80 in *Historical Studies VII*. London: Routledge & Kegan Paul.

Jupp, P. J. (1973) *British and Irish Elections 1784–1831*. Newton Abbot: David & Charles

John Coakley

Jupp, P. J. (1986) 'Ireland', pp. 100–9 in R. G. Thorne, *The History of Parliament: The House of Commons 1790–1820. I. Introductory Survey*. London: Secker & Warburg, for the History of Parliament Trust

Laffan, Michael (1999) *The Resurrection of Ireland: The Sinn Féin Party, 1916–1923*. Cambridge: Cambridge University Press.

Lampson, G. Locker (1907) *A Consideration of the State of Ireland in the Nineteenth Century*. London: Archibald Constable & Co.

Lipset, S. M. and Stein Rokkan (1967) 'Cleavage structures, party systems and voter alignments: an introduction', pp. 1–64 in S. M. Lipset and Stein Rokkan (eds), *Party Systems and Voter Alignments*. New York: The Free Press.

Lyons, F. S. L. (1951) *The Irish Parliamentary Party 1890–1910*. London: Faber & Faber.

MacIntyre, Angus (1965) *The Liberator: Daniel O'Connell and the Irish Party 1830–1847*. London: Hamish Hamilton.

Mackie, Thomas T, and Richard Rose (1991) *The International Almanac of Electoral History*, 3rd edn. London: Macmillan.

Mair, Peter (1987) *The Changing Irish Party System*. London: Frances Pinter.

McCracken, J. L. (1971) *The Irish Parliament in the Eighteenth Century*. Dundalk: Dundalgan Press.

McDowell, R. B. (1952) 'Irish political parties in the age of reform', pp. 109–38 in *Public Opinion and Government Policy in Ireland, 1801–1846*. London: Faber & Faber.

McHale, Vincent and Sharon Skowronski (1983) *Political Parties of Europe*. Westport, CT: Greenwood Press.

Michels, Robert (1915) *Political Parties: A Sociological Study of the Oligarchical Tendencies of Modern Democracy*. London: Jarrold.

Mitchell, Arthur (1974) *Labour in Irish Politics 1890–1930: The Irish Labour Movement in an Age of Revolution*. Dublin: Irish University Press.

Mitchell, Arthur (1995) *Revolutionary Government in Ireland: Dáil Éireann 1919–22*. Dublin: Gill & Macmillan.

Norman, E. R. (1965) *The Catholic Church and Ireland in the Age of Rebellion 1859–1973*. London: Longman.

O'Brien, Conor Cruise (1957) *Parnell and His Party 1880–90*. Oxford: Clarendon.

O'Brien, Joseph V. (1976) *William O'Brien and the Course of Irish Politics 1881–1918*. Berkeley, CA: University of California Press.

O'Ferrall, Fergus (1985) *Catholic Emancipation: Daniel O'Connell and the Birth of Irish Democracy*. Dublin: Gill & Macmillan.

Reynolds, James A. (1954) *The Catholic Emancipation Crisis in Ireland, 1823–1829*. New Haven, CT: Yale University Press.

Roberts, Michael (1986) *The Age of Liberty: Sweden 1719–1772*. Cambridge: Cambridge University Press.

Rokkan, Stein (1970) 'Nation building, cleavage formation and the structuring of mass politics', pp. 72–144 in *Citizens, Elections, Parties: Approaches to the Comparative Study of the Processes of Development*. Oslo: Universitetsforlaget.

Sartori, Giovanni (1976) *Parties and Party Systems: A Framework for Analysis.* Cambridge: Cambridge University Press.

Sinnott, Richard (1995) *Irish Voters Decide: Voting Behaviour in Elections and Referendums Since 1918.* Manchester: Manchester University Press.

Smith, William Stooks (1973) *The Parliaments of England from 1715 to 1847.* 2nd edn, ed. F. W. S. Craig. Chichester: Political Reference Publications.

Thornley, David (1964) *Isaac Butt and Home Rule.* London: Macgibbon & Kee.

Walker, B. M. (1973) 'The Irish electorate, 1868–1915', *Irish Historical Studies* 18 (71): 369–406.

Walker, B. M. (1978) *Parliamentary Election Results in Ireland, 1801–1922.* Dublin: Royal Irish Academy.

Walker, B. M. (1981) 'Party organisation in Ulster, 1865–92: registration agents and their activities', pp. 191–209 in Peter Roebuck (ed.), *Plantation to Partition: Essays in Ulster History in Honour of J. L. McCracken.* Belfast: Blackstaff.

Walker, B. M. (1989) *Ulster Politics: The Formative Years, 1868–86.* Belfast: Ulster Historical Foundation and Institute of Irish Studies, Queen's University of Belfast.

Walker, B. M. (1996) 'The 1885 and 1886 general elections: a milestone in Irish history', pp. 15–33 in *Dancing to History's Tune: History, Myth and Politics in Ireland.* Belfast: Institute of Irish Studies, Queen's University of Belfast.

Wende, Frank, ed. (1981) *Lexikon zur Geschichte der Parteien in Europa.* Stuttgart: Kröner.

Whyte, J. H. (1958) *The Independent Irish Party 1850–59.* London: Oxford University Press.

Whyte, J. H (1960) 'The influence of the Catholic clergy on elections in nineteenth-century Ireland', *English Historical Review* 75 (295): 239–59.

Whyte, J. H. (1965) 'Landlord influence at elections in Ireland, 1769–1885', *English Historical Review* 80 (317): 740–60.

Williams, T. Desmond (1984) 'O'Connell's impact on Europe', pp. 100–6 in Kevin B. Nowlan and Maurice R. O'Connell (eds), *Daniel O'Connell: Portrait of a Radical.* Belfast: Appletree Press.

CHAPTER ELEVEN

Funding for referendum campaigns: equal or equitable?

RICHARD SINNOTT

—

Introduction

Writing about communications and community in Ireland, Brian Farrell noted the difficulties involved in bringing about and sustaining popular participation in politics: 'Participation in decision-making is a proclaimed aim and purpose of democratic society. It cannot be achieved easily. It requires encouragement – not least from the elites' (Farrell, 1984: 121). This statement applies with particular force to popular participation in decision-making through referendums. As a political scientist and current affairs journalist and broadcaster, Brian has witnessed almost 30 Irish referendums. These have covered a wide range of issues, many of them of quite a fundamental character, including, *inter alia*, the issues of divorce, abortion, the death penalty, the constitutional position of the Catholic Church, proportional representation, the definition of the national territory and the related claim to sovereignty over the territory of Northern Ireland, joining the European Economic Communities in the first place and taking each subsequent step on the road to supranational integration. Popular participation in deciding complex issues such as these needs to be nurtured. However, the way in which Irish elites can go about encouraging and supporting such participation underwent fundamental change in the mid-1990s. The change originated in a series of court decisions on the use of publicly funded resources in referendums.

In brief, the High Court and the Supreme Court have interpreted the constitution as prohibiting the use of publicly funded resources to support referendum campaigning unless the resources are divided equally between the 'yes' and 'no' sides.[1] A recent report on the referendum process by the All-Party Oireachtas Committee on the Constitution reluctantly endorsed this view, recommending that there should be public funding for referendum campaigning and that such funding should be divided equally between those in favour and those opposing the proposal. However, the All-Party Committee's report clearly indicates that this recommendation was not actually the preferred position of the majority of the Committee and was only made because of the constitutional constraints resulting from the McKenna judgement. The Committee's report states that the majority felt that 'the issue of funding should be decided on the basis of what was equitable rather than what was equal' but 'did not believe in pressing their view to a referendum proposal at this stage' (All-Party Oireachtas Committee on the Constitution, 2001: 6).

This chapter considers the issue of whether the allocation of public funding in support of campaigning in a referendum should be equal or equitable.[2] It begins by examining the evidence regarding the extent and the impact of people's knowledge and understanding of the issues at stake in the two referendums on the Treaty of Nice. This leads to the conclusion that public funding for referendum campaigning is indeed necessary. In order to determine whether such funding should be allocated on an equal or on an equitable basis, the chapter examines two models of the referendum process – the separation of powers model underlying the judgements of the courts that suggests equal allocation and a structural-functional model that suggests equitable allocation. It concludes that the structural-functional model provides a more comprehensive account of the referendum process and one that is more conducive to encouraging and supporting popular participation in referendums. The chapter then argues that the structural-functional model of the referendum, with its implicit endorsement of equitable rather than equal funding, may well be compatible with the constitution in virtue of an article that deals with referendums but that, surprisingly, has not been invoked in the debate so far (Article 27). The chapter concludes by advocating equitable rather than equal funding, acknowledging the implication that, if the argument regarding the constitutional recognition of a special role for elected representatives in Article 27 were to be rejected, it would be necessary to hold a referendum on how referendums should be conducted!

The view of the courts and response of the policy makers

One can summarise the courts' interpretation of the constitutional provisions for the conduct of referendums as follows: (1) in a referendum the people are the exclusive decision-makers;[3] (2) the people are entitled to reach their decision free from unauthorised interference;[4] (3) the government may not spend public money to support one side of a referendum campaign as this would be contrary to principles of fairness and equality;[5] (4) political parties have no constitutional role in the referendum process[6] and (5) in the context of a referendum campaign, the national public broadcasting service (RTÉ) may not allocate free broadcast time to political parties on a proportional basis.[7]

The main direct consequences of these judgements have been (a) an end to the practice of governments spending public money on campaigns in support of their proposals for constitutional change; (b) the abandonment by RTÉ of party political broadcasts during referendum campaigns and (c) the establishment of successive referendum commissions with varying terms of reference to assist in putting the issues in a referendum before the people.

Under the 1998 Referendum Act, the Referendum Commission has five members: a former Supreme Court or High Court judge, or a current High Court judge, who is nominated by the Chief Justice and acts as chairman, the Comptroller and Auditor General, the Ombudsman, the Clerk of the Dáil and the Clerk of the Seanad. The Commission was given three main functions in the 1998 Act: (1) to prepare a statement containing a general explanation of the referendum proposal and statements of the arguments for and against the proposal, which statements must be 'fair to all interests concerned'; (2) to publish and distribute such statements by means that 'the Commission considers most likely to bring them to the attention of the electorate'; and (3) to foster and promote and, where appropriate, to facilitate debate or discussion in a manner that is fair to all interests concerned' (Referendum Act, 1998, section 3.1). Following publication of the All-Party Oireachtas Committee report referred to above, the Referendum Act 2001 abolished the Commission's functions of preparing and publishing arguments for and against the proposal and of fostering and promoting debate and added the function of promoting public awareness of the referendum and encouraging the electorate to vote (Referendum Act, 2001, section 1). The act did not, however, provide any public funding for the referendum, other than that provided for by the now neutral activities of the Referendum Commission.

These policy responses indicate a marked reluctance on the part of the authorities to go down the route of equal allocation of publicly funded resources to the 'yes' and 'no' sides in a referendum campaign. The pragmatic reason for this reluctance is starkly illustrated in the case of the 1998 referendum on the Good Friday Agreement. The proposed constitutional changes, which had been agreed to by the Irish government as part of the negotiations that brought an end to almost three decades of violent political conflict in Northern Ireland, were supported by all the political parties, including Sinn Féin and by virtually all relevant groups and organisations in the state.[8] The only organised opposition came from a very small number of extreme nationalist groups, several of which had close ties to paramilitary organisations that were not part of the 'peace process' and had not committed themselves to the ceasefire that was central to that process. Thus, equal allocation of public funding or of publicly funded air-time to the 'yes' and 'no' sides in that referendum would have involved allocating equal and, presumably, substantial campaigning resources to very small and very unrepresentative groups of political extremists. This would have been so even if the legislation were to stipulate that the funding be given to 'umbrella groups' on each side. While this might be regarded as a special and once-off case, there is an underlying problem-in-principle involved. The underlying problem is that the entities entitled to equal funding under the McKenna judgement (or under any equal allocation provision) are abstractions, being simply the positive and negative responses to the referendum proposal. But funding can only be allocated to real organisations or groups and, in making such an allocation, some account must be taken of the representativeness of the groups in question. But this is to anticipate the argument. The next step is to examine the extent and the impact of the electorate's knowledge and understanding of the issues in the two referendums on the Treaty of Nice in order to illustrate the problems that can arise even in referendums on major national issues.[9]

Communication and knowledge in the referendums on the Treaty of Nice

Ireland has had six referendums dealing with ratification of EEC/EC/EU treaties, starting with the referendum on the EEC accession treaty in 1972. Five of these referendums have produced substantial 'yes' votes (ranging from 83.1 per cent in 1972 to 61.8 per cent in 1998). The remaining referendum (the first referendum on the Treaty of Nice) produced a 'yes' vote of only 45.7 per cent, yielding a clear 'no' majority of 54.3 per cent. In order to make an assessment of the quality of the referendum process as it relates to European issues, however, it is necessary to look at these 'yes' and 'no' proportions in the context of the behaviour of the electorate as a whole, in other words, taking account of abstainers as well as 'yes' and 'no' voters (see Figure 11.1). With a turnout of

71 per cent in 1972, Irish European referendums started rather well. However, in the very next European referendum (on the Single European Act in 1987), participation took a serious knock, dropping to only 44 per cent. Turnout recovered somewhat (to 57 per cent in 1992) and this was more or less maintained in the referendum on the Treaty of Amsterdam in 1998.[10] But then, in the first referendum on the Treaty of Nice (2001), turnout dropped dramatically – to 34 per cent. The evidence indicates that the abstention came disproportionately from the 'yes' side. Indeed, such was the impact of differential abstention that the 'no' side won by a comfortable margin despite the fact that, as a proportion of the electorate, its vote dropped from 21 per cent in 1998 to 19 per cent in 2001 (see Figure 11.1). In the second referendum on the Treaty of Nice, turnout recovered but only somewhat, reaching just under 50 per cent.

The experience of the first Nice referendum was not a happy one. By referendum day, a mere eight per cent felt they 'had a good understanding of what the treaty was all about' and a further 28 per cent felt that they

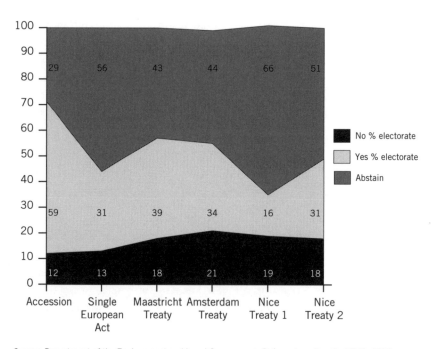

Source: Department of the Environment and Local Government, Referendum Results 1972–2002

Figure 11.1 **Referendums on European issues in Ireland: 'yes', 'no' and abstention as proportions of the electorate, 1972–2002**

'understood some of the issues but not all that was involved' (see Figure 11.2). Thus, almost two thirds of people felt either that they were 'only vaguely aware' of the issues (28 per cent) or that 'did not know what the Treaty was about at all' (35 per cent). Nice2 brought about substantial improvement in people's subjective sense that they understood the issues. The proportion claiming to have a good understanding of what the Treaty was all about went from eight per cent to 22 per cent; additionally, the proportion claiming to understand some of the issues but not all went from 28 per cent to 39 per cent. On the other side of the scale, the proportion who where only vaguely aware of the issues involved dropped slightly while the proportion who felt they did not know what the Treaty was about at all dropped sharply – from 36 to 16 per cent. Overall, there was a 25 percentage point improvement in the level of people's positive assessment of their understanding of the issues between Nice1 and Nice2.

The fact that communication and campaigning in the first Nice referendum left something to be desired is confirmed by respondents' less than enthusiastic evaluations of a wide array of sources ranging from the media

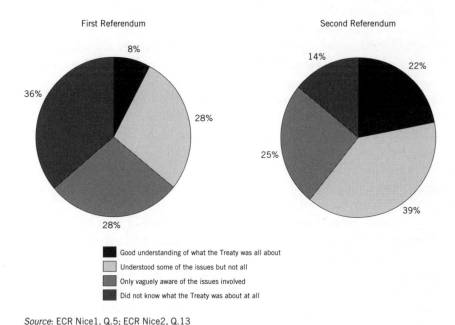

Source: ECR Nice1, Q.5; ECR Nice2, Q.13

Figure 11.2 **Perceived level of understanding of issues involved in the first and second Nice Treaty referendums**

(television, radio and newspapers) to the campaigns on each side, to informal discussions (see Figure 11.3). In Nice1, none of these sources was found to be of value by even half the respondents. The sources of information found to be most valuable were television news and current affairs programmes (45 per cent), discussion within families and among friends and colleagues (43 per cent), radio news and current affairs (42 per cent) and the newspapers (40 per cent). The leaflets and brochures circulated by the parties and organisations campaigning on each side come in a good way behind the media, the 'no' campaign (31 per cent) being a tiny fraction ahead of the 'yes' campaign (28 per cent) in this respect. Given its assigned role (in the first Nice referendum) as an even-handed purveyor of information and arguments that were meant to state both sides of the issue with equal force, one would have expected the activities of the Referendum Commission to have been found to be valuable by both 'yes' and 'no' voters. Accordingly, one would expect it to have a higher rating than either of the partisan campaigns. In the light of this expectation, a positive rating of 30 per cent for the Referendum Commission in Nice1 (see Figure 11.3) must be regarded as evidence of failure on the part of the Commission in carrying out the admittedly very difficult task given to it by the 1998 Referendum Act.

Positive evaluations of two key types of communication – through the media (television, radio, newspapers) and through interpersonal discussions – rose by more than 20 percentage points between Nice1 and Nice2 (see Figure 11.3). A more modest but significant improvement also occurred in the evaluation of the advertisements and leaflets issued by the Referendum Commission (now armed with a new and more realistic brief) and in evaluation of the government's White Paper and/or the summary of the White Paper. On the other hand, the rating of other sources of information, for example leaflets and brochures distributed by the Yes and No campaigns, the offices of the European Commission and European Parliament and posters in public places either remained static or declined somewhat.

The public's lack of confidence in its grasp of the issues was a major contributor to the unprecedentedly high level of abstention that characterised the first Nice referendum and that played such a large role in the defeat of the proposal to ratify the treaty. In responses to an open-ended question on reasons for not having voted in Nice1, by far the most frequent subjective explanation given was lack of information and lack of understanding of the issues (see Table 11.1). Forty-four per cent of Nice1 abstainers explained their non-voting in these terms. In Nice2 the proportion citing lack of knowledge or lack of information or understanding as their reason for not voting fell by almost half

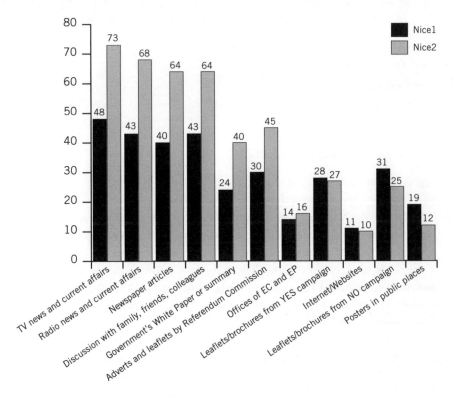

Source: ECR Nice1, Q.4; ECR Nice2, Q.11

Figure 11.3 **Evaluation of sources of information in the Nice referendum – percent very valuable plus somewhat valuable (in descending order of size of increase between Nice1 and Nice2)**

(from 44 to 26 per cent). Lack of information also affected the direction of choice of those who voted. This was particularly marked in Nice1 when 39 per cent of 'no' voters cited lack of information as their reason for voting 'no'. As Table 11.1 shows, this proportion fell to 14 per cent in Nice2.

The impact of low levels of understanding and of inadequate communication on the behaviour of the electorate is confirmed by multivariate statistical analysis. This shows that, controlling for the effect of habitual abstention and of a wide range of socio-demographic and attitudinal factors, non-voting in the first Nice referendum was influenced most of all by the feeling of not understanding the issues. A sense of not understanding the issues also contributed to abstention in Nice2. Analysis of the Nice2 data also indicates that low levels of

Table 11.1 **Lack of understanding/information as perceived influences on voting behaviour in the first and second Nice referendums**

Lack of understanding/information as reason . . .	Nice1	Nice2
. . . for abstaining	44	26
. . . for voting 'no'	39	14
n =	930	618

Source: ECR Nice1, Q.3; ECR Nice2, Q.4

objective knowledge of European Union affairs and low levels of attention to news about politics increased the rate of abstention.[11]

People's confidence in their grasp of the issues increased substantially between Nice1 and Nice2. At the end of the process, however, significant proportions of the electorate still felt did not understand the issues and this feeling contributed to keeping turnout below the 50 per cent mark in Nice2. The multivariate analysis of the determinants of *how* people voted in Nice1 confirmed that lack of understanding of the issues was the most important factor contributing to the 'no' vote.

In sum, levels of knowledge and the level of turnout were pretty appalling in the first Nice referendum and were the main factors leading to the 'no' outcome. Levels of knowledge and understanding were better in the second Nice referendum, but lack of knowledge and understanding was a still a problem and one that contributed to what can only be seen as a worryingly low level of turnout. All of this points to the need to re-examine the referendum process in order to see what might be done to improve its capacity to handle complex issues and to mobilise widespread and well-informed participation by as large a segment of the electorate as possible. Public funding of referendum campaigning is one of the obvious measures that might be introduced to tackle the problem. But this proposal raises the issue of whether such funding should be equal or equitable. Viewing the referendum process from the perspective of different models of the political system suggests different answers to this question.

The referendum process in alternative models of the political system

The key point of departure of the various court judgements relating to the conduct of referendums is the tripartite distinction between legislative, executive and judicial powers. The judgements then extend this distinction and the associated principle of the separation of powers to include referendums, the people being seen as performing a legislative function in which the executive in particular must not 'interfere'. The principle of non-interference in the performance of their legislative function by the people also applies to the Oireachtas, its function being limited to passing the referendum bill. As noted above, the courts also make clear that political parties have no de jure role in the referendum process.

While the separation-of-powers model is obviously at the core of the system of government laid down in the constitution, its extension to cover the referendum process is problematic. The problem is that, in applying a strict separation-of-powers principle to the exercise of the legislative function by the people, the argument excludes a series of other functions that are essential if the referendum process is to work effectively. In contrast to this truncated view of the referendum, a 'structural-functional' model of the political system and of the referendum process gives a much more comprehensive picture. The structural-functional model incorporates the idea of legislative, executive and judicial powers and the idea that these functions can be performed by different institutions or structures but goes on identify a number of other essential functions. The full range of functions in a political system and the main structures involved in the performance of each function in the Irish political system are set out in Table 11.2,[12] which shows that the legislative, executive and judicial powers or functions are replicated in the structural-functional model as rule-making, rule application and rule adjudication (see items 1 to 3 in Table 11.2). However, before rules can be made, still less applied or adjudicated on, there are several intermediate functions that must be performed. First of all, interests must be articulated, that is needs, demands, opinions, beliefs and positions

Table 11.2 **The structural-functional model of the political system**

Functions	*Structures*
1. Interest articulation	Interest groups and political parties
2. Interest aggregation	Political parties and inter-party coalitions
3. Political communication	The Dáil, the media, political parties, interest groups
4. Political recruitment	Political parties and interest groups
5. Political socialisation	Families, peer groups, schools, the media, political parties
6. Rule making	The Dáil, the Government, the people (in a referendum)
7. Rule application	The Government and the Civil Service
8. Rule adjudication	The Courts

must be put forward, promoted, argued for and defended. Then, this diverse range of interests must be aggregated into alternative proposals and packages within which compromises are reached and on which decisions can be made.

The function of interest *articulation* is normally performed by interest groups[13] and, to a lesser extent, by small political parties; the function of interest *aggregation* is normally performed by large or at least fairly large political parties and is also performed by inter-party coalitions. Since the functions of interest articulation and interest aggregation must be performed in the course of a referendum debate, it follows that interest groups and political parties have key roles to play in the referendum process. Just as, prior to legislation being enacted by the Oireachtas, groups and parties state their position and argue their case, so, prior to the performance of the rule-making function by the electorate as a whole in a referendum, it is essential that the interests involved be articulated and aggregated and this can be done most effectively by the relevant interest groups and by the political parties.

Political communication is the third additional function posited by the structural-functional model. This function is normally carried out by the Oireachtas and its individual members, by the political parties and by the media. Political communication becomes particularly important when the constitution puts the electorate as a whole centre-stage and assigns to it a rule-making function. In the light of this, proposals for the funding of referendums should recognise the role of the legislature as a whole, of the individual members of the legislature, of political parties and of the media in performing the communication function in a referendum context.

Finally, the structural-functional model points to two further functions, namely political recruitment and political socialisation. People must be recruited to perform various roles in the political process. There is perhaps a tendency to think of political recruitment as recruitment of activists, of candidates for office and of office holders, but the fact is that citizens also must be recruited as voters. This voter recruitment function is performed by interest groups and by political parties. Not only must people be recruited into various political roles, they must also be socialised, that is, they must learn what is necessary for the effective performance of their role. In general this kind of learning takes place in families, in peer groups, in schools, through the media and through exposure to the activities of political parties and interest groups. The function of political socialisation or learning is as important in referendums as it is in the political process in general and the referendum process should be designed in a way that facilitates its effective performance.

One can summarise the above argument as follows. When applied to referendums, the traditional separation-of-powers model of the political system tends to cut the people off from the institutions and structures of government and politics and to emphasise a principle of non-interference in the decision-making process being undertaken by the people. In the main, this was the model which, perhaps inevitably, informed the Supreme Court and High Court judgements in the McKenna and related cases. An alternative and more realistic approach is to see the referendum in the context of a more comprehensive 'structural-functional' model of the political system. This model draws attention to the essential role of groups, of political parties, of the Oireachtas and its individual members and of the media in ensuring informed and knowledgeable participation by the voters in the performance of their rule-making function. In recognising the essential roles that political parties and elected representatives play in the referendum process, the structural-functional model would favour a proportionate or equitable rather than an equal allocation of funding in support of campaigning in referendums.

It may be argued that this is all very well in terms of a political science understanding of the political system and of the referendum process, but that the fact remains that any proposal regarding the referendum process must stay within the constraints of the existing provisions of the constitution as interpreted by the courts. Otherwise, those proposing a change to the rules governing referendums would have to persuade the voters to change the constitution. Before accepting that the constitution would have to be changed to accommodate equitable rather than equal allocation of funding in support of referendum campaigning, it is perhaps worth exploring what might be interpreted as implicit support in the constitution for the notion of equitable funding. The argument that such support exists is based on what can be seen as an implicit constitutional reference to the role of Dáil deputies and of political parties in the referendum process. The reference occurs in Article 27.

Dáil deputies, political parties and the referendum process: the implications of Article 27

Article 27 of Bunreacht na hEireann allows for a bill to be referred to the people on the grounds that the bill 'contains a proposal of such national importance that the will of the people thereon ought to be ascertained' (Article 27.1). The referral has to be initiated by a majority of the Seanad supported by at least one third of the Dáil and takes the form of a request to the President to decline to sign the Bill until the will of the people in regard to it has been ascertained. The possibilities and procedures set out in Article 27 are complex but the key provision in the present context is simple: if the President decides that the will of the people on the bill in question ought to be ascertained, this can be done *either* by holding a referendum within a period of 18 months after the President's decision *or* by 'a resolution of Dáil Eireann passed within the said period after a dissolution and re-assembly of Dáil Eireann' (Article 27.5.1.2).

Given that the purpose of Article 27 is to ascertain the will of the people on a matter of major national importance, it is surely very significant that, in certain circumstances, power is given to a Dáil majority to decide what the will of the people is. This power of decision is given to the Dáil only when an election has intervened between the President's decision in favour of ascertaining the will of the people and the passing of the Dáil resolution. The fact that the will of the people on a Bill can be ascertained by resolution of the Dáil following an intervening general election implies that the candidates in the election, individually or collectively, would have put the matter in question to the people in the election campaign. If indeed the matter were one of major national importance, they would presumably have campaigned vigorously on the issue. It is on this basis that the election result and a subsequent resolution by the Dáil can be taken as expressing the will of the people and as the equivalent of a referendum. Under the Electoral Act, 1997, such campaigning would be, in part, publicly funded and such funding would be broadly in proportion to the electoral strength of the political parties.[14]

All of this surely implies that, in a case in which the alternative (referendum) route is taken under Article 27, the Dáil and its members, individually or grouped according to their positions on the referendum issue, would have a right to put their arguments to the people in the referendum, to campaign vigorously on the issue and, under present legislation, to receive proportionately allocated assistance from public funds in order to do so. It would be strange indeed if, under Article 27, ascertaining the will of the people via one route (an election and a Dáil decision) involved extensive publicly funded campaigning while such publicly funded campaigning were to be regarded as unauthorised interference if the process of ascertaining the will of the people took the other (referendum) route.

The question then is whether or not this implicit proportionately publicly funded role for elected representatives in the referendum process is confined to referendums held under Article 27. At first sight, it might appear that the role is so confined since Article 27 does not apply to bills to amend the constitution. Article 27 is quite explicit on this point; its opening sentence states: 'This article applies to any Bill, other than a Bill expressed to be a Bill containing a proposal for the amendment of this Constitution . . .'. Furthermore, the article in the constitution that lays down how referendums are to be conducted (Article 47) applies different decision-making rules to constitutional referendums and to Article 27 referendums: a straightforward absolute majority rule to the former and a blocking qualified majority rule to the latter.[15] However, these are the only differences between the two kinds of referendums specified in the constitution. The first difference is necessary to close off what would otherwise have been a way of avoiding the referendum as the only means of amending the constitution. The second is a highly specific variation in how the outcome of each type of referendum is decided. Neither of these provisions in any way implies that the conduct of the referendum ought to be different depending on whether the referendum is about amending the constitution or about ascertaining the will of the people on an issue of major national importance. There is, in short, nothing in Article 27 or in Articles 46 and 47 to suggest that the constitution envisages two different kinds of *referendum process*. Rather, there is in the constitution a single referendum process specified in a single article (Article 47) that must be followed both in the case of an amendment to the constitution and when the President decides to refer a Bill to the people under Article 27, unless, in the latter case, the alternative means of ascertaining the will of the people (a general election and a vote by the Dáil) occurs within an 18-month period following the President's decision. It would seem therefore that, although Bills containing proposals for the amendment of the constitution are, for a particular and obvious reason, excluded from the purview of Article 27, the implications of Article 27 for the actual conduct of referendums apply as much to referendums on proposals to change the constitution as to referendums on Bills referred to the people. In short, on this reading of Article 27, the constitution implicitly envisages a role for members of the Dáil and for Dáil candidates, and, by implication, for political parties in referendum campaigning.[16] Moreover, given the current provisions for public funding of election campaigns, there is no reason to suppose that the campaigning role in question could not be supported from public funds, with such public funds being allocated proportionately, i.e. equitably between parties and TDs.

Richard Sinnott

Conclusion

Evidence from the two referendums on the Treaty of Nice indicates substantial problems in the level of engagement of the electorate in the referendum process and in the amount of information and understanding that the citizens bring to bear in performing their constitutionally prescribed decision-making role. In the case of the first referendum on the Nice Treaty, this resulted in an extremely low turnout that was a major factor in the victory of the 'no' side. It also resulted in a tendency, among those who did vote, to vote 'no' on the basis that they did not understand the issues. While the second Nice referendum represented an improvement in these respects, it still involved quite extensive feelings of confusion regarding the issues, confusion that contributed to keeping turnout on a vital national issue under 50 per cent. This confusion and the (relatively) low turnout in the second Nice referendum persisted despite a major effort by the political parties and the various campaign groups and organisations to get their message across. In the case of the pro-Treaty parties and groups, this quite exceptional effort was a result of the realisation that lack of knowledge and low turnout were prime causes of the defeat of the Nice Treaty on the first occasion. Since there is no guarantee that efforts of this magnitude and intensity will be produced in future referendums on this or on other issues, the relatively successful experience of the second referendum on the Treaty of Nice in fact reinforces the argument regarding the need for public funding to support campaigning in referendums.

The courts have said that such funding should be allocated on an equal basis between the 'yes' and the 'no' sides. This argument is based substantially on viewing the referendum process in terms of the traditional, tripartite, separation-of-powers model of the political system. An alternative model of the political system and of the referendum process draws attention to the need for the performance of the functions of interest articulation, interest aggregation, political communication, political recruitment and political socialisation in the referendum process and recognises the role of the Dáil, the political parties, interest groups and the media in performing these functions. By implication, the structural-functional model would support proportionate or equitable allocation of campaign funding to political parties and elected representatives. It is arguable that such an allocation of funding is in fact compatible with the constitution in so far as Article 27 implicitly envisages a very significant role for the Dáil, for elected politicians and, by implication, for political parties in the referendum process, a role that might well be defined in terms of several of the key functions just listed.

In sum, the arguments presented in this chapter suggest that funding in support of campaigning in referendums should be allocated on a proportional basis to the political parties in the Dáil or, if the parties are internally divided on the referendum issue, to the prevailing majority and minority on the issue in the Dáil. The arguments in this chapter would also support the previous practice of RTÉ in allocating free broadcast time to political parties on a proportional basis. While this chapter has focused mainly on the issue of allocating public funding to political parties and elected representatives, the arguments also support the allocation of funding and other public resources (e.g. free broadcast time) to interest groups. In general, funding for interest groups should be allocated on an equal basis between the 'yes' and the 'no' camps, with the proviso that, in order to ensure that such funding would only go to bona fide interest groups, the allocation would be made on the basis of applications to an independent referendum commission. Many of the details of this alternative approach to the funding of the referendum process, such as the details of the role of an independent referendum commission, remain to be filled in. However, the evidence and arguments presented suggest that proceeding along these lines is desirable in terms of improving the quality of participation in the referendum process and is compatible with the provisions of the constitution. Finally, if proceeding along these lines were, at the end of the day, to be found to be incompatible with the constitution, consideration should be given to amending the constitution in the interests of encouraging maximum popular participation in decision making on what are often quite fundamental issues.

Notes

1 The main cases have been McKenna *v* An Taoiseach (no. 2) [1995] 2IR 10; Hanafin v An Taoiseach [1996] 2 IRLM 171; Coughlan *v* Broadcasting Commission and RTÉ [2000] 3 IR 1.

2 In the Committee's view, an equitable approach would start by dividing the total funding into two equal segments. One segment would then be divided among the parties in the Oireachtas in proportion to their size (if parties were not united on the issue, this could presumably be in proportion to the size of the 'yes' and 'no' groups in the Oireachtas). The other segment would be divided equally between the pro and anti groups outside the Oireachtas.

3 'The role of the People in amending the constitution cannot be overemphasised. It is solely their prerogative to amend any provision thereof by way of variation, addition, or repeal or to refuse to amend. The decision is theirs and theirs alone' Hamilton CJ [1995] 2 IR 41.

4 '. . . the People, by virtue of the democratic nature of the State enshrined in the Constitution, are entitled to be permitted to reach their decision free from unauthorised interference by any of the organs of State . . .' Hamilton CJ (ibid.)

5 '. . . the use by the Government of public funds in a campaign in favour of a "yes" vote was contrary to the requirement of "fair procedures" and an infringement of the concept of equality' Hamilton CJ [1995] 2 IR 41–2.

6 'So far as the instant case is concerned the political parties are in the same position as the Government in that they are not assigned by either the Constitution or the Laws for the time being in force any role in the submission of the proposal for the decision of the People' (Carney, J., unreported, High Court, 24 April 1998, 14).

7 'In my view a package of uncontested or partisan broadcasts by the National Broadcasting Service weighted on one side of the argument is an interference with the referendum process of a kind contemplated by Hamilton, C.J. as undemocratic and is a constitutionally unfair procedure' (Carney, *ibid.*, 16–17)

8 The referendum proposal was supported by 94.4 per cent of the voters.

9 These two referendums are chosen for detailed consideration because of the availability of substantial bodies of data on voter attitudes and behaviour in them. The data derive from special surveys carried out on behalf of the European Commission Representation in Ireland (for details see Sinnott, 2001 and 2003; for an overview of Irish referendums, see Sinnott, 1995 and 2002).

10 As the referendum on the Treaty of Amsterdam was held on the same day as the referendum on the Good Friday Agreement, the 56 per cent turnout cannot be regarded as an unambiguous indicator of the underlying propensity of the electorate to turn out to vote in European referendums.

11 For details of the multivariate analyses in question see Sinnott, 2001 and 2003.

12 The structural-functional model of the political system was first elaborated in the 1960s, most notably in Almond, Gabriel and Bingham Powell, Jr (1966), and it gave rise to considerable debate, in particular about the merits of 'systems analysis' and of 'functionalism'. Much of this debate was a distraction from the main contribution of the categorisation, which, while not providing a final answer, was to take political analysis that vital step beyond the formal-legal limits of the traditional, constitutional approach. As Jean Blondel remarks (1990: 20), the categorisation was 'both ingenious and, as a first approximation, valuable'.

13 The term 'interest group' is used here in the broad sense, i.e. as including any group (other than a political party) that either on an ad hoc or on an ongoing basis seeks to promote a particular interest, principle or cause.

14 The Electoral Act, 1997 makes provision for the reimbursement of the election expenses of candidates at Dáil general elections and by-elections; reimbursement is subject to a certain vote threshold and to a monetary ceiling. The Act also makes provision for payments to political parties for administration, research, education and training, policy formulation and the co-ordination of the activities of the branches and members of the party. The Act specifies that these latter payments (to political parties) shall not be applied to election expenses or to furthering any particular outcome at a referendum. This latter restriction does not affect the

argument put forward here; for the purpose of the argument, it is sufficient that the election expenses of candidates (both party and non-party) are reimbursable.

15   In the case of an article 27 referendum the bill in question is only vetoed if a majority of voters vote against it and 'if the votes so cast against its enactment into law shall have amounted to not less than thirty-three and one third per cent of the voters on the register' (Article 47.2.1)

16   This role would approximate to the desideratum identified by Mr Justice Barrington when, in the Hanafin case, he argued that 'Politicians who think that the constitution should be amended have the right and duty to attempt to persuade their fellow citizens to adopt the proposed amendment. It appears to me that they are entitled to do this individually, as private citizens, or collectively as members of a political party or of the government. The problem is that anything they do collectively as members of the government is likely to cost money and, almost inevitably, this will be taxpayer's money. In McKenna (No. 2) however, this Court decided that the government by spending funds on a one-sided professional advertising campaign designed to persuade the voters to vote for the government's proposed amendment to the constitution has exceeded the limits of its discretion and had been unfair to those taxpayers who opposed the introduction of divorce' ([1996] 2 IRLM., 210–11).

Bibliography

All-Party Oireachtas Committee on the Constitution (2001) *Sixth Progress Report: The Referendum*. Dublin: Stationery Office.

Almond, Gabriel and G. Bingham Powell, Jr. (1966*) Comparative Politics: A Developmental Approach*. Boston: Little, Brown.

Farrell, Brian (1984) 'Communications and community: problems and prospects", pp. 111–21 in Brian Farrell (ed.), *Communications and Community in Ireland*. Dublin and Cork: Mercier.

Blondel, Jean (1990) *Comparative Government: An Introduction*. London: Philip Allan.

Sinnott, Richard (1995) *Irish Voters Decide: Voting Behaviour in Elections and Referendums Since 1918*. Manchester: Manchester University Press.

Sinnott, Richard (2001) 'Attitudes and Behaviour of the Irish Electorate in the Referendum on the Treaty of Nice: Results of a survey of public opinion carried out for the European Commission Representation in Ireland', http://europa.eu.int/comm/dg10/epo/flash/fl108_v2_en.pdf.

Sinnott, Richard (2002) 'Cleavages, parties and referendums: Relationships between representative and direct democracy in the Republic of Ireland', *European Journal of Political Research* 41: 811–26.

Sinnott, Richard (2003) 'Attitudes and behaviour of the Irish electorate in the second referendum on the Treaty of Nice: Results of a survey of public opinion carried out for the European Commission Representation in Ireland', http://www.euireland.ie/TreatyofNice(2) report.pdf.

CHAPTER TWELVE

Before campaigns were 'modern': Irish electioneering in times past

DAVID M. FARRELL

—

In recent years, there has been a veritable growth industry in the study of campaigns and their modernisation (Bowler and Farrell, 1992; Butler and Ranney, 1992; Gunther and Mughan, 2000; Swanson and Mancini, 1996). Studies have shown how electioneering by parties and (especially in the USA) candidates has changed in terms of the three 'Ts' of technology, technicians and techniques. By the turn of the millennium the talk was of how election-eering had entered a new phase of modernisation, referred to variously as 'stage 3' (Farrell and Webb, 2000), 'digital age' (Farrell, 2002), 'post-Fordist' (Denver and Hands, 2002), or even 'post-modern' (Norris, 2000). The implication is that the parties and candidates have moved to a stage beyond the 'TV-age' of cen-tralised, standardised, one-size-fits-all national campaigns; they are embracing the new media technologies – especially those centred on the world wide web and the internet – and running campaigns which differ in some quite fundamental ways from those of a mere ten or twenty years before. This shift from 'modern' to 'post-modern' campaign styles is summarised in the last two columns of Table 12.1, and it has already been explored in some detail in a number of recent studies (most notably, Farrell and Webb, 2002; Norris, 2000).

Research on individual Irish elections, particularly in the *How Ireland Voted* series, would place Irish campaigns somewhere in between the modern and post-modern stages (most recently, see Holmes, 1999). Certainly, the general consensus has been that Ireland entered 'modernity' in the last quarter of the twentieth century, the entry marked most dramatically by the Fianna Fáil elec-tion campaign of 1977, an election much written about by Brian Farrell, among others (Farrell, 1978a, 1978b; Farrell and Manning, 1978; also Corr, 1977). By the time of the subsequent Fine Gael campaign of 1981 (Farrell, 1986), it was evident that the parties' campaigns had shifted up a gear, moving away from a

Table 12.1 **Three stages in the development of election campaigning**

	'Pre-modern'	*'Modern'*	*'Post-modern'*
1. Campaign preparations	Short-term; ad hoc	Long-term; specialist committee established 1–2 years in advance of election	'Permanent campaign': establishment of specialist campaign departments
2. Campaign organisation	Decentralised Local party organisation Little standardisation Staffing: party/candidate-based, voluntary	Nationalisation, centralisation Staffing: party-based, salaried professional	Decentralisation of operation with central scrutiny Staffing: party/candidate-based, professional, contract work; growth of leader's office
3. Agencies, consultants	Minimal use; 'generalist' role Politicians in charge	Growing prominence of 'specialist' consultants Politicians still in charge	Consultants as campaign personalities International links 'Who is in charge?'
4. Sources of feedback	Impressionistic, 'feel' Important role of canvassers, group leaders	Large-scale opinion polls More scientific	Greater range of polling techniques Interactive capabilities of cable and internet
5. Use of media	Emphasis on 'direct' Direct=party literature, posters Indirect=little use of public relations, etc	Emphasis on 'indirect' Direct=advertising campaigns Indirect=public relations, media training, press conferences	Emphasis on 'direct' Direct=targeted ads, direct mail, cable TV, internet Indirect=as before
6. Campaign events	Public meetings; local events	TV debates; press conferences; emphasis on party leader and tour	As before; events targeted more locally

Source: Based on Farrell (1996)

'pre-modern' form and embracing what were then the new – predominantly TV-centred – technologies.

When making the argument that party campaigns strategies and tactics have changed and become more 'professional' a major problem is that, with few exceptions (e.g. Wring, 1995), little evidence is given of the way campaigning actually used to be. It is difficult to counter the argument that perhaps things have not changed quite so dramatically, that perhaps there never was a pre-modern campaign Golden Age (Bartels, 1992; Dionne, 1976). Evidence in support of this point is available from looking at the first election campaigns in the new Irish Free State. In the late 1920s, Cumann na nGaedheal employed the O'Kennedy–Brindley advertising agency to promote its image while in government and during the two 1927 campaigns.[1] In a 1929 by-election, the advertising agency designed a glossy pamphlet for distribution, and on polling day, copies of another leaflet were dropped from an aeroplane.[2]

Throughout the 1920s both Fianna Fáil and Cumann na nGaedheal made use of the sort of campaign gimmickry more usually associated with recent campaigns, including the distribution of badges and flags, and the composing of campaign songs (Moss, 1933: 130).[3] In the 1932 election, Cumann na nGaedheal distributed a 160-page handbook among party canvassers, entitled *Fighting Points for Cumann na nGaedheal Speakers and Workers.* In the 1933 election, the party produced a film of the party leader, W. T. Cosgrave, making a campaign speech and this was distributed across the country (Moss, 1933: 193). In another election in the 1940s one party fitted an aeroplane with a microphone and flew it around the country calling for votes (McCracken, 1958: 85).

There would appear to be grounds, therefore, for arguing that campaigning has changed little from the styles and strategies followed in the 1920s.[4] But such a conclusion would be premature. In a number of fundamental ways election campaigns generally have undergone great change, and while today we might dispute the degree to which Irish parties have entered a post-modern stage of campaigning, there is little doubt that they have left far behind their pre-modern stage. Certainly by the 1980s it was clear that, for the better-endowed parties at any rate, the election campaign was characterised by the following six features (see column two of Table 12.1): (1) long-term preparation, (2) centralised campaign organisation and an emphasis on standardisation of campaign materials, (3) the prominent role of campaign specialists and agencies, (4) use of opinion polls for objective campaign feedback, (5) an emphasis on press advertising and media relations, and (6) an emphasis on party leaders and press conferences. As this chapter will show, in each of these respects, Irish election campaigns looked very different in times past.

This chapter focuses on the shift from pre-modern to modern campaigning in Ireland. Making use of archival material and some background interviews, it highlights just how much Irish elections changed in the latter part of the last century through an exploration of six main features of party campaign strategies and tactics in the pre-modern age.[7] The focus is on Fine Gael's campaigns, for the most part in the 1950s–1960s; but the pre-modern campaign styles can even be traced through to the party's disastrous 1977 campaign. In short, the aim of the chapter is to assess how well Ireland 'fits' into the individual cells of 'pre-modern' campaigning listed in Table 12.1.

Campaign preparations

In comparative accounts of contemporary election campaigns, it is apparent that one of the main features of a well-designed campaign is careful and long-term planning and preparation. It has been a requirement for some time that campaign organisations are established long in advance of the anticipated election: in recent years, it has reached a stage where a good campaign is seen as one that is in a state of perpetual readiness – the 'permanent campaign' of Sydney Blumenthal (1982). Clearly, this is one area where we should expect to see a big difference in the campaign styles of yesteryear, and in this respect Fine Gael certainly does not disappoint.

There is clear evidence that Fine Gael's campaigns of old were notable for their lack of preparedness. Campaign planning tended to follow a standardised basic model. There were prima facie indications that attention was paid to campaign preparations. Generally, there was some sort of backroom standing committee that started meeting a few months before the expected election. A central feature of the committee's work was liaising with the party's advertising agency. A closer examination of the evidence reveals a number of shortcomings, however, in these preparations, at least when compared with contemporary experience. For instance, the pre-campaign contacts with the advertising agency appear for the most part to have involved discussions on likely costings for the advertising campaign and estimates on the numbers and range of advertisements to be produced.[6] It is difficult to see these contacts as strategic in nature: there was little by way of innovation in the development of new advertising techniques; the slogans tended to be singularly uninspiring and repetitive across the various elections (e.g. in 1954, 'There is going to be a new government'; in 1965, 'It's time for a change').[7]

Table 12.2 **Fine Gael campaign plan notes, 1954**

Plan of Campaign, 1954

[Handwritten across the top] Appeal for funds, workers, etc. for Friday in 3 dailies

1. Posters – very urgent – David Allen[1] (F. J. Mullen)

2. Newspaper advertising campaign: allocation (no country papers?), dates, sizes (conference with Mr. Padbury and Senator Hayes), illustrations (blocks). Query – Evening Papers. Themes of advertisements. Policy? Specific Item, e.g. Civil Servants.

3. Election Address in Draft – Monday?

4. Handbills in Draft. Repeat of existing ones? 120,000 cost of living handbills, also stencils for constituencies, cost: £1 each, i.e. £40.

5. Points for Speakers (Árd Fheis Digest for General – plus stencilled points).

---

1   David Allen Outdoor Advertising.
Source: Fine Gael/UCD archives, P39/BF7(p)

Of greater significance is the actual nature of the campaign plans that were drawn up by the standing committee. It is hard to conceive of these in any way as strategic or tactical plans for an election campaign; rather, they tended to take the form of an aide-mémoire of tasks that needed to be fulfilled. Tables 12.2 and 12.3 provide two examples of what the party then meant by campaign preparations. In 1954, last-minute notes were hastily produced to guide the general secretary and his (sole) secretary on what had to be set in motion for the campaign. It is clear that these notes were written *after* the election had been announced. By the early 1960s the party had gone one step further. The notes were no longer produced at the last minute;[8] however, they still represented little more than a set of guidelines on what had to be done in the event of an election being called.

The practice of minimalist campaign preparations was to continue right through to Fine Gael's disastrous 1977 campaign, when the party leader and Taoiseach, Liam Cosgrave, announced an election against the advice of his

Table 12.3 **Fine Gael campaign plan notes, 1963**

Notes in the Event of a General Election (18 June 1963)

1. Issue a general warning order.

2. Prepare and issue a schedule of conventions for selection of candidates.

3. Decide on campaign programme:

   a. Press conferences announcing policy and issues to be put before the people.

   b. Decide action to be taken regarding:
      – public meetings and rallies.
      – television appearances.
      – use of radio.
      – President's Tour of the country.

   c. Finance – collections at Church Gates or House-to-House.
      General – issue of election collection circular seeking funds all over the country.

   d. Publicity:
      – Advertisements.
      – leaflets.
      – specimen election addresses.
      – posters with general appeal.
      – David Allen's sites.
      – CIE sites.
      – Points for Speakers.

Source: Fine Gael/UCD archives, P39/BF34(I)

most senior advisers, without any early warning to the party organisation, and without even commissioning a pre-campaign poll. A series of successful by-elections and a carefully crafted constituency boundary re-division – which was designed to deliver a gerrymander for the party (but which failed miserably to do so; see Sinnott, 1993) – gave the party leadership (false) confidence, which in part helps to explain why so little attention was paid to campaign preparation. There were no fundraising or membership drives, no organisational reviews. In line with the practice of earlier election campaigns, an ad hoc standing committee started meeting from April 1977, a few short months before the election, and far too late to initiate any major campaign preparations. In short, the degree of party preparation in 1977 was little different from that of a decade earlier (Table 12.3).

Campaign organisation

As Table 12.1 shows, the nature of the campaign organisation is one area of campaigning which is undergoing quite radical reform in the current shift from modern to post-modern campaigns. Equally there were some important organisational changes in the pre-modern to modern stages of campaign development. Modern campaigns have been characterised by a heavy emphasis on nationalisation, standardisation and professionalisation. By contrast, in the pre-modern age the catchwords for campaign organisation were decentralisation, little standardisation and volunteerism. Once again, the Fine Gael campaigns of times past fit this picture perfectly.

At this stage, Irish party headquarters were very under-resourced (e.g. Manning, 1999: 330; more generally, Chubb, 1959). The tendency was to leave the constituencies to run their own separate campaigns: there was little by way of central control, little attempt to standardise campaign material and messages across the country. This can be illustrated by two examples. First, the number of posters distributed by the Fine Gael headquarters to the constituencies was very small (a mere 84 posters per constituency in 1954, 250 in 1961; in 1965 less than 12,000 leader posters were printed for nationwide distribution).[9] In the 1954 election, one constituency organisation wrote to headquarters asking to buy some extra posters, but without success. In his reply, the general secretary wrote: 'I am sorry we cannot do more to help you from here, but in the general election everything is decentralised'.[10]

Second, what help the standing committee did provide tended to be in the form of vague guidance to the constituencies on their local publicity; there was no effort at standardisation. For the most part, headquarters gave only rough suggestions about style, which the constituencies were at liberty to ignore. For example, in 1961 the general secretary sent a memo to the local party organisations on 'constituency publicity'. In this he suggested: 'the Election Address (for free post) should consist of a short letter to the electors from the candidates; some points from Fine Gael Heads of Policy, selected by yourself, suitable to your constituency; one or two slogans and brief biographical notices of each candidate with photograph where possible'.[11] In another memo during the same campaign, the general secretary provided some advice on poster design: 'All your posters should give in large characters the names of your candidates, your main idea must be to "sell" your candidate to the media'.[12] During the 1969 election, the General Secretary wrote to the constituency organisations regarding local postering: 'I enclose herewith a copy of our Fine Gael Will Win poster, a supply of which has already been issued to your constituency. It is suggested that, for designing local posters for use in your constituency, you use the top portion of this poster, and have the candidates names printed underneath, instead of the words "Will Win".'[13]

Organisational decentralism and lack of effort at standardisation were still apparent in the 1977 Fine Gael campaign. For instance, five days *after* the election was called, the General Secretary, J. W. Sanfey, wrote to constituency secretaries asking them to provide details on their requirements for election literature.[14] Three days later, in a letter to each constituency director of elections – and where there was none, to each candidate – Sanfey wrote: 'Constituencies which have not yet done so should immediately inform headquarters of the following: (a) the location and full address of election headquarters with telephone numbers if available; (b) the name and address of the director of elections with the phone number.'[15]

Agencies and consultants

The growing prominence of campaign consultants and specialist agencies is central to the contemporary campaign: these are the 'campaign warriors' who fight the fight of the parties and their leading candidates (Thurber and Nelson, 2000). In his work on political consultants in the USA, Larry Sabato draws a useful distinction between a 'generalist' consultant, who tends to be a 'jack of all trades', and a 'specialist' consultant, who focuses on just one part of the overall campaign. According to Sabato (1981: 9), '[w]hile almost all of the early consultants were generalists, most consultants today are specialists'. This argument can be applied to an examination of the agencies and specialists employed by parties in most countries (Bowler and Farrell, 2000; Farrell et al., 2001). In the case of Fine Gael, it is apparent that there have been a number of phases in the incorporation of consultants and agencies into its electioneering. In the first instance, the party had long-term arrangements with an advertising agency, but the work required of the agency tended to be limited and quite basic. As we move into the 1960s and 1970s there are signs of Fine Gael requiring a more active role from its advertising agency. This can be seen as the stage of what Sabato would call 'general' consultancy, when the advertising agency was being called upon to carry out a wide range of different functions. The shift to specialised consultancy in Fine Gael would have to wait until 1981 (Farrell, 1986).

Throughout most of the 1940s and 1950s, Fine Gael employed the services of Padbury's advertising agency.[16] By the end of the 1960s, however, senior members of the party were stressing their deep disquiet at the quality of the party's advertisements in comparison to 'the high standard of material now being used by our opponents'.[17] As one politician put it in a letter to the General Secretary about the party's campaign in a recent by-election:

> The Election Address was like an Obituary Notice. The Headquarters canvassing cards were delivered weeks late. There were four different types of canvassing cards in circulation. The poster was a failure . . . At the time that I expressed my displeasure with poor advertising, I was informed that steps would be taken to replace Padbury's with a progressive advertising agency. I don't know what has been done in this regard.

This letter and other complaints provoked a reaction from headquarters. Soon after, in a period of organisational review, the party changed agencies, signing a new contract with Arks. This agency made much of its available client services which covered 'advertising, marketing and public relations in all their aspects. We regard it as our duty to assist and advise our clients in the general development of the presentation and sales of their products and in making the best use of their appropriation'. The party and new agency enjoyed a brief honeymoon period. In Arks, Fine Gael apparently benefited from 'a very enthusiastic team' whose 'enthusiasm is certainly reflected in the quality of the work they are producing'.[18]

It is clear that Arks had a very 'generalist' role to play. Fine Gael set in train a process of revising party logos, colours, and printed material, paying close attention to developments at the time in Fianna Fáil advertising.[19] Arks were not solely involved in clearing up Fine Gael's printed communications. With the arrival of television in the 1960s, attention also had to be paid to preparing the party's principal politicians.[20] Arks were responsible for arranging special training courses, editing the politicians' scripts, dressing them,[21] and liaising with RTÉ. For the most part, however, these 'training courses' appear to have been one-off and rather superficial events, very different from the type of media training which politicians currently undergo.

Evidently Arks had a crucial role to play in Fine Gael's first steps towards organisational and communication revival. Much was expected of them, and the strains soon showed. In early 1969 – within only a few months of signing the contract with Fine Gael – Arks decided to end the relationship on the grounds that the 1968 referendum campaign (on the proposal to change the electoral system) had been far too disruptive. The agency took the decision 'that we cannot, in future, handle political advertising for any party'. No amount of persuasion by Fine Gael could get Arks to change their mind. As an alternative, Fine Gael employed the services of Kenny's Advertising for the 1969 election campaign. However, by the time of the 1973 election Fine Gael was again using Arks and was to continue to do so into the 1980s.[22] Whether the party was always in a position to make optimum use of its advertising agency is a moot point. For instance, the party's principal Arks contact in the 1970s refers, in a private interview, to how disorganised the Fine Gael campaign was in 1977. He claims to have received little guidance from the party, and there was evidence of personal disagreements over strategy between senior representatives of the party.

The only slight shift towards a more specialised role for campaign agencies was in 1973, when Fine Gael started to make use of the Market Research Bureau of Ireland (MRBI) for market research. But even here, as we shall see next, there are serious doubts over the degree to which MRBI had much influence on the nature and style of electioneering deployed by its client.

Sources of feedback

No self-respecting political campaign of today can do without high quality, objective feedback (Rose, 1967). More than anything else this signifies the shift from treating politics as an exercise in promoting party ideology, in which politicians presented their wares and the voters either supported them or not, to politics as a marketing exercise, in which party strategists market-test policies and image and the party and its leadership adapt as necessary to suit the whims of the electorate.

Polling came late to Irish politics. Politicians and journalists alike were reluctant and slow to make use of market research techniques that were seen as commonplace in the USA and Britain. As recently as 1973, for instance, prominent newspaper articles were warning of the dangers of inaccurate poll predictions.[23] And in the mid-1970s, Brian Farrell (1978: 128) observed of the media that they 'remain fundamentally suspicious of survey methods, doubtful of their accuracy, and wary of the reluctance of professional pollsters to predict precise results'. Also relevant, of course, was the fact that, until relatively recently, there was a general lack of available agencies to carry out such research. At the start of the 1960s, Gallup – which then had offices in Dublin – appears to have been the only agency available to carry out political opinion polling. The country's two leading indigenous agencies were not set up until a few years into the decade: MRBI in 1962 and Irish Marketing Surveys (IMS) in 1963. According to John Meagher (1983) of IMS, the first survey of political attitudes was commissioned by the *Irish Press* in July 1961, dealing with attitudes relating to Ireland's first application for EC membership. Labour was the first party to commission a poll (from Gallup) before the 1969 general election (see Whyte, 1974). This was to be the only national poll ever commissioned by Labour on its own. In the 1970s, benefiting from its coalition links with Fine Gael, it shared access to the latter's MRBI polls.

Fine Gael's records reveal some fascinating insights regarding the introduction of market research into Irish politics. Not surprisingly, the party relied for a long time on impressionistic sources and intuition. The 1965 election provides a good example of an attempt by some in the party to move towards more objective data gathering, albeit then a somewhat amateur exercise. Midway through the election the party received a report from a party activist, which was described as 'our usual mid-campaign survey'. The sample consisted of voters who were selected 'with considerable precision to represent, as far as possible, various sections . . . The reporters are extremely experienced and can spot a committed party man a mile away'.[24] The report, which had a number of recommendations on how the party might alter its campaign to counter a likely Fianna Fáil victory, was immediately dispatched by the general secretary to James Dillon, the party leader. There is no indication that any further attention was paid to its contents.[25]

It was not until early 1971 that Fine Gael first entertained the idea of commissioning its own market research. In his memoirs, Garret FitzGerald (1991: 77ff.) writes of how in late 1967 he had been appointed to a Fine Gael electoral strategy committee to examine the party's policies and tactics. One key area of discussion was the possibility of merger or alliance with Labour. (This was the period of Fine Gael's social democratic 'Just Society' policies.) The matter was discussed at some length between both parties at the highest level. After more than a decade in opposition, Fine Gael clearly gave serious thought to the possibility of forming some sort of arrangement with Labour. In

February 1971, at the request of party leader Liam Cosgrave, the General Secretary wrote to Arks asking for advice on whether and how the party might assess public opinion on the matter via market research. Arks replied several days later with a short document entitled 'The Use of Market Research by Fine Gael'.[26] This argued that market research was expensive and, to save money, the party should consider whether it might best be arranged via the party machinery – a curious argument for a professional advertiser to make.

In 1973 Fine Gael finally started to commission its own market research, from MRBI, an agency which has continued to provide data and advice to the party ever since. By doing so, Fine Gael appears to have gone quite far in switching towards more scientific voter feedback, and in this area the party was certainly ahead of Fianna Fáil. However, as the evidence from the 1977 campaign shows, the party may have been prepared to commission research, but there are doubts about the extent to which it was actually prepared to make use of it. Fine Gael's first private poll was taken one day after Cosgrave called the election. Nine days later the managing director of MRBI presented the findings to a startled gathering of party strategists. The poll predicted a Fianna Fáil landslide: Fianna Fáil had 58 per cent of the vote; Fine Gael 25 per cent; Labour 10 per cent.[27] The findings of the poll were kept quiet so as not to dampen morale, and there was still a belief that the gerrymandering of constituencies would make all the difference. A bullish confidence was maintained. Two days after the findings of the first poll were known, the party's director of election sent a memo to the local party organisations stating:

> We have always known that our opponents would mount a massive campaign against us, but the signs are that victory can be ours. . . Our opponents have mounted such a campaign at the beginning that they appear to be running out of steam. Nevertheless we must be on guard against their ability to put on an extra burst of activity in the closing days of the campaign.[28]

Fine Gael's advertising throughout the 1977 campaign gave every impression of following whims rather than research recommendations. The emphasis was on continuity: 'Ireland is now back on the road to steady economic recovery. The good work should not be interrupted'. Slogans tended to be long-winded: 'Now you've got a good government. Keep it'; 'Keep the winning team. Let the good work continue'. This last full-page advertisement, which appeared in the newspapers on the final weekend of the election, featured photographs of all the Fine Gael ministers and a large photograph of Cosgrave. It ignored the fact that neither the ministers nor Cosgrave were scoring well in the opinion polls, that these were not the areas to lay stress on (Farrell, 1978a: 118).

Use of media

A useful distinction can be drawn between two main forms of campaign communication: direct communication, where the party has complete control over the presentation of its campaign messages (e.g. in posters campaigns or through purchasing advertising space), and indirect communication in which the party's messages are mediated through the established media (e.g. press coverage of campaign events).

As Table 12.1 shows, not only have there been shifts over time in the *types* of media used in campaigns (e.g. from an emphasis on posters, to newspaper ads, and now direct mail), there have also been shifts in the *form* of communication (as shown by the varying emphases on direct and indirect communication). In pre-modern campaigns the form of communication was predominantly direct, with little use of press relations or media training. We saw above how Fine Gael's advertising agency, Arks, did implement some media training in the 1960s, but this appears to have been small scale and rather rudimentary. One episode in 1977 graphically illustrates the Fine Gael leadership's attitude at the time to the importance of press relations. The day the election was called a young university economist, Moore McDowell, telephoned party headquarters and volunteered to help in the campaign. The following day he was interrupted during a game of squash and invited in to meet Cosgrave who gave him a choice of two jobs, either to co-ordinate the leader's tour or to handle press relations. McDowell opted for the former, as he had no experience of press relations. But a day or two later the party contacted him again and asked him to be the press officer. He was given an empty room in Leinster House, where he had to wait several days for a telephone to be installed and to receive an assistant.

In pre-modern labour-intensive campaigns, the main types of media deployed tended to rely heavily on the use of volunteer activists for the distribution of campaign messages. The emphasis, therefore, was on party literature that could be handed out door-to-door, and on posters for hanging on lampposts. Table 12.4 provides rare financial indicators of the changing emphases in types of media used by Fine Gael across two campaigns. As we see, in its 1966 presidential campaign, the bulk of Fine Gael's campaign expenditure was on literature (37.4 per cent), far more than what it spent in its 1981 parliamentary

Table 12.4 **Fine Gael campaign expenditure, 1966 presidential election and 1981 general election: percentage breakdowns**

	1966	*1981*[1]
	(%)	(%)
Posters	18.4	5.1
Advertising	27.8	60.6
Literature	37.4	4.5
Merchandising	0.2	10.8
Staff	1.6	1.9
Communications (general)	6.9	2.5
HQ Budget Internal	4.2	4.4
Tour	3.5	10.2

1   These are proposed expenditures drawn up (in March 1981) for a May election. In the election post-mortem Fine Gael strategists were happy to report that they had not had any major budgetary overrun. These estimates, therefore, can be treated as an accurate indicator of actual expenditure.
Sources: Fine Gael, *1st Draft Work Book, February 1968: Feasibility Study and Plan* (confidential internal document); Fine Gael headquarters' files, 10 March 1981.

election campaign (4.5 per cent). Similarly, the party spent far more on posters (18.4 per cent versus 5.1 per cent). By contrast, the amount spent on press advertising in 1966 was less than half the 1981 figure (27.8 per cent versus 60.6 per cent).

Campaign events

Campaigns were very different in '[the] pre-television age, [when] most politicians could travel the country without being recognised' (Manning, 1999: 111), and this is shown vividly by Fine Gael's preparations for its leader's tours throughout the pre-modern period. A schedule would be drawn up, but always at the last moment. There was no advance team to go ahead of the leader and pave the way, no entourage to accompany the leader. The preparations consisted of a one-page memo outlining where the leader was to be from one day to the next. This was then circulated to the constituency parties together with a covering letter from the general secretary asking for the necessary arrangements to be made to receive the leader. This was the practice for all the campaigns in the period. For example in the 1961 Irish election – a year after J. F. Kennedy's triumphant campaign for the American presidency – the Fine Gael General Secretary, in a letter on 16 September to the party's representative in the Galway constituency, wrote:

> This is to inform you that the Standing Committee have arranged that Mr James Dillon [the party leader] will address a meeting in Galway City on Tuesday 26th September at 8 pm. I shall be glad if you will please ensure that all the necessary arrangements will be carried out for the meeting, including the provision of a platform or lorry, an efficient loudspeaker, a Chairman, and a National Flag. It is important to have the meeting advertised locally and to have some kind of slogan-poster on the lorry.[29]

Two days later, the general secretary wrote again, requesting that the local representative meet the party leader at a city centre hotel. He continued: 'We are not sure exactly where the meeting is to be held, so I think the best arrangement would be for you to contact him at the Hotel'.[30] As this example shows, the party leader was literally on his own on the campaign trail. No campaign bus was provided; there were no advisers; advance planning was minimal and haphazard. Once the leader had set off on his tour of the constituencies, he was not easily contactable. For example, during the 1965 election, a local party volunteer wrote to the General Secretary seeking information on the route the party leader would take through his area. The General Secretary replied: 'I am unable to contact [the party leader] at the moment as he is moving around the country on his tour'.[31] This is a far cry from the use of beepers, mobile phones and palm organisers in today's campaigns.

The situation was little changed in 1977. As before, the leader's tour was arranged in a very ad hoc manner during the campaign. Journalists and the constituency organisations were usually given only one day's warning of the leader's movements. There was no specially equipped bus, no detailed logistical plans. In time-honoured fashion, the party's General Secretary sent a standard memo at very short notice informing local party workers of Cosgrave's impending visit and advising them: 'You should make arrangements to make the maximum use of his visit.'[32] In the event, the leader's tour was cut short when Cosgrave was diagnosed with a bad case of laryngitis, and he was prescribed bed rest (an episode which, in its own way, speaks volumes about the state of personality-driven politics in the Fine Gael of the 1970s).

Conclusion

In a number of respects, Irish electioneering in the new millennium bears some similarity to the campaigns of times past. Church-gate meetings still take place, particularly in rural areas; the parties still rely heavily on volunteer activists to distribute leaflets and knock-up voters; poster-wars continue apace on lamp posts the length and breadth of the country. An external observer having a relatively superficial glance at a contemporary Irish campaign could be forgiven for thinking that little has changed from the time when campaigns were being observed by the likes of Moss in the 1930s (Moss, 1933), McCracken in the 1940s (McCracken, 1958), Chubb in the 1950s (Chubb, 1959), or even as recently as Farrell in the 1970s (Farrell, 1978a, 1978b; Farrell and Manning, 1978).

But such an observer would be mistaken. As this chapter has shown, in terms of six main features of electioneering, Irish electioneering has gone through some important changes from pre-modern times when (1) campaign planning varied from non-existent to last-minute and sporadic; (2) campaign organisations were sparse, voluntary efforts with little scope for standardisation of messages; (3) minimalist and 'generalist' use was made of advertising agencies; (4) feedback, such as it was, was haphazard and based more on intuition than science, (5) there was little if any engagement with the national media; and (6) campaign events were local affairs with little if any focus on the party leader. From the late 1970s onwards, Irish campaigns changed utterly, and they have changed in much the same way as campaigns have been modernising in the rest of the world's demo-cracies. While perhaps not yet 'post-modern', the contemporary Irish campaign is certainly more modern than in times past.

Notes

1 On the 1927 elections, see O'Kennedy (n.d. [1927?]). Cumann na nGaedheal stopped using its advertising agency in 1932, 'since the headquarters staff was quite capable of doing the work themselves' (Moss, 1933: 125). The O'Kennedy–Brindley agency was acquired in the 1980s by London-based Saatchi's, and most recently has worked on Fianna Fáil campaigns.

2 NLI, LO p117 (107 and 108).

3 On the use of campaign posters in Ireland in the early 1930s, see Keogh (1983).

4 In this context, it is worth noting John A. Murphy's (1969) comments on the Cumann na nGaedheal campaigns of 1927–32. He contrasts the imagination and professionalism of that period with the aloofness and 'ad hocary' of Fine Gael campaigns in the 1940s.

5 Archival material used in this chapter was gathered from the following sources: the National Library of Ireland, University College Dublin Archives Department (Fine Gael party

files), and the Fine Gael party. Interviews were conducted with the following people involved particularly in the 1977 campaign: J. W. Sanfey, general secretary; Moore McDowell, press officer; a representative from the Arks advertising agency (anonymous); Jack Jones, Market Research Bureau of Ireland. A senior executive of RTÉ was also interviewed about television coverage of Irish elections in the 1960s.

6 For example, see the account of publicity preparations in the 1961 election post-mortem by the Fine Gael general secretary on 4 October 1961 (Fine Gael/UCD archives, P39/BF34(a)).

7 Fine Gael/UCD Archives, P39/BF7; P39/BF8(j)/1.

8 It is worth noting that the 1963 plans were retyped verbatim in early 1965 for use in that election (Fine Gael/UCD archives, P39/BF34(l)).

9 Fine Gael/UCD Archives, P39/BF7(m), P39/BF39(a), P39/BF34(i).

10 Fine Gael/UCD Archives, P39/BF7(f).

11 Fine Gael/UCD Archives, P39/BF11(c).

12 Fine Gael/UCD Archives, P39/BF39(a).

13 Fine Gael Headquarters Archives, letter by the General Secretary to the constituencies, 28 May 1969.

14 Sanfey to each constituency secretary, 30 May 1977 (Fine Gael headquarters' archives).

15 Sanfey to local organisations, 2 June 1977 (Fine Gael headquarters' archives).

16 For background on Padbury's, see Padbury (1945).

17 Fine Gael/UCD Archives, P39/TC8/7(a). The following discussion is based on material from this source.

18 Letter from Arks to the Fine Gael General Secretary in April 1968.

19 See the letter from Richie Ryan, TD to Arks in April 1968 in which he enclosed samples of Fianna Fáil material and requested that Arks try to come up with similar quality material.

20 The Fine Gael archives reveal how seriously the party viewed the introduction of television. As early as 1961 the party's general secretary (together with his counterparts from the other parties) was receiving communications from RTÉ producers requesting negotiations 'concerning the conditions under which political viewpoints and political personalities will be featured' (Fine Gael/UCD archives, P39/TC6/15(b)). This was to lead to a series of negotiations between party whips and television executives (private interview with a senior RTÉ executive).

21 '(a) The suit should if possible be a medium grey without a pattern rather than a plain black. (b) The shirt should be either cream, light blue or light grey, again without a pattern, and definitely not white. (c) The tie should again be plain, and not of any shiny material such as silk.'

22 Precisely why Arks changed its mind is unclear. The Fine Gael Archives reveal that Arks were working for the party again in early 1971.

23 B. Kavanagh in *The Irish Times*, 23 February 1973; F. Kilfeather in *The Irish Times*, 27 February 1973; *Irish Independent*, 27 February 1973.

24 No further details were given on sampling.

25 Fine Gael/UCD Archives, P39/BF34(l).

26 Fine Gael/UCD Archives, P39/TC8/8(j).

27 In later polls the Fine Gael–Labour coalition was seen to close the gap, but the Fianna Fáil lead appeared unassailable (Smith, 1985: 139 ff.).

28 Ryan to each constituency director of elections, 6 June 1977 (Fine Gael headquarters' archives).

29 Fine Gael/UCD Archives, P39/BF39(c).

30 *Ibid.*

31 Fine Gael/UCD Archives, P39/BF34(k).

32 Sample letter from Sanfey to local party organisations, Fine Gael headquarters' archives.

Bibliography

Bartels, Larry M. (1992) 'The impact of electioneering in the United States', in David Butler and Austin Ranney (eds), *Electioneering: A Comparative Study of Continuity and Change.* Oxford: Clarendon.

Blumenthal, Sydney (1982) *The Permanent Campaign.* New York: Simon & Schuster.

Bowler, Shaun and David Farrell (eds) (1992), *Electoral Strategies and Political Marketing.* Basingstoke, Macmillan.

Bowler, Shaun and David Farrell (2000) 'The internationalization of campaign consultancy', in James Thurber and Candice Nelson (eds), *Campaign Warriors: Political Consultants in Elections.* Washington, DC: Brookings Institution.

Butler, David and Austin Ranney (eds) (1992) *Electioneering: A Comparative Study of Continuity and Change.* Oxford: Clarendon.

Chubb, Basil (1959) 'Ireland, 1957', in David Butler (ed.), *Elections Abroad.* London: Macmillan.

Corr, F. (1977) 'The selling of Fianna Fáil', *Irish Marketing Journal,* July.

Denver, David and Gordon Hands (2002) 'Post-Fordism in the constituencies? The continuing development of constituency campaigning in Britain', in David Farrell and Rüdiger Schmitt-Beck (eds), *Do Political Campaigns Matter? Campaign Effects in Elections and Referendums.* London: Routledge.

Dionne, E. J. (1976) 'What technology has not changed: continuity and localism in British politics', in Louis Maisel (ed.), *Changing Campaign Techniques: Elections and Values in Contemporary Democracies.* Beverly Hills: Sage.

Farrell, Brian (1978) 'The mass media and the 1977 campaign', in Howard R. Penniman (ed.), *Ireland at the Polls: The Dáil Elections of 1977.* Washington DC: American Enterprise Institute.

Farrell, Brian (1978a) 'The Irish general election, 1977', *Parliamentary Affairs* 31(1).

Farrell, Brian and Maurice Manning (1978) 'The election', in Howard R. Penniman (ed.), *Ireland at the Polls: The Dáil Elections of 1977* Washington DC: American Enterprise Institute.

Farrell, David (1986) 'The strategy to market Fine Gael in 1981', *Irish Political Studies* 1: 1–14.

Farrell, David (1996) 'Campaign strategies and tactics', in Lawrence LeDuc, Richard G. Niemi and Pippa Norris (eds), *Comparing Democracies: Elections and Voting in Global Perspective.* Thousand Oaks, CA.: Sage.

Farrell, David (2002) 'Campaign modernisation and the West European party', in Kurt Richard Luther and Ferdinand Müller-Rommel (eds), *Political Parties in the New Europe*. Oxford: Oxford University Press.

Farrell, David and Paul Webb (2000) 'Political parties as campaign organisations', in Russell Dalton and Martin Wattenberg (eds), *Parties Without Partisans: Political Change in Advanced Industrial Democracies*. Oxford: Oxford University Press.

Farrell, David, Robin Kolodny and Stephen Medvic (2001) 'Political parties and campaign professionals in a digital age: political consultants in the US and their counterparts overseas', *Press/Politics* 6: 11–30.

FitzGerald, Garret (1991) *All in a Life: Garret FitzGerald, an Autobiography*. Dublin: Gill & Macmillan.

Gunther, Richard and Anthony Mughan (2000) *Democracy and the Media*. Cambridge: Cambridge University Press.

Holmes, Michael (1999) 'Organisational preparation and political marketing', in Michael Marsh and Paul Mitchell (eds), *How Ireland Voted, 1997*. Oxford: Westview/PSAI Press.

Keogh, D. (1983) 'De Valera, the Catholic Church and the "Red Scare", 1931–1932', in J. P. O'Carroll and J. A Murphy (eds), *De Valera and His Times*. Cork: Cork University Press.

Manning, Maurice (1999) *James Dillon: A Biography*. Dublin: Wolfhound Press.

McCracken, J. L. (1958) *Representative Government in Ireland: Dáil Éireann, 1919–48*. London: Oxford University Press.

Meagher, John F. (1983) 'Political polling in the Republic of Ireland', in Robert Worcester (ed.), *Political Opinion Polling: An International Review*. London: Macmillan.

Moss, W. (1933) *Political Parties in the Irish Free State*. New York: Columbia University Press.

Murphy, John A. (1969) 'The Irish party system, 1938–51', in K. Nowlan and T. D. Williams (eds), *Ireland in the War Years and After, 1939–51*. Dublin: Gill & Macmillan.

Norris, Pippa (2000) *A Virtuous Circle: Political Communications in Postindustrial Societies*. Cambridge: Cambridge University Press.

O'Kennedy, B. (n.d. [1927?]) *Making History: The Story of a Remarkable Campaign*. Dublin: O'Kennedy-Brindley.

Padbury, F. (1945) 'Art in advertising', *The Bell* 10 (5).

Rose, Richard (1967) *Influencing Voters: A Study of Campaign Rationality*. New York: St Martin's.

Sabato, Larry (1981) *The Rise of Political Consultants: New Ways of Winning Elections* New York: Basic Books.

Sinnott, Richard (1993) 'The electoral system', in John Coakley and Michael Gallagher (eds), *Politics in the Republic of Ireland*, 2nd edn. Dublin: Folens/PSAI Press.

Smith, R. (1985) *Garret: The Enigma: Dr Garret FitzGerald*. Dublin: Aherlow.

Swanson, David and Paolo Mancini (eds) (1996) *Politics, Media and Modern Democracy: An International Study of Innovations in Electoral Campaigning and Their Consequences*. Westport, CT: Praeger.

Thurber, James and Candice Nelson (eds) (2000) *Campaign Warriors: Political Consultants in Elections*. Washington, DC: Brookings Institution.

Whyte, John (1974) 'Ireland: Politics without Social Bases', in Richard Rose (ed.), *Electoral Behavior: A Comparative Handbook.* New York: Free Press.

Wring, Dominic (1995) 'From mass propaganda to political marketing: The transformation of Labour Party election campaigning', in Colin Rallings, David Farrell, David Broughton and David Denver (eds), *British Elections and Parties Yearbook, 1995.* London: Frank Cass.

CHAPTER THIRTEEN

The parliamentary lobby system

STEPHEN COLLINS

—

In 1992 RTÉ's political correspondent, Sean Duignan, switched sides and went to work as government press secretary for the newly appointed Taoiseach, Albert Reynolds. Despite his long experience as a political journalist, Duignan was astonished at how much attention his political masters paid to the media: 'I had been long enough around politicians to appreciate the massive importance they attached to the media. However, it was not until I actually found myself inside the tent that I felt the full seismic force of this awesome phenomenon. The reality is that where politicians are concerned – not just Albert Reynolds but all politicians – the media is a constant all-consuming obsession' (Duignan, 1995: 7).

The early years

The obsession with how they are perceived by the media, and the techniques of 'spinning' may be relatively new phenomena, but Irish politicians have always been acutely aware of the importance of image (see also chapter 12 in this volume). Indeed, during the War of Independence, Sinn Féin placed a huge emphasis on propaganda, and this weapon was every bit as important as the gunmen unleashed by Michael Collins. The propaganda campaign was carried on through the Irish, British and international newspapers and Sinn Féin valued the impact of film and newsreel. For instance, the effect on the population of 'sack of Balbriggan' by the Black and Tans, reportedly re-enacted for the newsreel cameras a few days after the actual event at the behest of the local IRA, had huge impact worldwide.

During the 1920s it can be argued that the government of W.T. Cosgrave lost influence because it did not pay sufficient attention to propaganda. Commenting in 1924 on the Cosgrave government's lack of skills in this regard,

Éamon de Valera remarked: 'They have no publicity department worth talking of. Any Government that desires to hold power in Ireland should put publicity before all.'[1]

De Valera took the ultimate step in following his own advice by founding the *Irish Press* in 1931 to ensure that Fianna Fáil has its own propaganda arm. While Cosgrave could generally rely on the support of Independent Newspapers and the *Cork Examiner*, he had no direct control over them. By contrast, de Valera ensured that he had a propaganda vehicle dedicated to his cause and under his control. During the 1930s, 1940s and 1950s the major newspapers made no bones about their political allegiance when it came to election time. The *Irish Press* backed Fianna Fáil to the hilt, the *Independent* tended to support Fine Gael, while *The Irish Times*, having lost its natural constituency of pro-union readers, tended to adopt a moderately liberal stance and gradually became sympathetic to the Labour Party.

Throughout this period, though, little attempt was made by politicians or parties to influence political journalists as a group. Individual journalists had their own contacts and allegiances but their job was to report events, not to interpret them. Whatever interpretation there was tended to be left to the editorial writers who were in a position to follow their proprietor's wishes. More importantly, the prevailing culture of the times simply did not allow working journalists to mingle on equal terms with senior politicians or civil servants. The notion that journalists should be briefed on a regular basis about the latest developments in government policy would simply not have occurred to a Taoiseach or his ministers. Neither would it have occurred to disaffected factions within government or opposition to try and use the media in pursuit of their objectives. One former civil servant, who worked in the system from the 1940s onwards, told me that it would simply have been unthinkable for political journalists to have been in a position to find out what was happening at cabinet and to report on it. In any case, political journalists did not really have an outlet for revealing much background information, even if they managed to obtain it. They were expected to quote people by name, and the notion of attributing news reports to anonymous government sources, or senior unnamed officials – now a standard and sometimes dubious practice – simply did not exist. The political journalist was expected to report rather than analyse or pontificate, and most newspaper reports emanated from Dáil debates and platform speeches.

With the establishment of the Free State, a formal system of reporting Dáil and Seanad proceedings was established by the newspapers. Just as the parliamentarians took their structures and institutions from the Westminster model so did the journalists. They reported on the proceedings of the two Houses in detail and probably knew far more about what was happening in the background than they were able or willing to report. The role of the journalists in this system is captured neatly by the Irish parliamentary party politician, John Pius Boland, who described the system in the House of Commons in the early years of the century:

> There is another group, Pressmen, who have a special entrée to the Lobby and flit at intervals from the Reporters Gallery to the Lobby to learn discreetly what is going on. A fine body of men who may be trusted to make no unfair use of what is imparted to them as confidential (Boland, 1943: 82).

Of course even in that more deferential age there was always room for a scoop. Robert Smylie, later editor of *The Irish Times*, pulled off a great exclusive in 1927 when he published the names of the potential Labour cabinet after the first election of 1927. He pieced together the names having rifled through the wastepaper basket in a room in the Powerscourt Arms Hotel in Enniskerry where the Labour leader, Tom Johnson, had conferred with two colleagues. Unfortunately for the value of the story Labour did not take over the reins of a minority government backed by Fianna Fáil as planned (Gaughan, 1980: 310).

The lobby system

The late John Healy is usually credited with bringing the media coverage of politics in Ireland into the modern era. In the early 1960s he introduced techniques of reporting that were novel and which helped to change the way things were done. In his groundbreaking 'Backbencher' column, which first appeared in the *Sunday Review* and later, when that newspaper closed, in *The Irish Times*, he bandied political gossip and intrigue to dramatic effect. Healy obtained the confidence of up and coming cabinet ministers like Charles Haughey, Donough O'Malley and Brian Lenihan, and he retailed their exploits with relish. In particular Healy established a rapport with Haughey and did everything he could to further his career, benefiting in turn from off the record briefings about discussions at cabinet.

However, Healy's column, which was written anonymously, represented just one strand in the changing attitude to the coverage of politics by the Irish media. By the mid-1960s the media were beginning to report political events in a less deferential way than heretofore. A new breed of political correspondents began to push out the boundaries. Arthur Noonan of the *Irish Independent*, Michael McInerney of *The Irish Times* and Michael Mills of the *Irish Press*, provided more detailed analysis of politics than their predecessors had done. They also conducted major interviews with the survivors of the older generation of politicians who had founded the state and who finally handed over the reins of power in the 1960s.

Mills in the *Irish Press* brought an independence and impartiality to the job that surprised colleagues. 'Tell the truth and be fair and provided you comply with these two requirements I'll stand over what you do', Mills was told by the proprietor of the *Irish Press*, Major Vivion de Valera, a Fianna Fáil TD and son of 'the Chief' (O'Toole, 1992: 97). Each man kept his side of the bargain, much to the surprise and indeed consternation of colleagues and Fianna Fáil TDs alike. Mills got a major scoop with the story of Sean Lemass's decision to resign as Taoiseach in 1966, and his reputation for inside knowledge, fairness and judgement grew over the years.

The opening of RTÉ brought a new dimension to political coverage. While the news reports were straightforward and dry, programmes like *7 Days* (fronted by Brian Farrell among others) brought a new dimension to political reporting. The political correspondents of the newspapers were given an opportunity, when they appeared on television in programmes such as *The Hurler on the Ditch*, to give a more frank and open account of what was happening than they did in their newspaper stories.

The political system was slow to react to the developments in the media during the 1960s. There was occasional fury in government at the irreverence sometimes shown by RTÉ, and while attempts were made to influence its coverage, no effort was put into revamping the antiquated structure of the Government Information Bureau which had not changed for decades. The head of the Bureau, who had the status of an assistant secretary in the civil service, supplied information to journalists on request; but there was little formal briefing, and political correspondents relied on their own sources and on Dáil debates for their reports.

In Britain at this time the relationship between the Government and the media had become quite sophisticated. As far back as the 1920s Ramsay MacDonald appointed a government press officer to brief the political correspondents, and a system of daily briefings at Downing Street had evolved by the 1950s (Harris, 1990). Such systematic briefing of political journalists by the government of the day did not happen in Ireland until after the 1973 general election when Fianna Fáil lost power after 16 continuous years in office. Perhaps because the party had been so successful up to this point, it did not see the need to change the way it dealt with the media.

When the Fine Gael–Labour government replaced Fianna Fáil in 1973, the Taoiseach, Liam Cosgrave, gave responsibility for the appointment of a new head of the Government Information Bureau to his Minister for Posts and Telegraphs, Conor Cruise O'Brien. The minister selected a dynamic RTÉ producer, Muiris MacConghail, who had considerable experience working in Britain. MacConghail introduced a new way of doing business between the government and the political correspondents. He instituted the practice of holding a daily briefing for the political correspondents in their room in Leinster House. These briefings were particularly interesting on the days on which cabinet meetings were held, as MacConghail had no compunction about discussing the cabinet agenda. In fact he brought the agenda to these briefings and went through the items one by one to provide either on the record information about decisions taken or background briefing about issues still outstanding. MacConghail's openness contrasted not only with the regime that had operated up to that time, but also with everything that came afterwards. It was the only time that political correspondents were briefed regularly and systematically on the basis of cabinet agendas. MacConghail, who had learned his trade as a journalist in the more open political system of Westminster, couldn't see what the fuss was about. He believed it was the right of the media to know what was going on and he trusted the senior political correspondents to deal fairly with the background information he gave them.[2]

One of the reasons the system worked was that MacConghail dealt with a small and tightly knit group of political correspondents who were good at their job. Mills was the doyen of the group by this stage. His colleagues were Dick Walsh of *The Irish Times*, Chris Glennon of the *Irish Independent*, Liam O'Neill of the *Examiner* and Seán Duignan and Donal Kelly of RTÉ. This small group had a powerful influence, not least because they were put in the picture by MacConghail. Of course, there were benefits for the government in having a well-briefed media, and the close contact between MacConghail and the political correspondents meant that the government knew immediately how the media were responding to its message. 'I knew what was going on in the press world through him [MacConghail]', said O'Brien later. 'He was very close to the ground, very bright' (Collins, 1996: 174).

Subsequent governments also relied on their press secretaries to keep them informed about how the media were taking the message, but none kept their side of the bargain by imparting information as openly as MacConghail. This period in the 1970s was probably the heyday of the lobby system, when political correspondents had a genuine access to information from government. Ultimately, however, it did not do the Cosgrave coalition any good, and Fine Gael and Labour were swept from office in the landslide of 1977, which only goes to show the limited benefit of good government–media relations – a point also stressed by Brian Farrell in his review of that period (Farrell, 1978). At the end of the day, the voters decide on the basis of underlying trends in economic and political life. Nevertheless, MacConghail is still proud of the work he did at that time and believes that it was a worthwhile exercise in itself.

MacConghail's immediate successors followed this lead, but none was given the same latitude by his political masters to keep the media as fully informed. Frank Dunlop, who took over the post when Jack Lynch returned to office in 1977, continued to provide systematic briefings, although he did not discuss the cabinet agenda in any detail. Peter Prendergast, who was in the post during the FitzGerald coalition of the 1980s, also provided comprehensive and detailed briefings about government policy particularly from the perspective of the Taoiseach.

An important change that occurred after MacConghail was that the press secretary was appointed by the Taoiseach directly and tended to see his role as being the Taoiseach's man. Peter Prendergast was briefed on cabinet matters by the Minister for the Public Service, John Boland, but in fact he was good at his job because of his close relationship with Garret FitzGerald to whom he had access at all times. The same was true of Frank Dunlop and Jack Lynch. When Charles Haughey replaced Lynch as Taoiseach, Dunlop was retained in the post but his effectiveness in the position declined because he did not have the same close relationship with the Taoiseach of the day. In fact on one occasion in 1982, Dunlop told the political correspondents that he could no longer guarantee that all the information he gave them was necessarily true. The clear implication was that he did not fully trust Haughey to tell him the truth. The political correspondents took due note of his warning and factored it into their dealings with him.

While the press secretary became the Taoiseach's mouthpiece, a position that has continued to the present, he has not developed into a political hit man or had the influence that his counterparts in Britain have had under different prime ministers. During the 1980s the House of Commons lobby was briefed by Margaret Thatcher's press secretary, Bernard Ingham, who regularly planted stories in the media designed to undermine certain ministers who were not wholly enthusiastic about her policies (Harris, 1990). More recently, Alistair Campbell virtually became Tony Blair's Svengali, and exercised an influence greater than that of most cabinet ministers.

This process has been facilitated by the arcane rules governing the lobby system in Britain that do not apply in Ireland. In Britain the accredited lobby correspondents are briefed in Downing Street at least once a day on a completely off the record basis. This means that the journalists are given information but they cannot attribute it to any official source and simply have to run it as fact if they want to use it. The Prime Minister's spokesman is thus able to plant stories in the media without having to take any responsibility for them. While everybody in the system knows where they have come from, the public is not let in on the secret.

In Ireland the system is quite different. The government press secretary is normally quoted as a 'Government spokesman' in reports of his briefings. In situations where he is willing to provide background information but does not want to be identified, the code 'government sources' is used, although journalists also use this term to cover other officials, or even ministers, who are willing to give them valuable information.

During the 1980s the lobby system in Leinster House was frequently criticised in the wider media. There was a widespread view that a privileged few in the system were getting inside information and that they were somehow involved in a conspiracy with politicians to limit the amount of information being put into the public domain. This was a distortion of the position, but it became a truism among the kind of journalists who are in thrall to conspiracy theory.

The lobby system in Leinster House began to change during the 1980s for a number of reasons. Firstly, the number of accredited political correspondents began to increase steadily. The Sunday newspapers appointed political correspondents to do more background analysis and to get news stories. The daily papers responded by appointing first one and then two or more deputies to each political correspondent so the numbers in the lobby rose from six to nearly 20 by the end of the 1980s.

As well as that, the return of Charles Haughey to office in 1987 marked a change in the relationship between the Taoiseach's office and the lobby. During his first term as Taoiseach in the early 1980s Haughey had come to loathe the political correspondents. Michael Mills had fiercely maintained his independence as political correspondent of the *Irish Press* and had made clear his deep suspicions about Haughey. Some of the other members of the lobby shared his attitude, and even though this view was not held universally, it coloured the relationship between Haughey and the correspondents.

The illegal tap placed on the phone of the *Sunday Press* political correspondent, Geraldine Kennedy, at the instigation of Haughey's Minister for Justice, Sean Doherty, marked the nadir of this relationship. Time and again Haughey tried to circumvent the lobby in the hope that he could get a better press by going over their heads, and sometimes he succeeded.

By the time Haughey returned to power in 1987 the lobby had changed. Mills had left to become the country's first ombudsman (see chapter 8 in this volume), and there were a number of new faces in the political correspondents' room. Haughey appointed the irrepressible P. J. Mara as his government press secretary, who used his charm to ensure that relations between his Boss and the lobby were kept on a reasonably cordial footing. Mara had already achieved a degree of fame, when acting as Haughey's press officer in opposition, by using the phrase 'Uno Duce, Una Voce' to describe his Boss's leadership style. Despite suffering a severe tongue lashing for his flippancy, Mara was not deterred. He subsequently took to referring to Haughey as 'The Caudillo' or, when the Boss was on the rampage, as 'El Diablo'. Despite the irreverence, Mara was extremely loyal to Haughey and he managed to establish a reasonable relationship between the Taoiseach and the media in the 1987–92 period. He persuaded the media to accept some of Haughey's ground rules. 'None of that old arms trial shite', he would warn journalists before they interviewed Haughey, and the admonition worked. Mara was also refreshingly honest about his own role. Once when a journalist, Emily O'Reilly, accused him of not revealing all he knew about Haughey, he responded tartly. 'Look, we are all big boys and girls here. I work for Charles Haughey and you all know that it is my job to give you information in a way that will show him in the best possible light. If you want to dig the dirt on Charlie that's your business, but don't expect any help from me.'

Mara's briefings, while hugely entertaining, were often short on detail because Haughey did not believe in telling the lobby very much. 'He told me to tell you that cabinet discussions are none of your business. When decisions are made you will be informed in due course', Mara told the correspondents on one occasion. He also made it quite clear that gathering information was as much part of his job as imparting it. 'What are the bastards in the poll corrs room saying', Haughey would inquire, and Mara would find out.

The benefit journalists got from the relationship was that Mara conveyed something about the atmosphere in government and the dynamic at work between individual ministers. In hindsight it is clear, of course, that journalists knew little or nothing about what was happening beneath the surface of the Haughey regime. There were occasional rumours about Haughey or Ray Burke but, despite the known excesses of the GUBU era, the media were unable or unwilling to check them out. It took the revelations of the judicial tribunals at the end of the 1990s to show the nature of the Haughey era for what it was.

The 1990s

When Albert Reynolds replaced Haughey as Taoiseach he tried a new experiment in dealing with the media. Reynolds was on good terms with a range of journalists. The gregarious Seán Duignan was astounded to discover that Reynolds personally knew more journalists than he did. The new Taoiseach also employed media guru Tom Savage of Carr Communications as an adviser who suggested that the Taoiseach should give the political correspondents a weekly on-the-record briefing. It seemed like a good idea at the time and in an ideal world would have worked to the advantage of both sides. However, on his first day in office Reynolds was presented with the intractable problem of the 'X case'. A practising Catholic and a conservative by nature on social issues, Reynolds found the problem a difficult one from a number of angles. He found himself at his weekly briefing being pressed again and again, particularly by the women political correspondents, on the issue about which he felt uncomfortable. Just as the issue began to die down he would find himself being pursued for an on-the-record comment that would ignite debate all over again. He soon came to dread the briefings, and they became less and less fruitful for both sides.

Reynolds's first government in coalition with the Progressive Democrats lasted less than a year and, when he formed his second government in coalition with Labour, the weekly briefing was dropped like a hot potato. Labour leader, Dick Spring, was if anything even more anxious than Reynolds to ensure that the new departure was strangled before it became an institution.

Both sides were at fault for the failure of an experiment that had the potential to give the political correspondents a unique insight into the operation of government. The journalists displayed their limitations by focusing almost entirely on getting a headline for the following morning's newspapers or a line for the next news bulletin, and showed little inclination to explore the issues of the day in a rounded fashion. It became a weekly briefing by the Taoiseach on the 'X case' and the abortion issue rather than a comprehensive run through of the broad range of issues facing the government.

For his part, Reynolds quickly discovered when he took office that the easy relationship he had enjoyed with most journalists no longer obtained. He was unused to the more combative style that characterises the relationship between Taoiseach and the media, and found it difficult to cope with it at times. So the attempt to provide a more open relationship between the lobby and the government failed. Ironically it happened just as Labour came into office with Fianna Fáil promising a new era of openness and transparency.

After the failure of the Reynolds experiment, the lobby system gradually became a less valuable vehicle for the transmission of information. There were a number of reasons for this. For a start, the numbers with access to the lobby continued to increase and this choked off the quality of information that was provided on a background basis. With so many journalists in competition with each other for stories, the old off-the-record rule withered away and successive press secretaries became less and less willing to risk frank exchanges with the lobby. Duignan and his successors in the post, Shane Kenny and Joe Lennon, did not have the luxury of dealing with a small tightly knit group and they also had to cope with the ever increasing demands of television, radio and the newspapers as the media began to fragment during the 1990s.

In recent years there has also been an increasing emphasis on 'spin', with governments attaching less importance to information and straightforward briefing. As part of this process, the Taoiseach and his ministers have employed a whole array of private media consultants who operate in the background and deal in selective leaking to journalists who are generally outside the lobby system. When Bertie Ahern took office in 1997, he established a 'media monitoring unit' in the Taoiseach's Department to keep tabs on every aspect of media coverage and to co-ordinate a response to negative stories and comment. The notion of 'prebuttal' (getting your retaliation in first) developed and came to have as much importance as that of rebuttal. Many political stories emerged without going near the lobby system, so designed to ensure that their sponsors left no fingerprints.

In any case, Fianna Fáil strategists had decided that the lobby was not as important as it had been cracked up to be. They decided to place a huge amount of emphasis on getting stories into the tabloid newspapers and cultivating the journalists who worked in them. A key part of the party's strategy in the 1997 election was getting its message across in the tabloids. Another important strand in the strategy was to get coverage on local radio, which had become important up and down the country. 'Forget about the *Irish Times* and RTÉ; *The Star* and local radio is where it's at', was the message.

While not entirely true, this approach did reflect changes both in the structure of the media and in the way journalists did their business. During the 1990s, photo opportunities and short doorstep interviews became much more important than long serious interviews or briefings. The clever manipulation of the modern media's voracious desire for fresh pictures and soundbites every few hours enabled senior politicians to pick the right moment to make an announcement or float and idea and then back off before the questioning got too rigorous.

The Dáil chamber is the only place where the Taoiseach and his ministers are subjected to serious questioning, but ironically Dáil proceedings have received less and less coverage from the media in recent years, even though the House has been opened up to live transmission on television and radio. Two decades ago a pool of up to 20 reporters covered the proceedings of the Dáil and Seanad in a systematic way, while a small elite group of lobby correspondents wrote about politics in general. Today that position has been completely reversed. There are now about 20 political correspondents competing with each other for stories but only five or so reporters to cover the proceedings of the Dáil. The inevitable result is that much of what happens in parliament is not reported at all. In fact politicians have a far better chance of having their views reported if they issue a press release than if they speak in the Oireachtas.

Former Taoiseach, John Bruton, expressed his frustration with this development in a letter to the *Irish Independent* in January 2002. He complained that his views on the abortion referendum had been misrepresented by the newspaper, even though he had made a clear statement of his position in the Dáil. 'This speech was not reported at all in your newspaper, or by any other. Of course, if one wants to say something that will stay confidential as far as Irish newspapers are concerned, the best place to say it is in the Dáil chamber.'[3]

As the coverage of the Dáil has declined and the lobby system has also become of less value in terms of providing inside information, a new form of life has evolved and thrived at the junction of politics, business and the media. This is the public affairs consultant or lobbyist who has begun to wield enormous influence, often on behalf of an anonymous client. Former government press secretaries like Frank Dunlop and P.J. Mara were among the pioneers of this way of life that has now become a feature of politics. Stories with an obvious political slant are planted in the media with the intention of influencing public policy on behalf of commercial clients. Quite often stories that are presented as sensational scoops are in fact part of the dirty tricks armoury deployed by the lobbyists and designed to discredit rivals of their clients.

Politicians and political parties regularly feature in this dirty war as powerful interests seek to discredit or influence government and opposition.

The fact that many lobbyists came from the world of politics and are engaged in the art of 'spinning' on behalf of their political connections as well as their commercial masters has muddied the waters even further. The emergence of the lobbyist has coincided with the rise of the judicial tribunals. In fact the McCracken tribunal, which began the process of investigating the slimy underbelly of politics, was an unintended result of this dirty war that has moved from the fringes and into the centre of political discourse.

The lobbyists have both thrived and been among the victims of the tribunal culture, sometimes attempting to influence the course of the tribunals through timely leaks and at other times featuring as subjects of investigation. There has been a shift in the centre of media power away from the political correspondents, as information of a political kind has emerged from a variety of other sources. The benefit of this is that more information about the murky side of political life than ever before has emerged into the public arena, but the downside is that journalists with little or no experience of politics and often no interest in it and no capacity for judgement, have been used by unscrupulous forces for their own ends.

These developments have taken place at a time when the coverage given to Dáil debates and legislation has declined to minimal proportions. There is now an unhealthy acceptance by journalists of 'spin', whether from straight political sources through the lobby or through the murkier world of the lobbyist. Of course there was always 'spinning' to some extent in the relationship between politicians and journalists, but the new development is the willingness of journalists to take the 'spin' and use it in their reports without attributing it to any source. By contrast, the media now provide paltry coverage to the forum where politicians deal in straight, unvarnished and attributable quotation – the Dáil chamber. A decade or two ago every TD who spoke in the Dáil was guaranteed a mention. Now there is no reporter on the gallery for most of the time.

The irony is that this has happened at a time when the Dáil was opened up to radio and television. The media convinced the politicians they would get more coverage if the microphones and the cameras were let in, but the opposite has happened. Dáil proceedings are transmitted at ungodly hours, where they are watched only by 'drunks and insomniacs', in Pat Rabbitte's famous phrase. The TV pictures are just used as soundbites for the nightly news.

In Britain a similar downgrading of parliamentary coverage has also occurred. This prompted the editor of the *Daily Telegraph*, Charles Moore, to decide that enough was enough. Noting that all the national papers in Britain had ceased to provide coverage of the proceedings of parliament, apart from the sneering columns of sketch writers, he decided that his paper would begin reporting proceedings again. His reasons were cogent:

> Just as political journalism grew with reporting Parliament, so there is a danger that it will diminish by not reporting it. The era of 'spin' is a reversion to a pre-democratic form of news, in which what is whispered is more important than what is publicly stated. This is the world of court favourites, rather than the world of representative government.[4]

Moore's strictures have a great deal of relevance to the media coverage of Irish politics. *The Irish Times* is the only newspaper that continues to provide a report of the Dáil and Seanad proceedings, and even then the coverage is shorter and much less comprehensive than it was a decade or two ago. While it is true that Dáil debates themselves have become much more bland, with the prepared script replacing the spontaneous speech, the trend has become a vicious circle and most politicians see little point in making substantial contributions to parliament.

In its current phase, the media coverage of politics often has less and less to do with fact and more with opinion and emotion. This has worked to the advantage of politicians who have mastered the art of manipulating the 'spin', while those who cannot, or will not, indulge in the game are regarded as not being media friendly and suffer as a result. John Bruton springs to mind as one notable politician who suffered in this manner. One astute British observer noted some years ago that political journalists do not normally seek to be fair or objective but to write copy that will be read or make programmes that will be watched. This is achieved by conveying a strong consistent message, not a subtle or balanced one: 'Hence in journalism, the quest is not for originality but for fashion: to be abreast of it, if possible to lead it, but not to be behind or out of tune with it' (Pimlott, 1992: 447).

While the media tend to reinforce political fashion, it does not dictate it, except when, as has happened in recent years, politicians abdicate responsibility and decide to follow the herd rather than risk unpopularity. The truly important politicians lead rather than follow fashion, at least for a time. In recent decades people like Sean Lemass, Garret FitzGerald, Albert Reynolds and even Haughey, to some extent, have directed events rather than followed in their wake.

Of course, the media do play an important role in building up or knocking down a politician's reputation, but in the final analysis it is the politicians themselves who dictate their own fate. The nineteenth-century British Conservative Prime Minister, Lord Salisbury, who was no mean political journalist in his younger days, had the following to say about the power of the media: 'These gentlemen of the press much exaggerate their own power . . . They bear much the relation to a man's unpopularity that flies do to a wound. If the wound exists, they can aggravate it and make it malignant, but they cannot make the wound' (Roberts, 1999: 311). The example of Charles Haughey immediately springs to mind. For all his claims about media vilification, journalists failed to wound him badly during his long and eventful career. When he was finally forced out of office he was actually given a sentimental farewell by the media. It was only when the sources of his wealthy lifestyle were exposed by the judicial tribunals that the media made a malignant meal of his self-inflicted wound.

Notes

1 Quoted by T. Ryle Dwyer, *Irish Examiner*, 8 March 2000.
2 Interview with the author, 1996.
3 Letter by John Bruton, TD to the *Irish Independent*, 15 January 2002.
4 *Daily Telegraph*, 16 October 1999.

Bibliography

Boland, John Pius (1943) *An Irishman's Day: A Day in the Life of an Irish MP*. London: Macdonald.

Collins, Stephen (1996) *The Cosgrave Legacy*. Dublin: Blackwater Press.

Duignan, Sean (1995) *One Spin on the Merry-Go-Round*. Dublin: Blackwater Press.

Farrell, Brian (1978) 'The mass media and the 1977 campaign', in Howard Penniman (ed.), *Ireland at the Polls: The Dáil Elections of 1977*. Washington, DC: American Enterprise Institute.

Gaughan, J. Anthony (1980) *Thomas Johnson, 1872–1963: First Leader of the Labour Party in Dáil Éireann*. Dublin: Kingdom Books.

Harris, Robert (1990) *Good and Faithful Servant: The Unauthorised Biography of Bernard Ingham*. London: Faber & Faber.

O'Toole, Michael (1992) *More Kicks Than Pence: A Life in Irish Journalism*. Dublin: Poolbeg Press.

Pimlott, Ben (1992) *Harold Wilson*. London: HarperCollins.

Roberts, Andrew (1999) *Sailsbury: Victorian Titan*. London: Weidenfeld & Nicolson.

CHAPTER FOURTEEN

The best newsmen we can expect?

JEAN BLONDEL

—

Studies devoted to the media are now legion. The subject of 'communication' has become a vibrant industry, whose tone is generally critical, often virulently so. Even if we leave aside the attacks which link the inadequacies of the media to the nature of capitalism, structures of mass communication are probably the most criticised of all the institutions which are involved in politics. The main objects of these criticisms are the undue interference of press barons or tycoons, chronic bias, the invasion of privacy, and reckless attempts to destroy political careers: no doubt, all of these sins are partly true; no doubt, too, they need to be qualified. Indeed, to compensate for these attacks, some studies have pointed out that, despite these failings, the media do fulfil a positive role by contributing to a better information of the mass public: television in particular has seemed by and large to increase information (Blumler, 1977; Negrine, 1989).

Meanwhile, studies of the media have tended to focus rather less on the journalists, on their careers, on their aspirations, and on their limitations. Some comprehensive works on communication do not even study journalists at all (e.g., Gurevitch et al., 1982; Axford and Huggins, 2001). Such a state of affairs is somewhat surprising: the press, radio, and television may be in part the product of their society as well as of their bosses; they are also what their personnel makes them. In particular, the news which the media carry is manifestly largely the result of what journalists feel they should, or wish to mention and of the way in which the items which they are presenting are being mentioned. Of this there is now no doubt: many journalists at least are aware of their responsibility. Yet the forms of what may be called the 'bias' of newsmen are still not a major preoccupation or a major source of analysis, although some studies have at least dipped into the matter (Golding and Elliott, 1979; Bennett, 1988): the characteristics of news journalism surely deserve to be examined with as much care as the general 'structural' characteristics of the media or the nature of 'communication processes' which have so far received most of the attention.

An analysis of the role and problems posed by journalism in the press, radio and television must start from the recognition that the field is dominated by two fundamental constraints, as well as a third characteristic which is difficult to circumvent. The two constraints are the enormous weight placed by *the present or the 'instant'* and *the need for drastic selection* among the items that are published or broadcast (Golding and Elliott, 1979: 17). The characteristic that is difficult to circumvent is the emphasis on *the role of top people* in what is being reported.

A day is an eternity in the context of the news media. Newspapers have to come out daily with reports of 'what happened' in the previous 24 hours; radio has to talk about what occurred in the last few hours; television has to mention and to show what the 'events' were during the same period. These constraints necessarily affect the way journalists look at their work and, indirectly, at the world. We may feel that the perspective is so short that it biases or limits reporting in a major way: the media have none the less to operate under these requirements whatever we think about them.

The second and indeed very insidious constraint comes from the obvious need for a rigorous selection of what is being presented to the public. The notion that a newspaper could give, as the *New York Times* still claims, 'all the news that's fit to print', either is utterly unrealistic and naïve or conceals selection under the expression 'fit to print'. This selection has, indeed, to be drastic, as so many elements of 'news' arrive on the desks of journalists and editors, but only a fraction can be chosen. Yet while a selection has to be made, the haste with which it has to take place, and therefore the arbitrariness with which it is completed, result in journalists being able to wield substantial power. They may sometimes wield this power unconsciously and almost mechanically: they wield it none the less. The consequence can be major distortions, misunderstandings, and, at a minimum, lack of proper informing of the public.

In the nature of things, too, the media are dominated by the further and related characteristic of having to report the actions of the rich and the powerful, i.e. those who take (or do not take although they are in a position to) the decisions which 'create' the news which journalists have to mention. This has the inherent drawback of tending to lead the media a little too far in the direction of the 'great men' theory of politics and society rather than towards the analysis of underlying trends: yet this bias is difficult to avoid, as journalists are almost condemned, in virtue of the nature of their job, to focus on the part played by 'key' decision makers. Indeed, this state of affairs creates another problem, which is perhaps more serious still: as journalists seek to obtain interviews from the rich and powerful, they are inevitably drawn to and often seduced by the kind of world in which those who are in power tend to live. They are, as a result, inclined to place great emphasis on the 'glamorous' part of political and social life, a characteristic that is not likely to produce, to say the least, truly healthy reporting.

The effect of these three elements – emphasis on the present moment, need for selection, and concentration on the role of top people – is naturally somewhat different in the case of each of the media. For instance, newspapers have greater opportunities to go back to the past, although some of the press appears to concentrate almost exclusively on the reporting of titillating daily events, largely non-political, but also occasionally political as well; moreover, foreign reporting is typically more spasmodic and therefore less governed by what might be called the '24 hour rule': it is also probably more subjected to the sharpness and even arbitrariness of selection. Radio, surprisingly perhaps at first sight, is perhaps the medium which is most constrained by the need to concentrate on the instant: the emphasis has to be on what occurred in the last few hours or even minutes; as a matter of fact, radio is the only communication mechanism where the news is still presented raw, so to speak, in particular by international services, these being characterised by a rather wide coverage based almost entirely on 'instantaneity'. Television is markedly constrained by the need to organise its images and, as a result, is highly selective while being somewhat less based on the instant: the rhythm is, as in the case of newspapers, the 24 hour cycle, during which the news, both oral and visual, is organised and put together in the same way as in a feature film.

Thus the instant dominates the media; the stress on the instant is in large part the cause or the rationale for selectivity, while there is heavy concentration on happenings among top decision makers and their immediate advisers. These constraints and characteristics render the profession of news journalism difficult; they also explain why the profession is in such a need of systematic and detailed examination. All newsmen have to accept these constraints. They in fact do; indeed they are largely socialised by them. Yet these characteristics are not in themselves the reason why there is often great unease about the way in which journalists conduct their business. The problems go beyond the constraints, however serious, which the profession imposes on journalists. They come from a somewhat peculiar approach to the news that may not perhaps have increased over the years but appears to be pervasive in the media, albeit to a somewhat different extent in different countries, in different organisations, and indeed in different media.

One of the problems stems from the way in which news journalists appear to place great emphasis on interpretation rather than on fact, as if their job was to give a point of view about events or, perhaps even in some cases, as if they did not realise that they were in a sense 'constructing' events rather than presenting them. Another problem comes from the apparent inability of journalists to give enough attention to what they should select and in many cases to show little interest in following up on stories which have been selected: thus an event is alluded to but its outcome is not mentioned later. A third and major concern stems from the fact that not just decisions or activities of top people are being stressed, but that the relationships between these top people are elevated to being a subject of major importance, even if, as in many cases, these relationships are only known indirectly and to an extent by hearsay.

These worries and concerns are so serious that they need to be systematically analysed and their impact assessed: in this chapter, naturally, only a preliminary examination is undertaken of the nature of the problems and of the dangers inherent in this way of approaching the news. It seems particularly apposite to do so in this volume, which is devoted to an academic political scientist who has played a major part in elevating journalism above the drawbacks from which it too often suffers.

Neither fact nor comment: interpretation

One of the problems of contemporary journalism – both written and spoken – is a tendency to develop a form of reporting which does not consist in reporting the facts alone. Ostensibly, it is not 'comment' in the sense which is conventionally given to the word, indeed by the journalists themselves: comment is likely to be described as a presentation of the views of the news media organisation, of a named journalist, or of someone invited to write or speak in the media. By and large, it seems that newsmen go in (perhaps increasingly, though the point needs to be established empirically) for 'interpretation' rather than 'facts'; such 'interpretation' is regarded as part of 'regular journalism' as it is not 'comment' in the conventional sense of the word.

There seem to be a number of reasons why 'interpretation' is preferred to 'factual' accounts. The first has to do with the point, which is frequently made, that it is extremely *difficult to determine what is 'fact'* if one is to be rigorous about the matter. It may be that journalists still, on the whole, do not subscribe to the view that facts are elusive; yet it seems unbelievable that discussions about 'facts', 'objectivity', and, on the contrary, the 'construction of reality', do not have at least a diffuse impact on the profession. Indeed, as is pointed out by W. Lance Bennett with respect to the USA, '[i]n recent years journalists have increasingly adopted the term "fairness" in place of the once-popular claim of "objectivity". Fairness seems to be a more reasonable reporting goal in light of all the obstacles to objectivity' (Bennett, 1988: 118). Without going as far as Boorstin, who claims that what journalists are concerned with are 'pseudo-events' (Boorstin, 1972: 16), it seems that newsmen are no longer in the business of being prepared to produce 'the facts' because they have become 'sophisti-cated' and realise, along the lines of what philosophers and sociologists have said repeatedly, that they could not 'give the facts' even if they wanted to. To this extent, therefore, journalists are far from being wholly to blame for having adopted a more 'adult' view of their role. By questioning whether 'reality exists', non-journalists have not merely given an excuse to journalists who might have been eager to abandon the straight jacketing imposed by facts. They have, in effect, socialised journalists into thinking that it was naïve on their part to believe that they could concentrate on 'the facts'. In this way, journalists have been allowed, almost encouraged, to give greater 'scope' to their relationship with their object of observation.

This situation is clearly unfortunate: for, while it is obviously true that, at some philosophical level, the concept of 'fact' cannot be given an objective definition, it is also obviously true that, unless we adopt a practical definition – inter-subjective rather than objective perhaps – it is simply impossible to operate any kind of information system. As journalists are not the object of the information system, but are the intermediaries through which information is being conveyed, there has to be such a practical definition of 'facts', and journalists have to be prepared to operate on the basis of that definition.

Yet, while many newsmen may be prepared to agree that such a definition has to be adopted, they may well also point out that difficulties remain because *reporting of the 'raw facts' can be useless* and even in some cases highly misleading. Let us take the example of an election. If the newspaper, or radio/television station were to give merely the raw data about the election, voters might be confused and, at best, wholly unable to draw any conclusion. To begin with, the results of any election must be compared with those of the previous election: thus the 'facts' of both elections must be published simultaneously; yet this may not always be entirely satisfactory as the parties may have changed to an extent and, in such a case, the changes have to be 'explained' – that is to say 'interpreted'. Nor is this the only problem: an election is a political event that has political consequences, such as providing the country with a new government. Readers, listeners, or viewers will therefore be correctly informed only if the characteristics of the parties are discussed: for instance, if there is typically a coalition government in the country, the audience has to be told which parties are likely to form a coalition together and which are not; this is clearly a form of interpretation.

Thus, merely in order to provide the necessary background for the understanding of the 'fact' of the election result, journalists appear justified in claiming that they have to give details about a variety of matters, going well beyond the apparent boundaries of the 'fact' which is being described. It is not that the journalist is deliberately wishing to go beyond these boundaries: it is that readers, listeners, or viewers who want to know the 'facts' also have to have at their disposal a variety of information around these facts in order to understand them. In such a situation, the 'interpretative' activities of the journalist consist in determining what are the pieces of information alongside the central 'fact' that are required for this central 'fact' to be intelligible. One might even add that, with society becoming more complex, such an 'interpretative' apparatus becomes increasingly necessary and indeed increasingly complex.

Journalists may or may not justify in this manner the bringing to the fore of a variety of points which are related to, but not directly part of, the 'fact' which is being examined: there is no doubt that in many cases such an 'interpretative' activity is required of journalists. Yet there is also no doubt that such an activity must be conceived restrictively if the requirements of a 'factual' presentation are to be maintained. Only if this is the case can journalists be regarded as being genuinely concerned with the dissemination of 'facts'. As with the practical definition of what 'facts' are, the definition of the necessary 'complements' has to be practical: it needs to be based, not on what philosophically or sociologically is or can be related to the primary object, but on what appears most likely to be related to this object. Journalists have to be trained to determine what the contours of these related 'complements' are: an understanding of the characteristics of political, social, and economic life will indeed provide a good understanding of these contours.

The problem, however, is that journalists are often not satisfied with the straight jacketing of the 'raw facts' and their 'ancillary components'. This is where the journalists' mission to 'present the facts' clashes with or is likely to be superseded by what many of them have tended to regard as their other, perhaps even nobler mission, that of *'uncovering' what is deliberately hidden* and 'investigating' what may be concealed. Such a distinction may be summarised in the contrast between the view that journalists should 'present' the facts and the view that they should 'establish' them. In the eyes of some at least, presenting the facts may not be regarded as a truly intellectual operation: it is merely to provide a record, even if one takes into account the need to decide about what 'complements' have to be added to the 'fact'. In this view, the presentation of news on radio, as it tended to be done in the past, can be regarded as being a 'low profile' activity that is not truly worthy of a 'real' journalist.

What a 'real' journalist should do, as the best of US journalism is held to have done in the past, is to look behind the facts and discover their underpinnings. Of course, such an 'investigative' journalism can be regarded as not being part of what the news is about; it may be considered as belonging more accurately to the documentary category. Yet the border between the two forms of journalism is not altogether clear cut; moreover, if investigative journalism is generally regarded as being 'nobler' or 'deeper' than 'factual' journalism, it is inevitable that some at least among those who are involved in factual journalism will want to emulate to an extent what their 'better' colleagues are doing. This may indeed be valuable for career purposes; it does in any case provide an element of individual involvement for the journalists who are concerned with the news, although the recipients may be somewhat confused as they may not be able to distinguish between what is presented as 'the news' and what is a detective-like inquiry on the part of the newsmen. Hence the almost pathological efforts to look for 'scandal politics' (Castells, 1998), and, if not, in a more general manner to emphasise what Moog and Sluyter-Baltrao call the 'deconstruction of politicians' marketing ploys' (2001: 38).

News journalism should on the contrary be concerned, obsessed almost, with the 'facts', whatever may be said about the 'reality' of the concept of fact. Only if they have such an obsession can the problems posed by 'interpretation' be overcome, as only in this case does it become possible for journalists to find guidance to decide whether they are straying too far away from the 'events' that they are reporting. Non-journalists must indeed collaborate in stressing the need for facts, instead of agonising about the question as to whether facts exist or not. There is here a parallel with the problems that comparative government has faced in the last decades, when it was suggested that there might be 'hyperfactualism', as Easton had once claimed, rather than recognising that what was missing in the discipline was a good factual base. Journalism has to provide facts to a public that is, in the nature of things, unable to obtain these facts: it entrusts journalists with the job of providing the facts for them. Journalists do not have the right to deceive the public in this regard: their 'mission' is not, in a 'nobler' manner, to provide guidance in opening the way to a mysterious domain which lies hidden behind what we think we are seeing; it is to inform us about the world around us. Many journalists are indeed wary of acting differently, as Golding and Elliott report (1979: 198). There is in reality no nobler mission than to inform. This means that journalists must not give in to what is always the easy penchant of human beings, to put themselves forward; they must, on the contrary, accept that their true role is to be continuously at the service of the public.

Silences, selection and the art of not pursuing stories to the end

Studies of journalists and of their approach to their job often emphasise, and indeed criticise, the fact that they are inclined to 'make the news' or that they create 'pseudo-events' rather than account for reality. This was the rationale for one of the very first studies of television 'news manipulation', that of K. and G. Lang, which was devoted to the reception given by the streets of Chicago to General MacArthur after he had been sacked by Truman in 1951 (Lang and Lang, 1953; Golding and Elliott, 1979). The idea is to see to what extent it is possible for journalists to create reality and to denounce such a development, echoed in the some of the book titles on the subject: e.g., *Making the News* (Golding and Elliott, 1979); *The Politics of Illusion* (Bennett, 1988). This problem draws Bennett to consider the problem of objectivity, although he does not conclude that bias is inevitable or objectivity impossible. On the contrary, he firmly makes the point, along lines analogous to what was suggested in the previous section, that 'a number of observers have argued persuasively that whatever the news is, it is not a spontaneous mirror of the world. Nevertheless, it would be a mistake to draw from the contradiction between journalism norms and practices the conclusion that neither the objectivity nor the reporting practices matter' (1988: 135).

Yet, even if objectivity is recognised as being 'possible', and indeed an ideal to be pursued, it remains that many of those who have studied journalists have emphasised the way in which news is 'made' by them: it is the active, one might say 'creative', part of journalism which has attracted attention. Indeed it is almost the only aspect of the activities of journalists that has, as if what was described earlier as 'interpretation' was stretched to a point at which reporting becomes difficult to distinguish from what would otherwise be described as 'imagination'. Journalists (or the media organisation to which they belong) can thus be accused of betraying the public. Indeed, in the US, codes of 'professional ethics' have been developed and have been a major subject of preoccupation (Rivers *et al.*, 1980).

While these descriptions of the 'imaginative' side of journalism have become fairly numerous and are indeed almost fashionable, little is said about what is probably more serious and undoubtedly much more common, namely the fact that many matters are not covered completely or at all, even in media which would claim to have a high respect for their 'news' function. One has, of course, to take into account not just differences between one organisation and another, but also differences from one medium to another: e.g., it is easier for newspapers to provide wide coverage than for television. Yet, when all these variations are taken into account, a huge number of matters are left aside and many of the matters that are alluded to are subsequently forgotten. While, as was pointed out in the introduction, selection is inevitable, its rather arbitrary character is not; nor is it imperative that an issue be dropped almost as soon as it has been mentioned.

The reason given as to why an issue is covered (or not) is likely to have to do with the question of *importance*, absolute or relative; yet the definition of importance is of course vague and subjective. As a matter of fact, this issue is not discussed much in the literature on journalism. The problem of importance is raised occasionally, however, but not really discussed (Golding and Elliott, 1979: 117–19). The concept is mentioned as if its content was self-evident: indeed, it is suggested that it constitutes the criterion used by journalists when they introduce an item despite the fact that it might not correspond to what (they feel) the audience wants. Speaking of television, Golding and Elliott state: 'items which may be boring, repetitive or non-visual must still be included despite audience disinterest. . . . Importance is often applied to political and foreign news. Both are assumed to be of greater interest to journalists than to their audience. Both are included however because of their unquestioned importance' (1979: 118).

It is remarkable that the expression 'unquestioned importance' should be used, as if it were ever the case that an item is, indeed, of unquestioned importance. Paraphrasing Pascal about truth, one could well say on the contrary that 'what is important on one side of the Pyrenees is unimportant on the other side'. It is manifestly the case that the home news of one country is not only not interesting but indeed regarded as not important, by and large, by the media of another country. This is the very reason why foreign news tends to be given low priority in most of the media, with the exception of the international news services of broadcasting stations.

The matter is compounded by the fact that the structure of the media in general is such that they are simply not equipped to cover events taking place abroad. This is particularly true of television, which is extremely reluctant to give space to items for which they have no visual backup; but it is also true of radio and newspapers, which are equally reluctant to mention problems occurring in countries in which they do not have correspondents. There is, curiously, a major reluctance to rely on agency reports, which at least radio and the press could use to a markedly larger extent: it is difficult to comprehend why radio stations or newspapers cannot elaborate on stories coming from agencies and it is therefore difficult to avoid the conclusion that they lack journalists competent to make sense of agency reports. For whatever reason, however, it is manifest that matters will be deemed 'more' important if they occur where the media organisation has, permanently or temporarily, correspondents: the argument is indeed circular, as the media organisation will indeed argue that it places correspondents or a crew where 'important' events occur. This state of affairs extends to regional and local matters as well as to international matters: in the case of the USA, it has been pointed out that 'almost all non-Washington news originated from the handful of cities where network station their crews' (Bennett, 1988: III, quoting Epstein, 1973).

A very strong plea has therefore to be made in favour of a wider definition of 'importance', one, for instance, which would consider what other people, in other countries, would feel is important. Yet the argument is presumably that, if space is given to a matter, something else would have to give way. This is true to a very limited extent only, for two reasons. The first is that much of the space in 'newspapers' and other media is devoted to matters which are not connected with news: there is indeed some evidence that the news content of the media is diminishing, as in the case of the *New York Times*, where, after changing its format in 1976, 'local and national coverage were down by II per cent and 30 per cent respectively, while society and "women's" sections surged by 80 per cent' (Bennett, 1988: 114, quoting Shapiro, 1976). The second reason is that the space given to news items can vary markedly and, one submits, many reports suffer from considerable 'padding', connected with the tendency, examined earlier, to 'interpret' rather than 'present' facts, a paradoxical situation at the time when, as we shall point out, the amount of space devoted to politics is reduced. 'Padding' is particularly noticeable in television, where points are typically stated by the station announcer, and indeed explained, only to be repeated by the correspondent on the spot; a similar tendency is noticeable in many radio stations, as well as in newspapers, where for instance the practice exists of writing a summary at the top of the article, only to have its contents repeated in the body of the article. If it were established that the number of column inches was severely restricted, much space would be freed to cover issues that are simply not covered at all. As a matter of fact, on the contrary (and this matter needs, of course, to be systematically examined empirically), it seems that articles are becoming longer, probably as a result of the growth of the 'interpreting' mode, rather than being crisper and more concise.

The matter is compounded by the other major failing of the media, namely the widespread habit of dropping issues before they are concluded. This occurs in two forms, technical and editorial. The first resembles what was pointed out earlier about foreign and local reporting, namely that reporting takes place, by and large, only if there are correspondents on the spot and that the 'importance' of an issue depends on whether the area is deemed to be worth having correspondents. There are naturally also roving correspondents who go to various hot spots as deemed necessary by the 'importance' of events. After a while, however, these correspondents leave the area, either because some other spot appears more 'important' or because it is felt by the media organisation that the audience's interest has flagged. In most cases, these developments occur in a joint, indeed even frenetic, manner: the various correspondents arrive and leave together, the announced departure of one of them being a signal to the others that they should be on the move.

The result is, naturally, that the story that was started is left suspended in mid-air, so to speak, as there is no one left to tell what subsequently occurs. This is particularly the case in relation to situations taking place in areas commonly regarded as remote. For instance, the civil war in Angola attracted major attention from time to time, but only from time to time; the same is true of the situation in Afghanistan. In the case of both these countries, after a period of intense interest displayed by the media, the subject was simply no longer mentioned at all: sets of events which were typically described (rightly) as tragic for the population and for the world have thus been allowed to go unreported. Indeed, events occurring in countries nearer the world 'centres' do not escape the same fate of being quietly forgotten by the media. The war in former Yugoslavia, for instance, attracted attention from time to time, but not continuously; the situation in Macedonia, after having been described as catastrophic, has ceased altogether to be reported.

While technical factors often account for the abandonment of an issue by the media, editorial reasons also play an important part. The justification given is likely to be the same as the one given earlier about the reasons why some questions are not mentioned at all, namely the absence of space. In the case of the abandonment of an item before its natural end, this justification takes also the more specific form that other items, deemed more pressing, have to be included, while it is probably also felt that the subject should be dropped because the public might become bored, however distant the solution of the problem may be and indeed perhaps even because the solution is very distant. Yet, in this case too, space could be allocated in a more parsimonious manner so that it does not become necessary to cease mentioning an 'older' item when a new one comes to the fore.

At the root of the problem are also probably the psychological habits of journalists. Journalists are interested in the instant: the present is their life. They – perhaps as much as the audience – become quickly bored by topics and wish to move on to another. There is thus a de facto collusion between the journalists and the media organisations, with the result that news coverage changes and that there is little chance that a subject will be fully treated or examined from beginning to end.

Rather than 'making' the news, then, the media and the journalists are probably more 'guilty' of 'not making' the news. Even moving between two neighbouring countries can result in such differences in the reports given by the media that it seems difficult to believe that the two areas are geographically contiguous and probably also culturally close. Not surprisingly, there is a real chasm between the news reported in countries that are distant from each other. Such a state of affairs is surely unacceptable in a world held to be gradually becoming one, as is equally unacceptable the continuous tendency of the media to abandon problems in mid-course, however serious and even tragic these problems may be. Efforts have to be made to reduce these defects, on the understanding that the need for some selection and the emphasis placed on the instant do not constitute satisfactory excuses for these defects. Nothing in these two 'constraints' obliges journalists to abandon problems before a solution is in sight, nor to be silent about questions which others deem important since they give them major space. Is it entirely unrealistic to hope that a television which is becoming world-wide – as distinct from a press which remains national or even regional – will induce journalists to provide a better coverage of 'important' news and to maintain this coverage so long as the news remains 'important'?

The obsession with the rich and powerful

Not surprisingly, as the news is about daily events, a major emphasis is placed on the persons who appear to be 'responsible' for these events. A party leader wins a general election; a minister introduces a reform; a dictator quells a rebellion with much blood spilled: these are 'facts'. Indeed, a concern for an examination of the 'underlying forces' that might also account for these events could be regarded as forms of 'interpretation' and should therefore be avoided. Yet, to begin with, pronouncements such as the ones which were just mentioned are at best 'short-cut' presentations, for only in rather particular cases is an individual truly and fully responsible for an event: it is therefore markedly more accurate to adopt a restrictive view about the direct involvement of an individual in the developments which are reported.

There is a further danger, namely that a general bias begins to emerge when individuals are linked to events repeatedly and almost systematically: what may have begun as the impression, superficial perhaps, but none the less apparently correct, that an individual is directly responsible for a given event becomes gradually an 'approach' to which the journalists become habituated at the same time as they habituate the public to this approach. Even if, 'in detail', so to speak, there is no or little 'interpretation' of the events concerned, there develops an 'interpretation' in bulk, as the causal relationship between events and individuals starts to be regarded as normal by the audience and indeed by the journalists themselves.

There are many aspects of such a 'personalisation' of the events that are recorded: three of these deserve particular attention. The first has to do with the belief that stories will make more sense if an 'abstract problem' becomes translated into a 'human' item. This type of argument appears particularly strongly in the case of television and radio, where it seems difficult to see a story 'pass' unless someone is physically involved. Hence the emphasis on interviews, which give greater concreteness to the subject that is being discussed. In itself, naturally, the interview is a valuable mechanism of communication: it does indeed render politicians and other members of elite groups more present and more natural; the public benefits manifestly from being able to read their reactions, hear their voices, see their traits.

Yet, quite apart from the fact that the 'facts' mentioned in an interview are far from being necessarily correct, interviews have to be done with considerable care as they personalise problems under discussion. Almost automatically, the case for or against a particular viewpoint becomes transformed into a matter of support for, or opposition to, a particular individual, or into a contention between two individuals. The goal that is immediately sought may be achieved in that the audience, especially in the case of television viewers, may be more entertained and therefore willing to listen more attentively; but it is questionable whether this is worthwhile in the long run. Does the personalisation of problems that occurs in the process truly ensure that the news is better understood or appreciated?

Thus the first consequence of the emphasis on individuals is an emphasis on interviews and other forms of personalisation. A further consequence follows. Turning the tables, politicians have been quick to see how they can use the media for their own purposes (as discussed already in chapter 13 in this volume). Thus the excessive importance given to individuals is often due to the top people themselves, since politicians and other influentials often 'feed' newsmen with information that they regard as advantageous to them. Clearly, top people exploit the desire of newsmen, and of television journalists in particular, to present personal stories on the grounds that these stories, as we just noted, are regarded as making the news more appealing. Meanwhile, for the politicians, the advantages are clear. At a minimum, they can expect in this way to be 'in the news': they remain in the public eye and avoid the risk of being forgotten. More subtly and more perversely, politicians can use the media for their own purposes, for instance to combat opponents indirectly, even without naming them, by suggesting that some policies, proposals, or points of view are absurd or unrealistic. Given that the media wish to present stories likely to create interest, the claim by politicians that they can make a 'revelation' will be difficult to resist, even if the foundations of such a 'revelation' are extremely shaky. Thus, in the last analysis, it is difficult to apportion blame: ostensibly, much of it has to be laid at the door of the politicians; however, by continually stressing personal matters, the media share at least a part of the responsibility: they open a road which the politicians are only too ready to use for their own purposes.

The combination of these two desires – the desire on the part of newsmen to add some personal angle to the items which they present and the desire on the part of politicians and other top people to be in the limelight – leads to the third, and unquestionably most serious, drawback of contemporary journalism, which has been described in French as the emphasis on the 'politicians' politics'. 'Politicians' politics' is different from personalisation in that its very substance is constituted by the views that politicians have of other politicians: conflicts are not about a policy, but about the relationships between politicians. Matters of this kind are provided in large part by the politicians themselves, of course, as they are eager to point to the differences between themselves and other politicians; but these items are also sought by the journalists, who interview politicians in order to find out about other politicians and about the problems which may arise as a result of conflicts between politicians.

'Politicians' politics' prevails more in some countries than in others, and on some occasions rather than others. Among western countries, Italy has probably been the one in which the emphasis on this aspect of political reporting has been the most prominent: it is, indeed, somewhat puzzling that so much space should be devoted in Italian television news on this aspect of politics as – in contrast to what has been noted so far about personalisation – 'politicians' politics' quickly becomes extremely complex and indeed Byzantine, difficult to follow unless one is close to the inner circle. 'Politicians' politics' is the 'kremlinology' of Western politics and only specialists can truly understand it. It is true that the presentation of politicians by journalists is often negative; as was noted earlier, the desire to 'investigate' results in many cases in the wish to 'uncover' scandals. Yet while doing so, journalists tend systematically to emphasise the role of personalities and thus in effect give a prominent place to those who are their true paymasters.

Italy is not the only country in which 'politicians' politics' is practised, at least episodically. For instance, in the UK, rumours of reshuffles give rise to a fever of this kind, in the press, but also on television, though less so on the main radio news. It is of course difficult to know how much of the discussions on these reshuffles are nourished, if not nurtured by the politicians themselves. Another example of 'politicians' politics' in Britain is provided by 'information' or 'revelations' relating to dissension within the political parties: for a very long period, such discussions centred on the Labour party; more recently emphasis has been placed on the Conservative party. Similar remarks could be made about many other countries.

'Politicians' politics' become a major subject of attention for the media as a result of the combination of two elements, the natural and common desire of journalists to give priority to conflicts among politicians and a degree of fragility of the 'political class'. The 'political class' has to be fragile, as journalists are not able to concentrate on the problems within that class unless the politicians themselves are unhappy about their relationships with each other, and in particular about the structure of power within the parties to which they belong or in the cabinet coalition which governs the country. It is therefore not surprising to see more emphasis on 'politicians' politics' in Italy than in, say,

Sweden, in the Fourth French Republic than in the Fifth, and, traditionally at least, in the British Labour Party than in the British Conservative Party.

The fragility of the political class thus becomes wholly associated with the fundamental eagerness of journalists to emphasise the personalisation of conflicts among politicians: one element feeds on the other. When the structure of authority within the parties declines, politicians are more willing to talk about what is going on within these parties; if they are unhappy about their fate, they are likely to want to play up this unhappiness. It is therefore easier for journalists to obtain the 'information' that they wish to obtain, 'information' which may well be at the level of gossip, with perhaps only a basic element of truth to which many embellishments are added. It thus becomes difficult to know who is responsible for what, especially because, in many cases, the origins of the 'information' cannot be reported, at least openly, though those who are 'in the know' are probably aware of its sources.

At one level, such a form of reporting can simply be dismissed as merely a game and therefore as not being detrimental to the health of the political system. One might merely dismiss this problem as unnecessary 'dramatisation'. Yet there is a serious danger in a situation in which the news is devoted to a substantial extent to such 'information'. The danger stems from the fact that, over time, newsmen, politicians, and indeed the public at large become corrupted. Newsmen are corrupted because they come to believe that the type of conflict which they report in this way is truly 'important': their discussions with politicians about other politicians make them feel that they are concerned with real power and are witnessing developments which may lead to a change of government, a change of leadership, perhaps a change of regime; it follows that all details must be recorded. In the process, journalists feel that their role is crucial as they reveal what would otherwise be hidden; coincidentally, one has to note that this kind of investigation may be rather popular both among journalists – since it takes place in the capital and is therefore rather less tiring to follow – and among the media organisations, since it is less costly than many other forms of reporting. Yet, as they are concerned with these matters, newsmen became increasingly estranged from policy making, from the life of the society, and indeed from political life outside the narrow circle of parliamentary and governmental groups.

Politicians become corrupted because the audience that they receive from the journalists – in effect the modern equivalent of a court – induces them to believe that they are not just important people but that they are conducting important business. The paradox – but also the worry – is that politicians come to have a highly inflated view of their own importance at the very moment when their behaviour, together with that of the journalists who are busily talking to them, renders politics trivial.

The public is also being corrupted since it is made to believe that such matters are the real stuff of politics. Admittedly, the public sometimes reacts, for instance by simply turning off: but this, too, amounts to a corruption, as what should have been a mechanism of information does not really inform. Indeed, the public may react more cynically by adopting a posture of disdain or dislike of the whole political class, a posture which may, when the political system is truly fragile, lead to a decline in support for democratic values and ultimately to the collapse of a regime.

This last development has not occurred in Western Europe since the Second World War: it is therefore perhaps believed a little too quickly that the countries of the area are immune from any resulting dangers; journalists are likely to believe that the media must not be diverted from their 'mission to inform the public' by the claim that the regime may be in trouble if they expose dissensions among the political class. The point is that this 'exposition' is, to a very large extent, 'voyeuristic'. There are problems among politicians everywhere, even when the structure of parties is not fragile: depending on the lens that is being used, these problems can be viewed as trivial, as medium-sized, or as really serious. Yet, at the same time, other problems that may affect the political system are not 'exposed' because journalists are busy reporting dissensions among the rich and powerful. From all points of view, the stress given by the newsmen to the role of personalities, to the conflicts among them, and to the possible outcome of these conflicts is 'dysfunctional', while being in no way a requirement for the existence of a healthy reporting in the countries concerned.

Conclusion

Despite the massive development of the media and, as a result, of the huge expansion of journalism in the West, the West does not have the best newsmen it could expect. Some of this is due to the structures of the organisations, to be sure: the fact that these structures are not being discussed here does not mean that they are not seriously affecting the form and content of the news. Much has been written about their effect; however, as was pointed out early in this chapter, the impression sometimes prevails that the ills resulting from the organisations are to an extent an excuse for not examining more closely the problems which are manifest in the profession of journalism.

These problems exist and they are serious. Much of the difficulty seems to stem from the fact that there is both a lack of modesty and a certain lack of training on the part of newsmen (Golding and Elliott, 1979: 181). It is worrying to discover that most journalists have not had any training in journalism, despite the existence of many schools. It is probably retorted that journalism requires a major versatility and that training is in essence too academic. The answer surely should not be that training should be by-passed: it should be improved and made relevant.

The view that training is not truly relevant is unfortunate as it is indicative of an absence of modesty on the basis of which it seems to be believed that newsmen can easily write or talk about any subject, at least any subject relating to politics and society. This view also suggests that newsmen can pass judgements about the political and social life of the countries about which they write or speak with a degree of assurance and superiority that would be laughable if it did not have serious effects on those who read or hear them. This does not mean that newsmen should not have a critical eye about what goes on; it means only that they should always ask themselves whether their role is truly to affirm in a peremptory fashion what is right and wrong, or whether it is not to describe, to the best of their ability, the situation as they see it. This last approach is surely the only one that respects the public and does not consider the audience as 'minors' who must be told what they should think about the information which is being passed on to them. Thus 'interpretation', the many silences about 'important' problems, and the too easy glamour obtained from concentrating on top people, are drawbacks which must be redressed: these drawbacks can indeed be redressed through better training and less assurance about one's ability to discover immediately what is right and wrong.

The job of a journalist is not improved if he or she looks at the problems of society from above. Journalism is not improved if journalists believe that they have a mission to 'reform' societies and to introduce their values in the context of the news reports that they offer to the public. This type of approach to the news has been characteristic, not of liberal societies, but of authoritarian states in which the news is used as a mechanism to spread points of view and values. The proper role of newsmen is to inform: this is the most difficult and therefore the noblest of tasks. On presenting an item newsmen must therefore always ask themselves whether, indeed, they truly inform and only inform. If they are able to do so, they show that they can truly exercise control on themselves and that they consider the audience as their equals and their friends.

Bibliography

Axford, B. and R. Huggins (2001) (eds) *New Media and Politics*. London: Sage.

Bennett, W. L. (1988) *The Politics of Illusion*, 2nd ed. White Plains, NY: Longman.

Blumler, J. (1977) *The Political Effects of Mass Communication*. Milton Keynes: Open University.

Boorstin, D. J. (1972) *The Image: A Guide to Pseudo-events in America*. New York: The Atheneum.

Castells, M. (1998) *End of Millennium*. Malden MA: Blackwell.

Curran, J. and M. Gurevitch (eds) (1996) *Mass Media and Society*, 2nd edn. London: Arnold.

Epstein, E. J. (1973) *News from Nowhere*. New York: Random House.

Ferguson, M. (ed) (1989) *Public Communication*. London: Sage.

Golding, P. and P. Elliott (1979) *Making the News*. London: Longman.

Gurevitch, M. (1982) *Culture, Society, and the Media*. London: Methuen.

Iyengar, S. (1991) *Is Anyone Responsible?* Chicago, Ill.: University of Chicago Press.

Jensen, J. (1990) *Redeeming Modernity*. London: Sage.

Lang, K. and G. E. Lang (1953) 'The unique perspective of television and its effect: a pilot study,' *American Sociological Review*. 18 (1): 3–12.

Moog, S., and J. Sluyter-Beltrao (2001) 'The transformation of political communication?' pp. 30–63 in B. Axford and R. Huggins, eds, *New Media and Politics*. London: Sage.

Negrine, R. (1989) *Politics and the Mass Media in Britain*. 2nd ed. London: Routledge.

Rivers, W. L., W. Schramm, C. G. Christians (1980) *Responsibility in Mass Communication*, 3rd edn. New York: Harper & Row.

Seymour-Ure, C. (1974) *The Political Effects of the Mass Media*. London: Constable.

Shapiro, F. C. (1976) 'Shrinking the News', *Columbia Journalism Review* 76: 23–4.

CHAPTER FIFTEEN

Government and broadcasting: maintaining a balance

PETER FEENEY

—

People base their political opinions on information.[1] In the nineteenth century with the growth of mass democracy such information came from friends, neighbours, families, the workplace, occasional attendance at political meetings, and from the print media. In the twentieth century the broadcast media, radio and television, have increasingly played a central role in the provision of political information.[2] It is no surprise, therefore, that politicians take broadcasting very seriously (see also chapters 12 and 13 in this volume). Since the beginning of an independent Irish state right up to the present day, government has exercised a degree of control over broadcasting incomparably greater than that exercised over newspapers and magazines. Of course, such a pattern of control is not unique to Ireland: the relationship between government and broadcasting has many parallels in other western European democracies. Inevitably there is a tension between government control and editorial independence in broadcasting. This chapter examines the experience in Ireland, concentrating on the period since 1961 when a national television service began broadcasting.

The early years of Irish broadcasting

Broadcasting in its broadest sense in Ireland started with the 1916 Rising, when the insurgents took over the Irish School of Wireless Telegraphy at the corner of O'Connell Street and Abbey Street in Dublin and began sending out information about the Rising to anyone who happened to be listening.[3] The first experience of political broadcasting was short lived as the city centre was reoccupied by British soldiers and the telegraphy service had to be abandoned.

With independence, the newly established Irish Free State was approached by various commercial groups seeking permission to broadcast radio in Ireland. The authorities received approaches from, amongst others, Marconi's Wireless Telegraph company and the Daily Express newspaper group. Not surprisingly the newly independent state had little enthusiasm for handing over broadcasting to British companies, even if it meant that the potential of broadcasting was not realised to any significant extent at all. A Dáil committee was established to make recommendations about a potential wireless service. That committee reported in 1924 in favour of a broadcasting service established and run by the post office. An alternative proposal to give the responsibility for the provision of a service to a company formed by various Irish interests in the electrical trade – who hoped to increase interest in the general public in purchasing wirelesses by establishing a popular radio service – was rejected. The new service was to be directly under the control of the Department of Posts and Telegraphs.

The Postmaster General, J. J. Walsh, was not keen on his new responsibility. Being of the opinion that broadcasting was not the sort of business that the solidly respectable post office should have much to do with, he did not relish the idea of his department being responsible for the control of both the content and the production of programmes. He asked how could his civil servants differentiate between rival organ grinders, rival tenors, not to mention rival politicians (Gorham, 1967: 16). But, despite the reservations of the Postmaster General, early radio broadcasters were to remain civil servants for nearly 35 years.

On 1 January 1926, 2RN – the first name given to Irish radio – started broadcasting. 2RN reflected the official ideology of the community it served: Irish language and culture played a central part in its limited output; dissension was kept off the airwaves. The Ireland of the 1920s to the 1940s was a conservative inward-looking society, in which the accepted ideology had a clear view of what constituted 'Irishness'. And the radio service largely reflected this. The Department of Posts and Telegraphs was zealous in its enthusiasm to limit any expansionist plans of the early broadcasters. Resources were tightly controlled. But despite the limited amount of programming, the number of wireless sets grew. 'Listening in' – the expression used – became a part of everyday life for many Irish people. Important work was done in the area of collection of folklore and the promotion of Irish music. At this stage, there was very little politics on the airwaves; indeed, initially, in response to fears of competition from the newspaper industry, there was virtually no news service on 2RN. Only one journalist was employed.

Irish radio was to wait for quite a number of years before the separation of broadcasting from government began to take place. In 1953 the Minister for Posts and Telegraphs, Erskine Childers, established the non-statutory Comhairle Radio Éireann. The function of this body was to advise the minister on radio broadcasting. It had no real powers, but at least it began the process of separating broadcasting from the civil service and ministerial control. Still, throughout the 1950s Radio Éireann remained locked in the pattern firmly established in the previous thirty years. While there was some increase in political comment, analysis and debate, significant change had to await the 1960s and the arrival of Irish television.

In the autumn of 1955, the BBC started transmitting television programmes from Northern Ireland, and people in the Irish Republic living along the border and down the east coast could receive these BBC signals. It was estimated that in 1959 there were 30,000 television sets in the Republic receiving BBC Northern Ireland and Ulster Television pictures. Naturally the demand for an Irish television service grew. Two arguments in favour of a national service were put forward. Firstly, the existing signals came from foreign sources and were likely to undermine national culture. Secondly, these signals were available only to those living in the north and east of the country. The majority could not receive any television signal at all.

The first television transmission from the Republic occurred in November 1955, when BBC television sent an outside broadcasting unit to Dublin to cover a boxing match between Ireland and England. Throughout the 1950s and even earlier, backbench Dáil deputies put down parliamentary questions to the Minister for Posts and Telegraphs to ascertain what was being done about the establishment of an Irish television service. The response invariably was that the government was keeping the situation under review. In 1957, the Minister for Posts and Telegraphs, Neil Blaney, announced in the Dáil that Ireland was to have its own television service. Initially the proposal was that the service was to be largely commercial in character, to be funded by advertising. The government was prepared to consider proposals from private interests who would be licensed to provide programming. Neil Blaney clearly did not expect there to be any link between the new television service and the long established radio service. In March 1958 the government established a television commission under the chairmanship of Mr Justice George D. Murnaghan. The commission's terms of reference included that no charge would fall on the exchequer, either capital or current, and that control was to be exercised by a public authority. The commission was also requested to enquire into what was the desirable relationship between radio and television.

This clumsily constructed commission, which had 20 members, reported in May 1959. It received applications for a licence from several British television companies, in many cases in conjunction with Irish companies. It also received an application from Gael Linn, as well as several representations from Radio Éireann. The final report was a confused document, which included a minority report and several stated reservations. But basically it recommended that a commercial company should have the right to make and broadcast programmes and that the company would be subject to a publicly appointed authority.

The government of Sean Lemass rejected the commission's findings, and in August 1959 it announced that a new semi-state company was to be established to run both radio and television. Significantly the Minister for Posts and Telegraphs, in giving his reasons for rejecting the recommendations, said: 'it would be difficult to exercise effective public control over a privately operated service' (quoted in McCaffery, 1991: 226).[4]

Broadcasting was to remain under government control, but with significant differences from the structure that had controlled radio for over 30 years. The 1960 Broadcasting Act led to the establishment of an authority that was responsible for the overall control and direction of radio and television broadcasting. The government would appoint the members of the authority, who would be the trustees of the public interest and would approve of overall policy. Broadcasters would no longer be civil servants. They would have the same status as members of other semi-state bodies such as Aer Lingus or the Electricity Supply Board. The structures adopted were very similar to those that had been put in place in the United Kingdom for the management of the BBC.

Broadcasting comes of age

The 1960 Broadcasting Act is substantially the body of legislation under which radio and television still operate today.[5] It has proved, by and large, to be a good piece of legislation, liberal in its ambition. Under the Act broadcasters are free of direct government control, the government appoints the authority, which is responsible for the broadcasting output. The authority is not involved in everyday matters; these are left to the full-time management of RTÉ. With the exception of the relevant government minister responsible for broadcasting who has some specific powers, politicians cannot 'constitutionally' involve themselves in programming issues.

The first broadcast by Telefís Éireann was on New Year's Eve 1961. In its early years, the output was received with great enthusiasm: indeed, the novelty of Irish television broadcasting itself guaranteed this enthusiasm. The arrival of a native television service was to have an enormous effect on social and cultural patterns (Farrell, 1984). But there were other important external forces operating towards change in society. The 1960s was a period of questioning attitudes towards authority and establishments everywhere. Television, and radio which was also affected by the more liberal atmosphere of the period, provided the vehicle for much of that change. In the early days television was a new and very welcome visitor in many people's homes. For those parts of the country that could not receive television pictures until the arrival of Telefís Éireann the service opened up new horizons and worlds. It gave access to a range of views and ideas that were ultimately to lead to considerable dissension and debate, even if initially these new ideas were rather uncritically embraced. Politicians, too, welcomed the new service: the novelty of appearing on television, and being recognised by their television appearances, was important to them.

The honeymoon did not last very long. Fairly quickly after the establishment of television, discontent began to be expressed. In the first months this discontent was largely about the small amount of Irish language programmes and what was seen as the excessive amount of American programming. The view was expressed that the new service was a threat to Irish culture. Rather than providing home produced programming which would enhance Irish culture, the television service was providing access to British and American values and attitudes through the large amount of imported programming.

Over and above such broad cultural issues, particular tensions between politicians and broadcasters were inevitable, and they were not long in coming. Such tensions were an indication that the independent journalistic function of the new television service was beginning to create a critical space between broadcasting and government. Inevitably the politicians who had created the television service and who may not have accepted the liberal political culture that informed the wording of the 1960 Broadcasting Act were going to resist the growing journalistic confidence of the television service. In 1964, Telefís Éireann transmitted a programme on the introduction of turnover tax (the predecessor of VAT). The government felt the programme had an anti-government bias. In 1965, the Minister for Posts and Telegraphs, Joe Brennan, said that he felt RTÉ was not fully aware of its obligation of impartiality.

In October 1966 the Minister for Agriculture, Charles Haughey, complained about the television news service juxtaposing a statement by him with a contradictory statement by the National Farmers' Association. Mr Haughey phoned the RTÉ newsroom to object, and subsequent bulletins did not carry the NFA statement. This incident led to the Taoiseach, Seán Lemass, making a statement in the Dáil, in which he said that RTÉ was set up by legislation as an instrument of public policy and as such was responsible to the government. He went on to say that to this extent the government rejected the view that RTÉ should be either generally or in regard to its current affairs and news programmes completely independent of government supervision. Many broadcasters felt that the 1966 Lemass statement went beyond the 1960 Broadcasting Act. But politicians clearly took the view that the provision of broadcasting was too important to be left entirely free of some form of government control. Politicians would have regarded the running of RTÉ as comparable to the running of the ESB, i.e. that a vital public service could not operate independently of govern-ment supervision. The tension between such a view and journalistic indepen-dence is at the centre of any understanding of the relationship between government and broadcasting.

There were more conflicts in 1966. A *7 Days* programme on the propor-tional representation electoral system was accused of bias and of unduly influencing the electorate before a referendum. Another *7 Days* programme on emigration aroused hostility. These programmes were popular with the ordinary public because there was a general wind of change about and television gave expression to this. Television programming also gave the impression that it was on the side of the viewer against those in power.[6]

In 1967 there were two incidents of political interference that led to disquiet amongst broadcasters. One was a decision by the minister for External Affairs, Frank Aiken, that an RTÉ news crew could not go to Vietnam. In that period western journalists were excluded from Vietnam, but the Vietnamese authorities decided to allow in an RTÉ crew on the grounds that Irish neutrality meant that they were more likely to be impartial. To have been given this permission was seen as quite a journalistic coup within RTÉ and the newsroom was hoping for a world exclusive story. Then Mr Aiken argued that the RTÉ crew would not be capable of presenting an unbiased report given the circumstances of their permission and that it was not in the government's interests for RTÉ to go to Vietnam (at the time the government was seeking US investment in Ireland and did not want to fall out with the US authorities). This thinking revealed a sense of commonality of interest between the national broadcasting service and government that was consistent with the views of Seán Lemass. It was a view that broadcasters would have to resist if RTÉ was to fulfil its impartial journalistic function.

The second incident that year raised many of the same issues. A bitter civil war was taking place in Nigeria, and Irish public opinion tended to sympathise with the breakaway region of Biafra. The government was concerned about the threat to Irish missionaries who were working in other parts of Nigeria if Irish public opinion became too pro-Biafran, and for this reason a current affairs crew was forbidden to travel to the region.

In 1968 the *7 Days* programme was transferred to the news division. Many broadcasters saw this as an attempt to increase the control over the programme. But, in fact, the programme was about to head into deeper conflict with government. In November 1969 it transmitted a programme on illegal money-lending in Dublin, in which it was alleged that the Gardaí were doing nothing about the problem. The programme was attacked by the Minister for Justice, Micheál Ó Moráin, who said that it presented a gross exaggeration of the problem. In a subsequent interview, the then Taoiseach, Jack Lynch, recalled his own response to the report:

[I]t was obviously very biased. It exaggerated the situation out of all proportion. It gave the impression that money lending was widespread throughout the city and county of Dublin. It suggested that it was in every housing estate in the city. It was suggested that there was such a degree of violence that it could not have gone unnoticed by the Gardaí. It referred to the fact that money was seen openly passing by illegal money-lenders to other people on the streets and that for money children's allowance books were being exchanged.[7]

The government went on to establish a public inquiry, which concentrated on the means the programme used in highlighting the incidence of illegal moneylending rather than the issue of illegal moneylending itself. While the RTÉ authority and management defended the programme, they did express doubts about some of the journalistic methods.[8] The politicians defended the tribunal by pointing to its findings that there was clear evidence of inconsistent and inaccurate research, that assertions had been made on insufficient evidence, and that levels of borrowing and violence had been exaggerated. Whatever the merits of the *7 Days* programme, many broadcasters regarded the tribunal as a watershed, arguing that television and radio in the years after the tribunal were more cautious, more self-censorial, and more likely to heed the attitude of politicians than before. The politicians, in the view of the broadcasters, had reasserted their control.

The Northern Ireland troubles and RTÉ

It was during this period that the single greatest factor affecting the relationship between government and broadcasting started to emerge. In 1968 political strife reappeared on the streets of Northern Ireland. For the next 25 years the Northern Ireland conflict was to become one of the main issues on news and current affairs programming on RTÉ radio and television. The emergence of armed militant groups and their associated political movements dedicated to overthrowing not just the state of Northern Ireland but also, in many instances, the political establishment of the Republic of Ireland meant that politicians were going to take a keen interest in the national broadcasting service's coverage of the Northern conflict.

In the early days of the civil rights marches and the one-sided responses of the Northern security forces, RTÉ's understanding of, and reporting on, what was happening on the streets of Belfast and Derry was conditioned by more than 50 years of simplistic history teaching. RTÉ's coverage, like that of the Republic's print media, assumed that right was on the Nationalists' side. As Loyalist extremists went on the rampage in 1969 it was not difficult to fall into the trap of identifying with one side only. RTÉ showed what was happening in Northern Ireland, and what it showed was often unpalatable – a high level of political violence just 60 miles north of the capital of the Republic. On several levels this could have a destabilising effect south of the border. It could win support for the IRA, it could lead to similar happenings in the south, and it could challenge the authority of the government. As the Lynch government wrestled with its own internal cabinet divisions over Northern policy, RTÉ brought the violence of the North to public attention.

In 1971 an RTÉ radio programme broadcast interviews with two members of the IRA. In his reaction to this in the Dáil, Jack Lynch said that it was not in the public interest that members of an illegal organisation should be permitted to use a service paid for by the taxpayers for publicising their activities. Mr Lynch believed that RTÉ was unbalanced in its analysis of what was happening in Northern Ireland, and he was supported in this view by the minister responsible for RTÉ, the minister for Posts and Telegraphs, Gerard Collins. Collins felt that the authority of the Irish government was being undermined by RTÉ giving excessive time to spokespersons for Sinn Féin. According to Collins, 'all serious-minded people were satisfied that those who advocated violence and the propagandists of the subversives and the men of violence were being given far too great a run in RTÉ. For instance, if the then Taoiseach, Jack Lynch, made a particular statement on something dealing with security he was immediately contradicted on radio or television by Ó Brádaigh or MacGiolla who had hot lines into the newsroom at that time.'⁹

In the autumn of 1971 the *7 Days* programme included interviews with senior members of the IRA, Seán MacStiofáin and Cathal Goulding. The government decided to act to curb what it felt to be the excessive attention paid by RTÉ to the IRA and Sinn Féin. Under section 31 of the 1960 Broadcasting Act, the Minister for Posts and Telegraphs had the power to direct RTÉ to refrain from broadcasting any particular matter or matter of any particular class. It was a very wide power that had not been used before, potentially permitting the minister to instruct RTÉ what it could and could not broadcast on any issue. Under this section, the minister issued in writing a directive to RTÉ 'to refrain from broadcasting any matter that could be calculated to promote the aims and activities of any organisation which engages in, encourages or advocates the attainment of any particular objective by violent means'. In its response, the RTÉ authority defended RTÉ's role and sought clarification, provoking the reaction from the minister that the directive spoke for itself and so no clarification was forthcoming. In their interpretation of this, the RTÉ authority proposed a ban on interviews or appearances on radio and television of known members of the IRA.

But the issue did not end there. In the late spring of 1972, Collins expressed in the Dáil his displeasure with RTÉ's handling of Northern affairs. He said that he was personally unhappy with the amount of publicity given to members of the IRA. A meeting between Collins and the RTÉ Authority in June 1972 did not resolve this. The issue then came to a head in November, when the Gardaí arrested Seán MacStiofáin, who was widely believed to be the chief of staff of the Provisional IRA. He immediately went on hunger and thirst strike. There were demonstrations in favour of MacStiofáin on the streets of Dublin. The *This Week* radio programme broadcast a paraphrased interview with MacStiofáin. The government was incensed at what they regarded as a breach by RTÉ of their section 31 directive, and the minister issued an ultimatum to the RTÉ authority, requesting that it consider what action to take. The authority met at great length and decided that, even though it felt poor judgement had been shown in transmitting the MacStiofáin interview, it could not dismiss any member of staff. Given the authority's decision, the government instead dismissed it, replacing it with an entirely new authority. While to people working in broadcasting this showed quite clearly who was ultimately in control of RTÉ, for the politicians it was a necessary step to protect the state from a paramilitary grouping that threatened the democratically elected government. RTÉ had, after all, been set up as an instrument of public policy responsible to the government.

From 1972 onwards the reporting of events in Northern Ireland would always take place within the context of a clearly established assertion of the limits of freedom that journalists working for the national broadcasting service could hope to enjoy. Restrictions under section 31 of the Broadcasting Act were to remain in place for over 20 years, and therefore coverage by broadcasters of Northern Irish affairs would never be as straightforward as for journalists working in the print media.

In 1973 after 16 years of Fianna Fáil single-party government, a new coalition government of Fine Gael and Labour was formed. In all subsequent general elections since then the outgoing government has always changed either through defeat or through new coalition arrangements. This instability in government contrasts with the years from 1957 to 1973. In terms of the relationship between government and broadcasting these regular government changes were to have significant effect.

In the period up to 1973 it was inevitable that there would be considerable tension between the ruling Fianna Fáil government and the broadcasters carrying out their legitimate journalistic function of analysing and criticising those in power. When those in power remain in power for long periods, a gulf with their critics is inevitable. But after 1973 those in power were likely to be in opposition after the next election. This meant a constantly changing body of politicians in government. In theory this could help RTÉ in its relations with government. The tension between government and broadcasters could be spread between all parties, thereby lessening personal animosities. But critics said that it could also mean that RTÉ might curry favour with all politicians, given that the make up of the next government could not be anticipated

In the 1973 coalition government the Minister for Posts and Telegraphs was Dr Conor Cruise O'Brien. Broadcasters welcomed his appointment: in opposition he was regarded as a liberal who would support the independence of broadcasting. While there were hopes that the section 31 directive might be dropped, instead Cruise O'Brien issued a more specific directive – something which the RTÉ Authority had been requesting. The new directive named the paramilitary organisations whose spokesmen were banned from radio and television interviews.

In one sense this made the life of RTÉ journalists easier. It was now clearer what could and could not be broadcast. Despite this greater clarity, however, RTÉ continued to issue internal guidelines that went further than the ministerial directive, for instance including 'representatives' of paramilitary organisations in the ban, and not just their 'spokesmen' as required under the directive. RTÉ played safe and took the view that all members of a banned organisation could be regarded as 'spokesmen'. It was clear that RTÉ was determined to observe the spirit as well as the letter of the directive.

Dr Cruise O'Brien was also responsible for the 1976 Broadcasting Amendment Act that restricted the power of the government to dismiss the RTÉ authority. Under the new act the government could only dismiss the authority with the approval of the two houses of the Oireachtas. This restriction on the power of the Minister for Posts and Telegraphs clearly signalled the potential independence of the RTÉ authority, although the extent to which it would act accordingly would depend on the calibre of individual members and the attitude of the authority's chairman. The 1976 Act also allowed RTÉ broadcasters to achieve impartiality in two or more related programmes rather than within each individual programme. In theory this allowed RTÉ to broadcast more opinionated programmes where balance could be achieved in a subsequent programme, although in practice RTÉ has seldom availed itself of this opportunity. This has at times led critics to suggest that RTÉ's programming lacks passion and commitment. However, opinion polls suggest that the public has great confidence in the balance and fairness of RTÉ's output,[10] and this perception could easily be lost if programming became too opinionated.

The establishment of new broadcasting networks

In the second half of the 1970s a campaign began to provide households that could only receive RTÉ with a choice of viewing. The number of households with access to British television was growing; however, a large number of homes could still not receive BBC or ITV pictures. Two views emerged: should the proposed new channel be given to RTÉ or should it be used to re-broadcast BBC Northern Ireland? Cruise O'Brien favoured what he called 'open broadcasting' where in exchange for the people of the Republic being given access to BBC Northern Ireland the people of Northern Ireland would be given access to RTÉ. He argued that both communities would benefit from exposure to each other's viewpoints. Others argued that it would be irresponsible of the Irish government to hand over a second channel to what was, in some people's eyes, a foreign country and that the second channel should remain in Irish hands.

RTÉ entered the argument, canvassing and lobbying for control of the second channel. They produced surveys that showed that the public would prefer a second channel scheduled by RTÉ, which would show the best of British television as well as material from other countries. The government ultimately agreed and RTÉ got its second channel. The debate showed that whilst it was quite clear that control of broadcasting still remained with government, RTÉ could use public opinion, as long as it retained the support of the public, to influence major decisions about future developments in broadcasting.

Another issue that arose in the 1970s was the growth of illegal local radio stations. Unlike the debate over the second television channel, public opinion on this issue was not on the side of RTÉ. These unlicensed broadcasts were seen to fulfil a broadcasting need that RTÉ could not fulfil. Although officially politicians could not approve of something that was illegal, in practice they found that local radio stations were a useful means of communicating with their electorate (Hall, 1993: 181–4).

In 1979 the government introduced legislation to suppress illegal broadcasting. But the popularity of some of the radio stations forced the government to bring forward a new framework that would incorporate independent local radio. Divisions within government as well as government changes caused by electoral defeat delayed the implementation of effective legislation. It was not until 1987 that the Minister for Communications, Ray Burke, successfully introduced a bill in Dáil Éireann that led to the establishment of the Independent Radio and Television Commission in 1988. This new body would regulate all broadcasting other than the broadcasting emanating from RTÉ. The licensing of new radio stations, and potentially also television stations, would not be in the hands of government but would rest with an independent commission. Two parallel bodies now existed, the RTÉ Authority and the IRTC, both appointed by government and both with the duty of overseeing all broadcasting in Ireland, and between them taking away from government all direct involvement in the running of broadcasting.[11]

However, the Minister for Communications still had very considerable powers over broadcasting and over RTÉ in particular, most notably over the television licence fee and the amount of advertising that RTÉ could carry. From the beginning, RTÉ television has received its income from these two sources. At its introduction in 1962, the licence fee amounted to £4 per annum. By 1986 it had risen to £62. With almost annual increases in the level of the television licence and annual growth in the number of households having a television set and a switching over from cheaper black and white licences to more expensive colour licences, RTÉ's income from licence fees grew at a rate well in excess of inflation. In addition, RTÉ was successful in gaining more and more revenue from commercial advertising. With this constantly increasing revenue RTÉ provided longer hours of television and radio (a separate radio licence had been abolished).

By the mid-1980s the government was concerned about the cost of broadcasting. Inflation was coming down. The prevailing economic thinking was much more critical of public bodies and their pricing policies, especially where the public body enjoyed a state licensed monopoly. The government ordered a consultants' report into the functioning of RTÉ by Stokes Kennedy Crowley, which reported in 1985. The commissioning of this report was again seen by some as evidence of an anti-RTÉ bias amongst politicians (Finn, 1993). Others viewed it simply as a necessary and long overdue attempt to make public bodies more efficient and cost conscious. The licence fee was frozen at its 1986 level. (There was only to be one increase in the following 14 years.) In addition, in the late 1980s Mr Burke capped the amount of income RTÉ could receive from radio and television advertising. He argued that RTÉ's position was so dominant in terms of its ability to raise revenue from advertising that local radio stations and the print media could not compete and that the marketplace in advertising had become distorted.

With the licence fee frozen and the ability to raise additional income from advertising cut off, RTÉ faced a future of, at best, stagnation. There was clearly some room for greater efficiency; the television industry worldwide was renowned for its restrictive practices. However, real growth looked impossible. In addition, in the early 1990s RTÉ television was coming under increasing pressure to commission out to independent production companies more of its programming budgets. The argument put forward was that as RTÉ had a monopoly of Irish originated television broadcasting, some diversity of editorial matter could best be achieved by switching resources to smaller independent production companies. Furthermore, it was argued that independent companies could make programmes more cheaply than RTÉ with its large overheads and permanent staff. Whatever the arguments about the economic issues, what was quite clear from the capping issue was that government still retained considerable control over broadcasting. If government could effectively determine RTÉ's income, it was inevitable that there would be reluctance within some areas of RTÉ to allow its programming to offend politicians. RTÉ felt itself to be vulnerable and had not always the appetite to assert its responsibility to editorial independence.

At each general election in the 1980s the pattern that began in 1973 of changing administrations continued, bringing new governments and new relationships between politicians and broadcasters. What was constant was the background of continuing political violence in Northern Ireland. Every administration throughout the period continued the restrictions imposed under section 31 of the Broadcasting Act. Most broadcast journalists argued that they could continue effectively to carry out their duties to provide information and background analysis to what was happening in Northern Ireland despite the restrictions imposed by section 31.

In the early 1980s there was a particularly tense period with members of the IRA dying on hunger strike in prison. Public opinion within the Republic switched towards a more hostile attitude to the British authorities. It was argued at the time that RTÉ was slow to perceive this change in public mood. The feeling was that RTÉ journalists had worked for so long under section 31 restrictions that they had lost touch with certain elements in political life on both sides of the Irish border. Most journalists in RTÉ continued to declare their opposition to what they regarded as censorship of their legitimate functions. Yet at the same time many felt that they were able, despite restrictions, to adequately report on what was happening in Northern Ireland. Critics argued that RTÉ increasingly only reflected a section of Irish life. The term 'Dublin 4' came to be used to reflect the view that RTÉ's reportage was restricted to a rather middle-class, capital-centred, pro-British and liberal view of Irish life.

The late 1980s was a period when government attempted to introduce domestic competition into the Irish television market. With the legitimisation of local radio, RTÉ radio faced commercial competition for the first time. The logic that applied to radio broadcasting was also used to argue the case for an alternative television service within the Republic. If RTÉ radio could face competition, why could not television face the same challenge? RTÉ defended its state-licensed monopoly by arguing that it already competed in an intensely competitive market with between 60 and 70 per cent of households having access to four terrestrial British channels and in many cases a whole range of satellite channels. None of these channels originated in the Republic, however, or scheduled its programmes to compete with RTÉ's two channels. With the approval of the Minister for Communications, the Independent Radio and Television Commission advertised for a licence to broadcast a third channel. The fact that it was government that guaranteed RTÉ's monopoly, and that the same government might decide that a competing channel could be introduced, showed clearly the dependency RTÉ had on its relationship with government.

In the event the company that won the licence for what became known as TV3 had its licence revoked by the IRTC when it could not satisfy the commission with its proposals for funding.[12]

The relationship between government and RTÉ throughout the 1980s and early 1990s was not significantly influenced by RTÉ's coverage of Northern Ireland. There were, however, episodes of tension between the two. For instance, there were tensions between the governments of Charles Haughey and RTÉ, with accusations of a bias against Mr Haughey within the national broadcasting service. In 1985 the Fine Gael-led government asked the RTÉ authority to postpone the appointment of a new Director General when the favoured candidate was felt to be unacceptable to the government. In the 1989 general election campaign there was some resentment within Fianna Fáil that RTÉ had been responsible for putting the issue of government health cuts on the agenda. But, overall, throughout this period there was no evidence of any public hostility between government and RTÉ. This situation contrasts markedly with the UK at the time, where Margaret Thatcher's government was openly hostile to the BBC (Barnett and Curry, 1994).

Critics of RTÉ will point to this absence of tension as an indication that RTÉ was too willing to curry favour with those in power. They point to what they perceive as a decline in the quality of programming and a general loss of nerve by RTÉ. Much of this criticism came from the print media whose favourable press of RTÉ in the 1960s and 1970s largely disappeared in the 1980s and 1990s. RTÉ, in its response, referred to the large increase in the number of hours of transmission on both radio and television and the much greater need to fight for an audience given the increasingly competitive environment and the relative swing towards dependency on revenue generated by advertising as opposed to licence fee income.

Another factor that was affecting the area of investigative journalism was the increasing threat of substantial damages being awarded in libel claims. Throughout the 1980s there was a growing realisation that individuals had the right to protect their good name against any section of the media, whether print or broadcast. Legal costs became an important consideration in the media generally. There were many calls from journalists for changes in the laws of defamation. In practice programme makers had to begin to use legal concepts of evidence before publication, and increasingly lawyers were involved in vetting controversial programming in advance of transmission.

With the formation of the Fianna Fáil/Labour coalition in January 1993, Michael D. Higgins was appointed to a new ministry, the Department of Arts,

Culture and the Gaeltacht, and given responsibility for broadcasting. He acted quickly to remove the limit on RTÉ's advertising revenue imposed by his predecessor. He also lifted the restrictions under section 31 of the Broadcasting Act that had been in existence for over 20 years. As part of the encouragement of the Republican movement to move away from military activity and engage in the political process, he allowed members of Sinn Féin to participate in radio and television programmes. This gesture was followed some months later by the British government, which removed similar restrictions.

As the decade unfolded the peace process in Northern Ireland brought to an end any tension that might have existed over RTÉ's coverage of Northern politics. The handshake between Taoiseach Albert Reynolds and the President of Sinn Féin, Gerry Adams, on the steps of government buildings symbolised a new era in Irish politics with the Republican movement receiving its legitimisation from the establishment. Having spent over 20 years being legally obliged to keep the Republican movement at a distance, RTÉ now found itself treating Sinn Féin as just another political party. The transition was not without its tensions within broadcasting. Practices and attitudes that had developed over two decades could not disappear overnight. But the tensions within RTÉ merely reflected a process that was happening throughout Ireland.

Michael D. Higgins was a very active Minister for Arts and Culture. He announced plans to establish an Irish language television service, Teilifís na Gaeilge. He also initiated a debate on the future of broadcasting which led to a green paper on broadcasting in May 1995. By the end of the decade, broadcasting stood on the threshold of the most radical change it has experienced since its inception. Much of this change was driven by developments in the technology of broadcasting, and at times the regulators and planners of broadcasting policy appeared to be chasing an industry that would not wait for the theory to catch up with the practice.

In June 1997 Fianna Fáil returned to government in coalition with the Progressive Democrats. Síle de Valera was appointed Minister of Arts, Heritage, Gaeltacht and the Islands. During her period of office TV3 began broadcasting, heralding the arrival of domestic competition in television broadcasting. She introduced a new regulatory body for commercial broadcasting, both radio and television, with the establishment of the Broadcasting Commission of Ireland, which replaced the IRTC. Under considerable pressure from RTÉ she awarded a licence fee increase of Ir£14.50. However, with the growth in competition, RTÉ's reliance on commercial sources for the majority of its funding remained a contentious issue. In part to address that issue, de Valera established in 2002 a

Forum on Broadcasting, whose terms of reference included the objective of fostering an environment that encourages the establishment and maintenance of high quality Irish radio and television services.

While the challenge for Irish broadcasters in the next decade is clear, the role of government in that process remains to be seen.

Irish broadcasting in the new millennium

The broadcasting environment of the new millennium is much changed from that of 40 years earlier when it was possible for governments to regulate and control television and radio. The availability of satellite television and the increasing use of digital technology have resulted in much television moving outside the control of national governments. Increasingly regulators are being asked not to control their national broadcasters, but rather to protect them from purely commercial multinational competition whose brief does not extend beyond the need to be profitable. The ability of any national government to assist their national broadcasters is limited both by an ideology which is favourably disposed to market forces and, within Europe, by European Union laws which do not allow the protection of the domestic market at the expense of other EU members. This coupled with developments in the technology of television will lead to many changes in the coming years.

So after almost eight decades of radio broadcasting and four decades of television broadcasting, how is the balance in Ireland between government and RTÉ? The degree of freedom which RTÉ enjoys is significantly different from that enjoyed by the print media. Factors which influence broadcasting in Ireland and determine the relationships with government include historical precedents such as the fact that RTÉ was established by government, that the state allowed RTÉ a monopoly in national television broadcasting for 35 years, that the level of income from licence fees is controlled by government, that the amount of time that RTÉ can give over to advertising is also controlled by government, and that the RTÉ authority is appointed by government.[13]

All of these factors influence RTÉ in its relationship with government. To balance this dependency, broadcasters are aware of their obligation to provide fair and objective programming which necessitates an independent stance that can at times bring RTÉ into conflict with politicians. If programming does not scrutinise those who hold public office, then programme makers are failing to justify the privileged position that has been created for them by those in public office. This conflicting relationship is at the centre of understanding the balance that must be maintained between broadcasters and politicians. Any assessment of how broadcasters have performed historically has to be understood within this context. Ultimately public service broadcasting is judged on its ability to deliver a service that is not provided by commercial broadcasting. In the news and current affairs areas, if public service broadcasting is to prosper it has to provide a service to viewers and listeners of independent journalism with an emphasis on fairness and objectivity, taking seriously its obligation to hold all vested interests up to public scrutiny, unafraid to criticise those in power, balanced in its approach to competing ideologies and placing in the centre of its schedules news and current affairs. Nothing less will suffice.

In addition to the historic relationship between broadcasting and government, there are also cultural factors that need to be taken into account in assessing RTÉ's performance over the last four decades. RTÉ is seen as a *national* institution and therefore is expected to reflect national values and aspirations. Viewers and listeners have different standards for RTÉ than they have for the print media or independent radio and television channels, which they see as operating entirely in the commercial marketplace. Because they pay a compulsory licence fee and because of the way in which RTÉ was created, the public regard RTÉ as in some way *theirs*, and therefore they expect RTÉ to reflect their values and attitudes. This may take the form of specific programming in support of cultural organisations. It may take the form of the public expecting RTÉ to adhere to certain standards of taste and decency (especially in relation to language, violence and the portrayal of sex). It may take the form of broadcasting events that are regarded as nationally important (even if, as in some cases, the potential audience is very small). It certainly takes the form of an expectation that RTÉ should provide a platform for fair public debate and argument when important national questions are being discussed.

This responsibility for providing an opportunity for fair debate sometimes can rest heavily on RTÉ. Because of its dominant position as the major broadcasting voice on Irish affairs, there is at times a conservative disposition within RTÉ which is reflected in the view that the role of broadcasting in public debate is too important and influential to risk getting it wrong. Programmes therefore often take a cautious approach to many topics. In the early years of television this conservative disposition would have found support amongst those broadcasters who had inherited the civil service ethos which carried over from Radio Éireann in the 1950s. But 40 years after the disappearance of the civil service broadcaster it is the sense of the weight of responsibility that induces caution.

This concern about getting it wrong was balanced by a sense of excitement in broadcasting. During the decades of the 1970s and 1980s when political life experienced considerable turmoil, with internal divisions within Fianna Fáil creating dramatic moments and frequent changes in government, the RTÉ studios, both radio and television, were at the very centre of political life. Much of the political drama of those decades unfolded on RTÉ airwaves, before RTÉ cameras, and in RTÉ studios. This brought a sense of excitement to news and current affairs broadcasting as moments in history seemed to be happening before the eyes and ears of the broadcasters.

This sense of broadcasting being at the centre of political life did not extend to events in Northern Ireland. Perhaps in part as a result of section 31 restrictions, there was always a feeling that RTÉ's coverage of political developments in Northern Ireland was less engaged and more peripheral. There was a feeling that RTÉ was *visiting* Northern Ireland and *reporting back* on events there. Perhaps more important than section 31 was the realisation that the two parts of the island of Ireland had separate broadcasting services with RTÉ *the* service for the Republic of Ireland and BBC Northern Ireland and UTV providing *the* services for Northern Ireland.

Interest groups who apply pressure on broadcasters to reflect their views on radio and television often use their perceptions of how fairly RTÉ has treated them as a means of generating attention and support for their causes. Broadcasters have come to expect their treatment of issues to become part of the political debate. Whether directed at opponents or the media, objective views about performance often do not play a significant part in the rhetoric of political life. This process inevitably makes broadcasting part of the political process, not just as a purveyor of debate but also as a participant in the debate itself. This apparent participatory role by what is widely regarded as the most powerful medium is fully realised by politicians who increasingly invest more and more resources into attempting to present the image they want of their performance and policies (see chapters 12 and 13 in this volume). The maintaining of the balance between politicians and broadcasters is part of a process that can never conclude. It is a central part of political life at the beginning of the twenty-first century.

I would like to finish with a visual image. In early October 2000 the Serbian people rebelled against the abuse of power of Slobodan Milosevic. The images from Belgrade made gripping television. First, the people stormed the parliament buildings; then they turned their anger on the Milosevic dominated Serbian television headquarters. The Yugoslav people understood the relationship between government and broadcasting and the need for distance between the two to allow impartiality and objectivity.

Notes

Brian Farrell, to whom this book is dedicated, has been a central figure in Irish broadcasting since the early 1960s. He has been a presenter of all the main current affairs television programmes. As well as this he has presented almost all election and referendum result programmes and has been the commentator on many major state occasions televised by RTÉ.

1   The first half of this chapter is based on an unpublished essay which provided the background for the script of a television documentary, *Lifting the Veil: The Politics of Television*, which was transmitted on RTÉ television on 16 November 1983. The author wrote and produced the documentary.

2   In a survey that RTÉ commissioned from MRBI in July–August 2000 (N = 1,000), 75 per cent of respondents said their main source of news and information was television; 10 per cent said radio; 11 per cent said newspapers (MRBI, 2000).

3   For the history of the first years of Irish radio see Gorham (1967).

4   I am grateful to Muiris MacConghail, former Controller of RTÉ television, for drawing my attention to this work. Chapter 5 of McCaffrey's dissertation gives a useful account of early tensions between government and broadcasters.

5   For a valuable account of the legal framework in which RTÉ operates, see Hall (1993).

6   For a view on the role of television current affairs on this issue, see Kelly (1984).

7   Jack Lynch interview in the RTÉ documentary, *Lifting the Veil: The Politics of Television*, 16 November 1983.

8   Donal Ó Morain, Tom Hardiman and John Irvine interviews in *ibid.*

9   Gerard Collins interview, *ibid.*

10   The MRBI poll (MRBI, 2000) showed that 78 per cent of respondents regarded RTÉ as balanced; only 12 per cent of respondents found evidence of bias.

11   The Flood Tribunal of Inquiry into Planning Issues has revealed a considerable amount of detail about the establishment of the first commercial national radio service, Century FM. The probity of the process has been questioned.

12   After lengthy court battles the TV3 Consortium had the IRTC decision revoked in 1995. TV3 came on air in late 1998 bringing the first domestic competition to RTÉ. TnaG (subsequently renamed TG4) is not in competition with RTÉ. There are plans to place TG4 on an independent statutory basis, but in the meantime it is under the umbrella of RTÉ.

13   From 1973 successive governments had appointed a member of RTÉ staff to the authority. In June 1995 this process was made more democratic when staff were allowed to vote for who they felt should be appointed as a member of staff to the authority. Betty Purcell, an editor of current affairs television programmes and a trade union activist, became the first member of the RTÉ authority to be appointed after such a process. In 2000 the practice of having an election was continued. The newsreader Anne Doyle was appointed to the authority after the staff had voted for her.

Bibliography

Barnett, Steven and Andrew Curry (1994) *The Battle for the BBC*. London: Aurum Press.

Farrell, Brian (ed.) (1984) *Communications and Community in Ireland*. Dublin: Mercier Press.

Finn, T. V. (1993) 'Thirty years a growing: the past, the present and the future of Irish broadcasting', *Irish Communications Review* 3.

Gorham, Maurice (1967) *Forty Years of Irish Broadcasting*. Dublin: RTÉ/Talbot Press.

Hall, Eamonn G. (1993) *The Electronic Age: Telecommunications in Ireland*. Dublin: Oak Tree.

Horgan, John (2001) *Irish Media: A Critical History since 1922*. London: Routledge.

Kelly, Mary (1984) 'Twenty years of current affairs on RTÉ', in Martin McLoone and John McMahon (eds), *Television and Irish Society: 21 Years of Irish Television*. Dublin: RTÉ/Irish Film Institute.

McCaffery, Colum (1991) 'Political Communication and Broadcasting: Theory, Practice and Reform'. Unpublished PhD dissertation, University College Dublin.

MRBI (2000) *RTÉ Corporate Reputation, 2000*. Dublin: Market Research Bureau of Ireland.

Brian Farrell's publications

1967

'Markievicz and the women of the revolution', pp. 227–38 in F. X. Martin (ed.), *Leaders and Men of the Easter Rising*. London.

1968

'The new state and Irish political culture', *Administration* 16 (3): 238–46.

1969

'A note on the Dáil constitution, 1919', *Irish Jurist* 4 (1): 127–38.

1970

'Dáil deputies: The 1969 generation', *Economic and Social Review* 1 (3): 309–27.

'Labour and the Irish political party system: A suggested approach to analysis', *Economic and Social Review* 1 (4): 477–502.

1970–71

'The drafting of the Irish Free State constitution', *Irish Jurist* 5 (1): 115–40; 5 (2): 343–56; 6 (1): 111–35; 6 (2): 345–59.

1971

Chairman or Chief? The Role of Taoiseach in Irish Government. Dublin: Gill & Macmillan.

The Founding of Dáil Éireann: Parliament and Nation-Building. Dublin: Gill & Macmillan.

'MacNeill in politics', pp. 181–97 in F. X. Martin and F. J. Byrne (eds), *Eoin MacNeill: The Revolutionary Scholar, 1867–1945*. Shannon: Irish University Press.

1973

Ed. *The Irish Parliamentary Tradition*. Dublin and New York: Gill & Macmillan/ Barnes & Noble.

'The paradox of Irish politics', pp. 13–25 in Brian Farrell (ed.), *The Irish Parliamentary Tradition*.

'The Patriot Parliament of 1689', pp. 116–27 in Brian Farrell (ed.), *The Irish Parliamentary Tradition*.

'The First Dáil and after', pp. 208–20 in Brian Farrell (ed.), *The Irish Parliamentary Tradition.*

1975

'The legislation of a "revolutionary" assembly: Dáil Decrees, 1919–1922', *Irish Jurist* 10 (1): 112–27.

'Irish government re-observed', *Economic and Social Review* 6 (3): 405–14.

1978

'The Irish General Election, 1977', *Parliamentary Affairs* 31 (1): 22–36.

'The mass media and the 1977 campaign', pp. 97–132 in Howard R. Penniman (ed.), *Ireland at the Polls: The Dáil Elections of 1977.* Washington, DC: American Enterprise Institute.

With Maurice Manning, 'The election', pp. 133–64 in Howard R. Penniman (ed.), *Ireland at the Polls: The Dáil Elections of 1977.* Washington, DC: American Enterprise Institute.

1982

'The 1982 General Election: campaign and analysis', pp. 136–41 in Ted Nealon and Seamus Brennan, *Nealon's Guide to the 23rd Dáil and Seanad.* Dublin: Platform Press.

1983

Seán Lemass. Dublin: Gill & Macmillan (Reprinted 1991).

'De Valera: unique dictator or charismatic chairman?', pp. 35–46 in J. P. O'Carroll and John A. Murphy (eds), *De Valera and his Times.* Cork: Cork University Press.

'Coalitions and political institutions: the Irish experience', pp. 248–62. in Vernon Bogdanor (ed.), *Coalition Government in Western Europe.* London: Heinemann.

1984

Ed., *Communications and Community in Ireland.* Dublin and Cork: Mercier Press.

'Communications and community: problems and prospects', pp. 111–21 in Brian Farrell (ed.), *Communications and Community in Ireland.* Dublin and Cork: Mercier.

1985

'Ireland: From friends and neighbours to clients and partisans: Some dimensions of parliamentary representation under PR–STV', pp. 237–64 in Vernon Bogdanor (ed.), *Representatives of the People? Parliamentarians and Constituents in Western Democracies.* Aldershot: Gower.

'The unlikely marriage: de Valera, Lemass and the shaping of Modern Ireland', *Etudes Irlandaises* 10: 215–22.

1986

'Politics and Change', pp. 143–51. in K. Kennedy (ed.), *Ireland in Transition: Economic and Social Change Since 1960*. Cork and Dublin: Mercier.

1987

With Howard Penniman (eds) *Ireland at the Polls 1981, 1982, and 1987: A Study of Four General Elections*. Durham, NC: Duke University Press.

'The context of the three elections', pp. 1–30 in Howard Penniman and Brian Farrell (eds), *Ireland at the Polls 1981, 1982, and 1987*.

'Government formation and ministerial selection', pp. 131–55 in Howard Penniman and Brian Farrell (eds), *Ireland at the Polls 1981, 1982, and 1987*.

With David M. Farrell, 'The general election of 1987', pp. 232–43 in Howard Penniman and Brian Farrell (eds), *Ireland at the Polls 1981, 1982, and 1987*.

'The Road from 1987: Government formation and institutional inertia', pp. 141–52 in Michael Laver, Peter Mair and Richard Sinnott (eds), *How Ireland Voted: The Irish General Election, 1987*. Dublin: Poolbeg.

1988

Ed. *De Valera's Constitution and Ours*. Dublin: Gill & Macmillan.

'From First Dáil through Irish Free State', pp. 18–32 in Brian Farrell (ed.), *De Valera's Constitution and Ours*.

'De Valera's constitution and ours', pp. 198–209 in Brian Farrell (ed.), *De Valera's Constitution and Ours*.

'The constitution and the institutions of government: Constitutional theory and political practice', *Administration* 35 (4): 162–72.

'Foreword', pp. v–xii in Charles Townshend (ed.), *Consensus in Ireland: Approaches and Recessions*. Oxford: Clarendon.

'Ireland: The Irish cabinet system: More British than the British themselves', pp. 33–46 in Jean Blondel and Ferdinand Müller-Rommel (eds), *Cabinets in Western Europe*. Houndmills, Basingstoke: Macmillan.

1989

With John Coakley, 'Selection of cabinet ministers in Ireland, 1922–1982', pp. 199–218 in Mattei Dogan (ed.), *Pathways to Power: Selecting Rulers in Pluralist Democracies*. Boulder, CO: Westview.

1990

'Forming the government', pp. 179–91 in Michael Gallagher and Richard Sinnott (eds), *How Ireland Voted 1989*. Galway: Centre for the Study of Irish Elections.

1992

'The government', pp. 151–66 in John Coakley and Michael Gallagher (eds), *Politics in the Republic of Ireland.* Galway: PSAI.

1993

'Cagey and secretive: collective responsibility, executive confidentiality and the public interest', pp. 82–103 in Ronald J. Hill and Michael Marsh (eds), *Modern Irish Democracy: Essays in Honour of Basil Chubb.* Dublin: Irish Academic Press.

'The government', pp. 167–89 in John Coakley and Michael Gallagher (eds), *Politics in the Republic of Ireland,* 2nd edn. Dublin and Limerick: Folens/PSAI.

'The formation of the Partnership Government', pp. 146–61 in Michael Gallagher and Michael Laver (eds), *How Ireland Voted 1992.* Dublin and Limerick: Folens/PSAI.

1994

Ed., *The Creation of the Dáil: A Volume of Essays from the Thomas Davis Lectures.* Dublin: Blackwater Press.

'The Parliamentary Road to Independence', pp. 1–14 in Brian Farrell (ed.), *The Creation of the Dáil.*

'The First Dáil and its Constitutional Documents', pp. 61–74 in Brian Farrell (ed.), *The Creation of the Dáil.*

Index

Ulster Unionist Party, 148
Ulster Unionists, 9, 28
Ulster Volunteers, 9
unemployment, 84, 92
United Irish League, 150
University College Dublin, 2–3
UTV, 233, 249

Vietnam War, 236

Walsh, Dick, 202
Walsh, J. J., 11, 232
War of Independence, 6, 48, 49, 58,
    62, 198
Whigs, 142
Whiteboyism, 12
women TDs, 14

X Case, 206